AN ALL-ROUND
MINISTRY

ADDRESSES TO
MINISTERS AND STUDENTS

C. H. SPURGEON

THE BANNER OF TRUTH TRUST

THE BANNER OF TRUTH TRUST
3 *Murrayfield Road, Edinburgh* EH12 6EL
P.O. Box 621, *Carlisle, Pennsylvania* 17013, *U.S.A.*

*

First published 1900
First Banner of Truth Trust edition 1960
Reprinted 1965
Reprinted in paperback 1972
Reprinted 1978
ISBN 0 85151 181 3

*

*Printed in Great Britain
by Hazell Watson & Viney Ltd
Aylesbury, Bucks*

CONTENTS

INTRODUCTION

WHILE C. H. Spurgeon is still remembered as a popular preacher, it has generally been forgotten that the influence he exercised on ministers and theological students was possibly an even greater factor in his life than his own personal ministry. That he organized a college, supervised the training of over 800 students, presided at an Annual Conference of ministers and regarded all this as his " life's labour and delight,—a labour for which all my other work is but a platform,—a delight superior even to that afforded by my ministerial success ",[1] these are facts which are little known today. The truth is that Spurgeon's views on the ministry and particularly on theological training have been very much overlooked since his death in 1892. At first sight it is hard to account for this when one remembers that for 37 years Spurgeon preached weekly to a congregation of some 5,000 people. Surely in days like these, when a decline in the power of preaching and in church attendance is so much in evidence, the opinions of such a man are worth knowing ?

But it is to be feared that this neglect of such an important aspect of C. H. Spurgeon is not merely accidental. It has arisen through definite historical

[1] *Autobiography*, Vol. III, p. 127.

circumstances. Since Spurgeon's day, *there has not been a college in England which has upheld the views which he advanced on theological training*. During the last years of his life he stood practically alone in his convictions on this subject and after his death the tide of opinion which he had so resolutely opposed carried all before it. " Today," the Modernist Baptist leader, Dr. T. R. Glover, wrote triumphantly in 1932, " if you want a real old obscurantist college, you have to found one." He had in mind a college such as Spurgeon's had been.

The best illustration of Spurgeon's views on preparation for the ministry is the history of his own college. Almost from the commencement of his ministry to London's vast multitudes in 1854, Spurgeon was burdened by the need for many more preachers of strong evangelical views. Moreover, he knew, as we often find him saying, that colleges had always played a vital part in the provision of such men: " Honorat, in the opening years of the fifth century, retired to the little island, near Cannes, which still bears his name; and attracted around him a number of students. The one best known to us is Patrick, the evangelizer of Ireland. . . . Thus did Honorat and Columba, in the olden days, and so did Wycliffe and Luther and Calvin, in the Reformation times, train the armies of the Lord for their mission. Schools of the prophets are a prime necessity if the power of religion is to be kept alive and propagated in the land."[1] " We talk of Luther and Calvin in the days of the Reformation, but we must remember

[1] *Ibid.*, p. 137.

that these men became what they were largely through their power to stamp their image and superscriptions upon other men with whom they came in contact. If you went to Würtemburg, it was not Luther only that you saw, but Luther's college, the men around him—the students all being formed into young Luthers under his direction. It was the same at Geneva. How much Scotland owes to the fact that Calvin could instruct John Knox ! How much have other nations derived from the little republic of Switzerland on account of Calvin's having the clear common-sense to perceive that one man could not hope to affect a whole nation except by multiplying himself, and spreading his views by writing them upon the fleshy tablets of the hearts of young and earnest men ! The churches seem to have forgotten this. It is nothing but sanctified common-sense that leads the church to the formation of a college. The Church ought to make the college the first object of its care."[1]

Spurgeon had not been preaching for long in London, so he tells us, when " several zealous young men were brought to a knowledge of the truth; and among them some whose preaching in the street was blessed of God to the conversion of souls."[2] The first of these " street preachers " was a young man named T. W. Medhurst. Apparently some of Spurgeon's congregation advised their pastor that Medhurst was untrained for such work, whereupon Spurgeon interviewed the young man and received the

[1] *The Life and Work of C. H. Spurgeon*, G. H. Pike, Vol.IV. p. 356.
[2] *Autobiography*, Vol. II, p. 147.

memorable reply, " I must preach, sir; and I shall preach unless you cut off my head." It was this that finally led Spurgeon to the practical decision that he must do something to fit such men for the ministry. Thus in 1855 (when Spurgeon was but twenty-one himself and when he had a thousand people who gave hopeful evidence of conversion seeking admission to New Park Street Chapel !), Medhurst began to come weekly to his pastor for several hours instruction in theology. He was boarded in the home of another minister and Mrs. Spurgeon meanwhile practised " the most rigorous economy in the household " to enable Spurgeon to support Medhurst out of his own salary ! In 1857 a second student was added; before long the number grew to eight, then twenty, and finally there were regularly between seventy and a hundred students, taking a two-year course, in the " Pastors' College " as it became known. By 1891, 845 men had been trained. Of these many broke up fresh ground and formed new churches in England, but others carried the Gospel to the ends of the earth, Morocco, the Falkland Islands, Tasmania, South Africa, the United States being among the many countries profited by their labours.

It might well be asked why Spurgeon should have thus formed a new college at a time when there were already a considerable number of Nonconformist colleges in existence—indeed not a few people asked this very question a century ago and thought his venture unnecessary, unconventional and divisive. Spurgeon's reply essentially was that there were no colleges which met the needs as he saw them, and that, in particular, he differed from the existing Nonconformist colleges in four respects:

First, with regard to the entrance of students into theological colleges, Spurgeon was convinced that no man should be accepted for training unless he was naturally *fitted to preach* and—as far as human eye could judge—divinely called to that office. No amount of mental ability or scholastic achievement could make up for the absence of this. " A low state of piety, a want of enthusiasm, a failure in private devotion, a lack of consecration,"[1] these were things not to be tolerated in would-be servants of Christ. Other college authorities might profess to hold this view, but Spurgeon found them sadly failing to apply it in practice. Our institution, he says, "aims to keep out of the sacred office those who are not called to it. We are continually declining candidates because we question their fitness. Some of these have education and money, and are supported by earnest requests from parents and friends; but all this avails them nothing."[2]

Secondly, as far as the curriculum of theological training is concerned, Spurgeon asserted that the place of prime importance should be given to *Biblical Theology*. " We have become daily more and more impressed with the conviction that theology should be the principal subject for instruction in a Theological College," so wrote George Rogers, the man whom Spurgeon chose as Principal of the Pastors'

---

[1] *The Sword and Trowel* (Spurgeon's monthly magazine), 1889, p. 311.
[2] *Ibid.*, 1887, p. 206.

College.[1] Moreover Spurgeon was careful to affirm what he meant by Biblical Theology. " We endeavour," he says, " to teach the Scriptures, but, as everybody else claims to do the same, and we wish to be known and read of all men, we say distinctly that the theology of the Pastors' College is Puritanic. We are old-fashioned enough to prefer Manton to Maurice, Charnock to Robertson, and Owen to Voysey. Both our experience and our reading of the Scriptures confirm us in the belief of the unfashionable doctrines of grace; and among us, upon those grand fundamentals, there is no uncertain sound."[2] " It must be frankly admitted," he writes, in explaining why he thought a new college necessary " that my views of the gospel and of the mode of training preachers were, and are, somewhat peculiar. I may have been uncharitable in my judgment, but I thought the Calvinism of the theology usually taught to be very doubtful, and the fervour of the generality of the students to be far behind their literary attainments. It seemed to me that preachers of the grand old truths of the gospel, ministers suitable for the masses, were more likely to be found in an institution where preaching and divinity would be the main objects, and not degrees and other insignia of human learning."[3]

There is no doubt that Spurgeon's opinions on this subject were greatly strengthened by his own personal experience. As is well known, he had

[1] *The Sword and Trowel*, 1866, p. 136.
[2] *Autobiography*, Vol. II, p. 149.
[3] *C. H. Spurgeon, His Life and Work*, R. Shindler, p. 134.

received no regular college training, but from his earliest days in his grandfather's manse at Stambourne, he had been grounded in Calvinistic theology, and when he began preaching in London he proved again (what most had forgotten since the days of Whitefield) that in that divinity lies the true power of a Gospel ministry. We find an interesting sidelight on this fact in a leading article in *The Times*, of April 13, 1857. The article dealt with the connection between strong doctrine and popular preaching, pointing to Spurgeon's extraordinary success as a proof. Eloquence that will move the masses, the writer said, requires not merely a loud voice but " proper material to exert itself upon. Nobody shouts out an axiom in mathematics; nobody balances probabilities in thunder. There must be a strong sentiment, some bold truth, to make a man shout. The doctrine of sudden conversion or of irresistible grace can be shouted; but if a man tried ever so hard to shout in delivering a moderate and sensible discourse on free-will, he would find himself talking quietly in spite of himself. A loud voice, then, must have ' loud ' doctrine to develop it. But the Church of England has rather a distaste for ' loud' doctrine; her general standard is opposed to it, her basis is a balanced one, mixing opposite truths, and qualifying what she teaches with judicious protests and disclaimers. She preaches Catholicity with a protest against Rome, and Protestantism with a protest against Geneva. This is very sensible . . . but it is not favourable to popular preaching."[1]

[1] *Autobiography*, Vol. II, p. 250–251.

This was but a partial understanding of the case, but at any rate it was a recognition of what Spurgeon always realized, namely that there is a far closer connection than men think between a minister's preaching and his theology. It was no mere theoretical interest in doctrine that led him to place the old divinity in the forefront of the college curriculum. " To be effective preachers you must be sound theologians," was the maxim he constantly gave his students.[1] " The buildings in which you will preach," he reminded them, " were erected as monuments to the power of the doctrines of grace. Mind you preach these doctrines in them. The doctrines some now preach could not build a mouse-trap."[2]

In the third place, Spurgeon differed from so many of his contemporaries (and ours !) with regard to the manner in which students should be trained. Instruction, he maintained, should be given in definite, *dogmatic* form. Tutors should not teach their students in that broad liberal manner which presents a number of " view-points " and leaves the ultimate choice to the student; rather they should forcibly and unmistakably declare the mind of God and show a determined predilection for the old theology, being saturated in it and ready to die for it ! [3]

Spurgeon never forgot the disastrous results which accompanied the " liberal method " of teaching at

[1] *Personal Reminiscences of C. H. Spurgeon*, W. Williams, p. 138.
[2] *Ibid.*, p. 170.
[3] *The Sword and Trowel*, 1871, pp. 227–228.

Philip Doddridge's Evangelical Academy at North-ampton. " Dr. Doddridge was as sound as he was amiable; but perhaps he was not always judicious; or more probably still, he was too judicious, and not sufficiently bold and decided."[1] The consequences of Doddridge's views on teaching came out clearly under his successor Dr. Ashworth. One of his pupils, Joseph Priestly—who became a great champion of Unitarianism among the Nonconformists—described the teaching policy in these words: " In my time the academy was in a state peculiarly favourable to the serious pursuit of truth, as the students were about equally divided upon every question of much impor-tance. Our tutors, also, were of different opinions, Dr. Ashworth taking the orthodox side of every question, and Mr. Clark, the sub-tutor, that of heresy, though always with the greatest modesty. The general plan of our studies, which may be seen in Dr. Doddridge's published lectures, was exceed-ingly favourable to free enquiry, as we were referred to authors on both sides of every question. In this situation I saw reason to embrace what is generally called the heterodox side of every question." Priestly was far from being alone in his choice and great harm was done.

The Principal of the Pastors' College, George Rogers, spoke for Spurgeon when he declared, " Calvinistic theology is dogmatically taught. We

---

[1] Cf. two articles on " The Down Grade " in *The Sword and Trowel*, 1887, pp. 122–126 and pp. 166–172, in which the decline of eighteenth-century Nonconformity is attributed largely to her theological colleges.

mean not dogmatic in the offensive sense of that term; but as the undoubted teaching of the Word of God. . . . We have no sympathy with any modern concealment or perversion of great gospel truths. We prefer Puritan to modern divinity. . . . We think it right to be informed of the ground and tactics of the adversaries of these main truths, in order to defend them when it is absolutely required, but not to be diverted from them."[1]

Yet it would be a great mistake to think that Spurgeon held that in the training of students a sound creed was everything. If the manner of instruction was to be dogmatic it was equally as important that it should be *fervent:* " Tutors should be what they wish their students to be; and what manner of men should ministers be ? They should thunder in preaching, and lighten in conversation; they should be flaming in prayer, shining in life, and burning in spirit. If they be not so, what can they effect ? If they be not spiritual Samsons how can the roaring lion be overcome ? How can the gates of hell be lifted from their hinges ?

" Provided that we know the truth and are confirmed in it by divine grace, it is yet no trifling work to pass on the heavenly treasure to those who are to become its guardians in the future. David had the ark of God in his land, but the Lord was not pleased with the manner of his moving it to its resting-place, and therefore, he made a breach upon him. The like may happen to us in handing over the truth of God to others: it is a delicate and difficult service.

[1] *Ibid.*, 1866, p. 136.

A man must first know the truth in his own soul before he can effectually transmit it to those who sit at his feet. Knowing it, he must live in the daily enjoyment of it. Only as the Holy Ghost over-shadows a man's mind can he influence other minds in a right manner. The spirit of the gospel must be in him as well as its doctrine."[1]

There is one final respect in which Spurgeon's views on theological training diverged from the conventional and prevailing outlook. He maintained that the all-controlling aim should be the preparation of powerful *preachers*. No matter what most other theological colleges might profess to have as their aim he saw that *in practice* the training they gave their students was not principally designed to make men mighty in the pulpit. Moreover Spurgeon, like one or two of his more clear-sighted contemporaries (notably John Angell James and Dr. John Campbell[2]), recognized the foremost cause of this state of affairs—it was the curse of " idolatry of intellect," the desire for academic prestige and the fear of losing intellectual respectability. By Spurgeon's day it had become fashionable for theological colleges to prepare students for London University degrees; he saw this for what it has proved to be—an invasion of the Church by the world, and an abandonment in practice of what should be the true aim of all ministerial training. Once let such procedure be adopted, and it is the death of the preparation of powerful preachers. Not that learning is a

[1] *Ibid.*, 1883, pp. 262–263.
[2] Cf. *The Banner of Truth*, 15th Issue, pp. 7–9.

hindrance to preaching, far from it; learning is essential to preaching, but *not* the kind of learning required by University degrees. " There is a learning that is essential to a successful ministry, viz. the learning of the whole Bible, to know God, by prayer, and experience of His dealings."[1]

Though he stood practically alone in this conviction, Spurgeon was ready to declare it in no uncertain terms: " Our men seek no Collegiate degrees, or classical honours,—though many of them could readily attain them; but to preach efficiently, to get at the heart of the masses, to evangelize the poor,— this is the College ambition, this and nothing else."[2] " The design of the Pastors' College has, from the beginning, been to help *preachers*, and not to produce *scholars*. Let the world educate men for its own purposes, and let the Church instruct men for its special service. We *aim* at helping men to set forth the truth of God, expound the Scriptures, win sinners, and edify saints."[3]

In an article in *The Sword and Trowel*[4] for January, 1866, George Rogers spoke clearly on this point, contrasting the aims of the Pastors' College with the prevailing tendencies of the age. " The literary attainments of our ministers, it has been said, must advance with the literature of the age. They must be prepared to stand in the foremost ranks of scholars and critics of their day. . . . A

[1] *Personal Reminiscences of C. H. Spurgeon*, W. Williams, p. 193.
[2] *Autobiography*, Vol. II, p. 149.
[3] *The Sword and Trowel*, 1889, p. 311.
[4] p. 42.

strong current, not of public opinion, but of effort on the part of the tutors and directors of our colleges, has of late years been accumulating in that direction. What has the result been ? Have the students that have passed through the new method of training been better preachers, more earnest, more eloquent ? Have they taken more commanding positions, and been more effective in their ministrations ? Have they more clearly and consistently interpreted and enforced the truths of God's Word ? We unhesitatingly answer, No !

" This effect, we grant, is not to be attributed to literature itself, but to the undue influence assigned it as a needful and primary element in the Christian teacher. Such a state of things might well lead us to pause, and to begin to think of retracing our steps, or at least to adopt some new method of collegiate training, better adapted to the real wants of the age."

In conclusion it is necessary for us to point out what connection all this has with this present book.

In 1865 Spurgeon originated an Annual Conference of the Pastors' College, to which all the pastors who had already been trained in the college were invited, the gathering being designed to provide a permanent bond of union between them. During his lifetime Spurgeon gave twenty-seven Presidential Addresses at the Conference, twelve of them being reprinted after his death in the form of this present book. In a Prefatory Note to the first edition it was stated that, " Mr. Spurgeon always regarded the Conference week as one of the most important in the whole year;

and he devoted much time, and thought, and care, and prayer, to the preparation of his Addresses to the hundreds of ministers and students who then gathered together from all parts of the kingdom."

Spurgeon, then, in preparing these Addresses could presuppose in his hearers a knowledge of the facts and principles we have narrated, for he was speaking to his sons in the faith—men who had been trained under his care. If he had been speaking to ministers who did not know his views on the foundation of *An All-Round Ministry* he would have found it necessary to say more, and had he been writing for ministers today doubtless he would have had some strong words to deliver on this theme. It is useless, he would have insisted, to expect ministers to be right, if the moulding influences which surround them in their student days are wrong! And if he felt theological colleges were failing in their aim a century ago what would he think of them now!

This book has some limitations from the fact that seventy years have passed since the last Address it contains was delivered.[1] Some allusions and illustrations are obviously out of date. But if the date of the book gives rise to some limitations, it also leads to some valuable benefits. The last thirty years of the nineteenth century witnessed a landslide in Evangelicalism; as Spurgeon wrote in 1887, " We are going down hill at break-neck speed."[2] If we

---

[1] The twelve Addresses in this book are printed in the order in which they were delivered—1872, 1874, 1875, 1877, 1880, 1881, 1882, 1886, 1887, 1888, 1889 and 1890.

[2] *The Sword and Trowel,* 1887, p. 122.

today are going to understand why the evangelical witness has reached such a low ebb, we need to go back to the last century and find out what happened. This book gives us many sidelights which will help us to do that, witness Spurgeon's remarks on the change of emphasis in Gospel preaching,[1] on aspects of " modern mission work,"[2] on the neglect of God's Sovereignty[3] and on the general decline in doctrinal purity. The last three chapters of this book were delivered while " The Down Grade "[4] controversy was at its height, and although the principles for which he then contended suffered a temporary eclipse, his " prophecy " on p. 360 is being fulfilled in our own times, " I am quite willing to be eaten of dogs for the next fifty years; *but the more distant future shall vindicate me.*" " It is in the truth that victory lies. In the long run it will beat policy; truth will beat superstition and overcome error "—*In Veritate Victoria !*

[1] p. 376.
[2] p. 297.
[3] p. 337.
[4] In 1887, Spurgeon, alarmed at the increasing spread of unbelief and heresy within the churches, called upon the Baptist Union for a declaration which would clearly state the beliefs of the denomination. As no such satisfaction was given, and Spurgeon's protests were regarded as unwarranted, he withdrew from the Union in October 1887. The Council of the Union in a " vote of censure " accepted his resignation and at the next annual meeting of the Union, on April 23, 1888, an overwhelming majority condoned the Council's action. This latter meeting is referred to by Spurgeon in a footnote on p. 282. " The Down Grade " was the name given by *The Sword and Trowel* to the landslide from orthodoxy; the controversy continued unabated till Spurgeon's death in 1892.

The greater part of this book, however, is not bounded by the historical setting. The spiritual factors necessary for a powerful ministry are as timeless as they were in the days of John Chrysostom, Hugh Latimer and George Whitefield. At a time when we are witnessing an increasing return to Reformed doctrine, there is great need for ministers and students to reconsider how this message should be preached again in converting power to the masses. There could hardly be a better guide on that point than C. H. Spurgeon.

IAIN MURRAY.

April, 1960.

FAITH.

NOW that the time has come for me to address you, my beloved brethren, may God Himself speak through me to you!

The subject which I have selected for this address is FAITH. As believers in Jesus, we are all of us of the pedigree of faith. Two lines of descent claim the covenant heritage. There is the line of nature, human efforts, and works, headed by Ishmael, the son of Hagar. We own no kindred there. We know that the highest position to which the child of the flesh can attain will only end in the command, "Cast out the bondwoman and her son: for the son of the bondwoman shall not be heir with the son of the freewoman." We, brethren, are children of the promise, born not after the flesh, nor according to the energy of nature, but by the power of God. We trace our new birth not to blood, nor to the will of the flesh, nor to the will of man, but to God alone. We owe our conversion neither to the reasoning of the logician nor to the eloquence of the orator, neither to our natural betterness nor to our personal efforts; we are, as Isaac was, the children of God's power according to the promise.

Now, to us the covenant belongs, for it has been decided—and the apostle has declared the decision in the name of God,—that "to Abraham and his seed were the promises made. He saith not, And to seeds, as of many; but as of one, And to thy seed, which is Christ. . . . And if ye be Christ's, then are ye Abraham's seed, and heirs according to the promise." —Gal. iii. 16, 29. We are altogether saved by faith. The brightest day that ever dawned upon us was the day in which we first "looked unto Him, and were lightened." It was all dark till faith beheld the Sun of Righteousness. The dawn of faith was to us the morning of life; by faith only we began to live. We have since then walked by faith. Whenever we have been tempted to step aside from the path of faith, we have been like the foolish Galatians, and we have smarted for our folly. I trust we have not "suffered so many things in vain."—Gal. iii. 4. We began in the Spirit, and if we have sought to be made perfect in the flesh, we have soon discovered ourselves to be sailing upon the wrong tack, and nearing sunken rocks. "The just shall live by faith," is a truth which has worked itself out in our experience, for often and often have we felt that, in any other course, death stares us in the face; and, therefore, "we through the Spirit wait for the hope of righteousness by faith."—Gal. v. 5.

Now, brethren, as our pedigree is of faith, and our claim to the privileges of the covenant is of faith, and our life in its beginning and continuance is all of faith, so may I boldly say that our ministry is of faith, too. We are heralds to the sons of men, not of the law of Sinai, but of the love of Calvary. We come to them, not with the command, "This do, and thou shalt live," but with the message, "Believe on the Lord Jesus Christ, and thou shalt be saved." Ours is the ministry of gracious faith, and is not after man, nor according to the law of a carnal commandment. We preach not man's merit, but Christ crucified.

The object of our preaching, as well as its doctrine, is faith; for we reckon that we have done nothing for sinners until, by the power of the Holy Ghost, we bring them to faith; and we only reckon that our preaching is useful to saints as we see them increase in faith. As faith is in our hand the power with which we sow, and as the seed we sow is received by us by faith, and steeped in faith, so the harvest for which we look is to see faith springing up in the furrows of men's hearts to the praise and glory of God.

Interwoven, therefore, with our entire spiritual life, and with all our ministerial work, is the doctrine and grace of faith; and, therefore, we must be very clear upon it,—that is a small business; we must be very strong in it,—that is the great matter. On that topic I will speak to you, praying earnestly that we may every one of us be, like Abraham, "strong in faith, giving glory to God," and, like Stephen, "full of faith and of the Holy Ghost."

Our work especially requires faith. If we fail in faith, we had better not have undertaken it; and unless we obtain faith commensurate with the service, we shall soon grow weary of it. It is proven by all observation that success in the Lord's service is very generally in proportion to faith. It certainly is not in proportion to ability, nor does it always run parallel with a display of zeal; but it is invariably according to the measure of faith, for this is a law of the Kingdom without exception, "According to your faith be it unto you." It is essential, then, that we should have faith if we are to be useful, and that we should have great faith if we are to be greatly useful. For many other reasons besides usefulness,—namely, even for our being able to hold our own against the enemies of the truth, and for ability to stand against the temptations which surround our office,—it is imperative upon us that we should have abundant confidence in the living God. We, above all men, need the mountain-moving faith, by which, in the old time, men of God " subdued kingdoms, wrought righteousness, obtained promises, stopped the mouths of lions, quenched the violence of fire, escaped the edge of the sword, out of weakness were made strong, waxed valiant in fight, turned to flight the armies of the aliens."

One of the brethren observed, at last night's meeting, that I confirmed you in the habit of saying, firstly, secondly, and thirdly. I must plead guilty to the charge, and follow the same method still; for I judge it to be no fault, but a practice helpful to the speaker in the arrangement and recollection of his thoughts, and profitable to the hearer in the remembrance of the sermon. We may risk being formal when to be formal is to be useful. Though not to be slavishly followed, the custom of announcing divisions in a discourse may be generally maintained, and we will maintain it, at any rate, to-day.

I.   I mean first to speak, concerning faith, under the head of this question,—WHEREIN AND UPON WHAT MATTERS HAVE WE, AS MINISTERS, FAITH, OR GREAT NEED OF IT?

First, we have *faith in God*. We believe " that He is, and that He is a rewarder of them that diligently seek Him." We do not believe in the powers of nature

operating of themselves apart from constant emana-
tions of power from the Great and Mighty One, who
is the Sustainer as well as the Creator of all things.
Far be it from us to banish God from His own universe. Neither do we believe in a merely nominal deity,
as those do who make all things to be God, for we
conceive pantheism to be only another form of
atheism. We know the Lord as a distinct personal
existence, a real God, infinitely more real than the
things which are seen and handled, more real even
than ourselves, for we are but shadows, *He* alone is
the I AM, abiding the same for ever and ever.

We believe in a God of purposes and plans, who has
not left a blind fate to tyrannize over the world, much
less an aimless chance to rock it to and fro. We are
not fatalists, neither are we doubters of providence
and predestination. We are believers in a God " who
worketh all things after the counsel of His own will."
We do not conceive of the Lord as having gone away
from the world, and left it and the inhabitants thereof
to themselves ; we believe in Him as continually pre-
siding in all the affairs of life. We, by faith, perceive
the hand of the Lord giving to every blade of grass its
own drop of dew, and to every young raven its meat.
We see the present power of God in the flight of
every sparrow, and hear His goodness in the song of
every lark. We believe that " the earth is the Lord's,
and the fulness thereof ; " and we go forth into it, not
as into the domains of Satan where light comes not,
nor into a chaos where rule is unknown, nor into a
boiling sea where fate's resistless billows shipwreck
mortals at their will ; but we walk boldly on,
having God within us and around us, living and

moving and having our being in Him, and so, by
faith, we dwell in a temple of providence and
grace wherein everything doth speak of His
glory. We believe in a present God wherever we
may be, and a working and operating God accom-
plishing His own purposes steadfastly and surely in
all matters, places, and times; working out His
designs as much in what seemeth evil as in that which
is manifestly good; in all things driving on in His
eternal chariot towards the goal which infinite wisdom
has chosen, never slackening His pace nor drawing
the rein, but for ever, according to the eternal strength
that is in Him, speeding forward without pause. We
believe in this God as being faithful to everything
that He has spoken, a God who can neither lie nor
change. The God of Abraham is the God and Father
of our Lord Jesus Christ, and He is our God this day.
We do not believe in the ever-shifting views of the
Divine Being which differing philosophies are
adopting; the God of the Hebrews is our God,—
Jehovah, Jah, the Mighty One, the covenant-keeping
God,—" this God is our God for ever and ever: He
will be our Guide even unto death."

Whether we be fools or not thus to believe in God,
the world shall know one day; and whether it be
more reasonable to believe in nature, or in powers
that operate of themselves, or to believe in nothing,
than it is to believe in a self-existent Being, we
shall leave eternity to decide. Meanwhile, to us,
faith in God is not only a necessity of reason, but the
fruit of a child-like instinct which tarries not to justify
itself by arguments, being born in us with our regenerate nature itself.

Next to this, our faith most earnestly and intensely fixes itself upon *the Christ of God*. We trust in Jesus; we believe all that inspired history says concerning Him; not making a myth of Him, or His life, but taking it as a matter of fact that God dwelt in very deed among men in human flesh, and that an atonement was really and truly offered by the Incarnate God upon the cross of Calvary. Yet, to us, the Lord Jesus Christ is not alone a Saviour of the past. We believe that " He ascended up on high," and " led captivity captive," and that " He ever liveth to make intercession for them that come unto God by Him." I saw, in the cathedral at Turin, a very remarkable sight, namely, the pretended graveclothes of the Lord Jesus Christ, which are devoutly worshipped by crowds of Romanists. I could not help observing, as I gazed upon these relics, that the ensigns of the death of Christ were all of Him that the Romish Church possessed. They may well show the true cross, for they crucify Him afresh; they may well pray in His sepulchre, for He is not there, or in their Church; and they may well claim His graveclothes, for they know only a dead Christ. But, beloved brethren, our Christ is not dead, neither has He fallen asleep; He still walks among the golden candlesticks, and holds the stars in His right hand.

Our faith in Jesus is most real. We believe in those dear wounds of His as we believe in nothing else; there is no fact so sure to us as that He was slain, and He has redeemed us to God by His blood. We believe in the brightness of His glory; for nothing seems to us so necessarily true as that He who was obedient unto death should, as His due reward, be

crowned with glory and honour. For this reason,
also, we believe in a real Christ yet to come, a second
time, in like manner as He went up into Heaven; and,
though we may not enquire minutely into times and
seasons, yet we are " looking for and hasting unto the
coming of the day of God," at which time we expect
the manifestation of the sons of God, and the rising of
their bodies from the tomb. Christ Jesus is no fiction
to us; and, with Dr. Watts, we sing,—

> " While Jews on their own law rely,
>   And Greeks of wisdom boast,
> We love th' incarnate mystery,
>   And there we fix our trust."

We have an equal confidence, beloved brethren, in
the Holy Spirit. We unfeignedly believe in His
Deity and personality. We speak of His influences,
because He has influences, but we do not forget that
He is a Person from whom those influences stream;
we believe in His offices, for He has offices, but we
rejoice in the Person who fills them, and makes them
effectual for our good. Devoutly would each one of
us say, " I believe in the Holy Ghost." Yet, my
brethren, do you believe in the Holy Ghost? " Yes,"
you say unanimously, spontaneously, and emphatically. " Yes," say I also; but be not grieved if I ask
you yet again if you verily and indeed believe in Him;
for there is a believing *and* a believing. There is a
believing which I have concerning a man, for which I
may have but slender grounds, and upon which I
would not risk a single penny of my substance; but
it is another form of believing in a man when I feel
that I could trust my very life with him, being assured
that he would be true to me, and prove both an able

and a willing helper. Have we such a reliance upon the Holy Ghost? Do we believe that, at this moment, He can clothe us with power, even as He did the apostles at Pentecost? Do we believe that, under our preaching, by His energy a thousand might be born in a day? If we all so believe, we are happy to be in such an assembly, for the majority of Christians, if under one sermon even a dozen persons were to cry out, " What must we do to be saved?" would exclaim exactly as the unbelieving Jews did, " These men are full of new wine." They would condemn the whole transaction as the result of dangerous excitement; they would never imagine it to be of the Lord. For this reason, I mournfully conclude that there is not, in the Church, such a belief in the Holy Ghost as there ought to be; and yet, as certainly as we hear the voice which saith, " Power belongeth unto God;" as surely as we hear the Divine voice of the Son, saying, " Ye believe in God, believe also in Me;" so truly does the third Person of the blessed Trinity claim our loving confidence, and woe be unto us if we vex Him by our unbelief! When we have a full faith in the Triune God, then shall we be " strong in the Lord, and in the power of His might."

Beside this, dear brethren, you and I believe in *the doctrines of the gospel*. We have received the certainties of revealed truth. These are things which are verily believed among us. We do not bow down before men's theories of truth, nor do we admit that theology consists in " views " and " opinions." We declare that there are certain verities,—essential, abiding, eternal,—from which it is ruinous to swerve. I am deeply grieved to hear so many ministers talk as if the truth of God were a variable quantity, a matter of daily formation, a nose of wax to be constantly re-shaped, a cloud driven by the wind. So do not I believe! I have been charged with being a mere echo of the Puritans, but I had rather be the echo of truth, than the voice of falsehood. It may be want of intellect which prevents our departing from the good old way; but even this is better than want of grace, which lies at the bottom of men's perpetual chopping and changing of their beliefs. Rest assured that there is nothing new in theology except that which is false; and that the facts of theology are to-day what they were eighteen hundred years ago.

But, in these days, the self-styled " men of pro-gress", who commenced with preaching the gospel, degenerate as they advance, and their divinity, like the snail, melts as it proceeds. I hope it will never be so with any of us. I have likened the career of certain divines to the journey of a Roman wine-cask from the vineyard to the city. It starts from the wine-press as the pure juice of the grape; but, at the first halting-place, the drivers of the cart must needs quench their thirst; and when they come to a foun-tain, they substitute water for the wine which they have drunk. In the next village, there are numbers of lovers of wine who beg or buy a little, and the dis-creet carrier dilutes it again. The watering is again and again repeated, till, on its entrance into Rome, the fluid is remarkably different from that which originally started from the vineyard. There is a way of " doctoring " the gospel in much the same manner. A little truth is given up, and then a little more, and men fill up the vacuum with opinions, inferences, speculations, and dreams, till their wine is mixed with water, and the water none of the best. Many preachers—and I speak it with sorrow,—have built a tower of theological speculations, upon which they sit, like Nero, fiddling the tune of their own philosophy while the world is burning with sin and misery. They are playing with the toys of speculation while men's souls are being lost.

Much of human wisdom is a mere coverlet for the absence of vital godliness. I went into railway carriages, of the first class in Italy, which were lined with very pretty crochet-work, and I thought the voyagers were highly honoured, since no doubt some delicate fingers had sumptuously furnished the cars for them; but I soon discovered that the crochet-work was simply put on to cover the grease and dirt of the cloth. A great deal of very pretty sentimentalism and religiousness that is now preached is a mere crochet-work covering for detestable heresies long since disproved, which dared not appear again without a disguise for their hideousness. With words of human wisdom, and speculations of their own invention, men disguise falsehood, and deceive many. Be it ours to give to the people what God gives to us. Be ye each of you as Micaiah, who declared, " As the Lord liveth, what the Lord saith unto me, that will I speak." If it be folly to keep to what we find in Scripture, and if it be madness to believe in verbal inspiration, we purpose to remain fools to the end of the chapter, and hope to be among·the foolish things of the world which God hath chosen to confound the wise, " that no flesh should glory in His presence."

Brethren, our faith also, resting upon the doctrines

of the gospel and upon the God of the gospel, embraces *the power of prayer*. We believe in the prevalence of supplication. I am afraid that this belief is going out of fashion in the so-called Christian world. The theory of some is, that prayer is useful to ourselves, but that it cannot be operative upon God; and much is said about the impossibility of the Divine purposes being changed, and the utter unlikelihood of a finite being affecting God by his cries. We also hold that the purposes of God are not changed; but what if prayer be a part of His purpose, and what if He ordains that His people should pray when He intends to give them blessings? Prayer is one of the necessary wheels of the machinery of providence. The offering of prayer is as operative in the affairs of the world, and the production of events, as the rise of dynasties or the fall of nations. We believe that God in very truth hearkens to the voices of men.

For my own part, if anyone should say to me now, " God does not hear prayer; such a notion is a piece of superstition;" I should reply to him, "Nay, sir, but with you I have no argument at all. The whole question is a personal one which concerns my own character,—am I an honest man or no? If I am a truth-speaking person, my testimony is worth receiving; and I solemnly declare that the Lord has heard and answered my prayers scores and hundreds of times, and that the answers have come so often and so singularly that they could not have been mere coincidences." I should not argue beyond this point, " Unless you are prepared to make me out to be a liar, you are as much bound to believe facts which I affirm that I have witnessed as I am to believe anything which you solemnly assert to be true."

Brethren, we ought not always to profess our ability to prove Scriptural truths to ungodly men, for many of those truths lie outside the region of their understanding. I should not try to prove to a blind man that the grass is green and the sky is blue, because he can have no idea of the proposition which I am proving. Argument in such a case is folly on both sides. To us, at any rate, prayer is no vain thing. We go to our chambers alone, believing that we are transacting high and real business when we pray. We do not bow the knee merely because it is a duty, and a commendable spiritual exercise; but because we believe that, into the ear of the eternal God, we speak our wants, and that His ear is linked with a heart feeling for us, and a hand working on our behalf. To us, true prayer is true power.

One other point, which I believe is essential to a minister's faith, is that we believe in *our own commission to preach the gospel*. If any brother here is not assured of his call to the ministry, let him wait till he is sure of it. He who doubts as to whether he is sent of God, goes hesitatingly; but he who is certain of his call from above demands and commands an audience; he does not apologize for his existence, or for his utterances; but he quits himself like a man, and boldly speaks God's truth in the Name of the Lord. He has a message to deliver which he must deliver, for woe is unto him unless he preaches the gospel! In the face of the Ritualists, who boast that they alone have the apostolical succession, we declare that ours is the true commission, and that their claim is false. We are not afraid to submit our claims to the test which the Lord Himself has appointed, "By their fruits ye shall know them." We believe that God has anointed us to preach the gospel, and we do preach it; but who will testify that these "priests" even so much as know the gospel? Under our word, the Spirit of God regenerates men, but He does not so work through these pretenders They do not even comprehend what regeneration is, but confound it with a ceremonial aspersion. Our gospel satisfies the heart, renews the nature, comforts the soul; but can these pretenders do so with their enchantments? If they be apostles, let them show us their signs. We claim to be the Lord's ministers, and our epistles of commendation are written upon many hearts.

Now, having detailed the great points of our faith, let me say, brethren, we believe, hence, on account of all this, that, notwithstanding the slenderness of our stores, *the Great Shepherd of the sheep will grant us an all-sufficiency with which to feed His people.* Believing in God All-sufficient, we expect to see our loaves and fishes multiplied; consequently, we do not lay by in store, but deal out at this present all that we have. I saw in Rome a fountain, which represented a man holding a barrel, out of which a copious stream of water was perpetually running. There never was much at any one time in that marble barrel, and yet it has continued to yield a stream for four or five hundred years. So let us pour forth from our very soul all that the Lord imparts to us. For twenty years and more, I have told out all I know, and have run dry every time, and yet my heart still bubbles up with a good matter. I know some brethren in the ministry

who are comparable to the great tun of Heidelberg
for capacity, and yet the people do not receive so
much gospel truth from them as from preachers of
very inferior capacity who have formed the habit of
giving out all they have. We believe that the Spirit
of God will be in us a well of water springing up unto
everlasting life, and we act according to that conviction. We do not expect to have much goods laid
up for many years ; but, as we live by daily bread, so
upon continually new supplies do we feed our people.
Away with the musty, worm-breeding stores of old
manna, and let us look up day by day for a fresh
supply !

Brethren, our faith discerns upon our side *unseen
agency*. While we are at work, God also is at work.
We do not reckon that the forces engaged upon our
side are confined to the pulpit ; we know that, all the
week long, God is, by care, and affliction, and trouble,
and sometimes by joy and consolation, making the
people ready to receive what He has charged us to
teach them. We look upon our congregations, and
perhaps are ready to cry in our unbelief, " Master,
what shall we do?" but our eyes are opened, and
we see horses of fire and chariots of fire round about
the prophet of the Lord ; mysterious agencies are co-
operating with the ministry of grace. When the
Mont Cenis Tunnel was being made, a party of
engineers worked from the Italian side for six years,
and expected at the end of that period to see an open
roadway through the mountain. They knew that the
work would take, at the rate they were going, twelve
years at least, and yet they knew it would be com-
pleted in six years, because there was another party,

on the French side, working to meet them; and, accordingly, in due time they met to an inch. I cannot understand these miracles of engineering, and do not know how two tunnelling parties manage to meet each other in the heart of an Alp; neither do I know how the Lord's work in men's consciences will fit in with mine, but I am quite sure it will, and, therefore, in faith, I go on working with all my might.

Faith leads us to believe in *difficulties being overruled to promote success.* Because we believe in God, and in His Holy Spirit, we believe that difficulties will be greatly sanctified to us, and that they are only placed before us as stepping-stones to grander results. We believe in defeats, my brethren; we believe in going back with the banner trailed in the mire, persuaded that this may be the surest way to lasting triumph. We believe in waiting, weeping, and agonizing; we believe in a non-success which prepares us for doing greater and higher work, for which we should not have been fitted unless anguish had sharpened our soul. We believe in our infirmities, and even glory in them; we thank God that we are not so eloquent as we could wish to be, and have not all the abilities we might desire, because now we know that " the excellency of the power " shall " be of God, and not of us." Faith enables us so to rejoice in the Lord that our infirmities become platforms for the display of His grace. Brethren, we believe that even our enemies shall, in God's hands, subserve our highest interests; they are yoked to the car of God. Perhaps, of all the powers which effect the Divine purposes in the world, no one does more than the devil himself. He is but a scullion in the Eternal's

kitchen; he unwillingly performs much work to which
the Lord would not put His own children, work which
is just as needful as that which seraphim perform.
Believe not that evil is a rival power of equal potency
with the good God. No, sin and death are, like the
Gibeonites, hewers of wood and drawers of water for
the Divine purposes; and, though they know it not,
when the Lord's enemies rave and rage most, they
fulfil His eternal purposes to the praise of the glory
of His wisdom and grace.

Further, brethren, we believe in *the gospel as God's
power to save.* We know that, for every case of
spiritual sickness, we have an infallible cure; we need
not say to any man, "We have no good news from
God for you." We believe that there is a way of getting at all hearts. There is a joint in every sinner's
harness, though he be an Ahab, and we may draw the
bow hopefully, praying the Lord to direct the arrow
through it. If we believe in God, nothing can be
too hard or too heavy for us. If I believe only in
myself, I feel that a hardened sinner may refuse
to listen to my reasoning, and may not be
moved by my affectionate address; but if I
believe in the Holy Ghost, I feel that He can
win a hearing, and carry conviction to the conscience.
We believe, brethren, in the power of truth. We
do not expect truth to be loved by all mankind; we
do not expect the gospel to become popular amongst
the great and the learned, for we remember that word
of the apostle, "Not many wise men after the flesh,
not many mighty, not many noble, are called;" but
we do not believe that the gospel has become decrepit
through old age. When the foolish wise men of this

age sneer at the old gospel, they render an uncon-
scious homage to its power. We do not believe that
our grand castle and defence has tottered and fallen
to the ground, because men say it is so. We recollect
Rab-shakeh, and how he reviled the Lord, and how,
nevertheless, it happened to the king of Assyria even
as the Lord said, "He shall not come into this city,
nor shoot an arrow there, nor come before it with
shield, nor cast a bank against it. By the way that he
came, by the same shall he return." We have seen
enough philosophies go back "to the vile dust from
whence they sprang," to know that the whole species
of them is of the order of Jonah's gourd. We, therefore, in confidence wait, and in patience bide our time.
We are sure of victory ere long.

If our gospel be true, it will yet come to the front,
and God will work for us; therefore are we "steadfast, unmovable, always abounding in the work of the
Lord." If we do not see souls saved to-day or to-
morrow, we will still work on. Ours is not the un-
requited toil of Sisyphus rolling uphill a stone which
will rebound upon us, nor that of the daughters of
Danaus who sought to fill a bottomless vessel. Our
work may no more quickly appear than the islands
which the coral insects are building below the blue
waves of the Southern sea; but the reef is rising, far
down the foundation of the massive structure is laid,
and its walls are climbing to the surface. We are
labouring for eternity, and we count not our work by
each day's advance, as men measure theirs; it is
God's work, and must be measured by His standard.
Be ye well assured that, when time, and things created,
and all that oppose themselves to the Lord's truth,

shall be gone, every earnest sermon preached, and every importunate prayer offered, and every form of Christian service honestly rendered, shall remain embedded in the mighty structure which God from all eternity has resolved to raise to His own honour.

II. Now, brethren, our second question will be, WHAT DOES OUR FAITH WORK IN US?

It works in us, first, *a glorious independence of man.* We are glad of earnest helpers, but we can do without them. We are grateful for our good deacons, but we dare not make flesh our arm. We are very glad if God raises up brethren in other churches who will fraternize with us, but we do not lean upon them. The man who believes in God, and believes in Christ, and believes in the Holy Ghost, will stay himself upon the Lord alone. He does not wish to be solitary, or to be singular, yet can he by himself contend for his Master; and when he has most human helps, he sedulously endeavours still to wait only upon God. If you lean upon your helpers when you have them, it may be that you will realize the terrible meaning of that ancient word, " Cursed be the man that trusteth in man, and maketh flesh his arm." As the apostle saith, " It remaineth, that both they that have wives be as though they had none ; " so may we say that it remaineth, that we who have zealous helpers be as though we had none, and to let our confidence in God be as simple, and our own selves be as free of all carnal confidence, as if we stood like Athanasius against the world, and had no one to speak a good word for us, or to bear a portion of our burden. God alone suffices to bear up yon unpillared firmament. He alone balances the clouds, and upbears them in the heavens. He kindles the lamps of night, and gives the sun his flames of fire. God alone is sufficient for us, and in His might we shall achieve the purpose of our being.

Further, true faith gives us *courage under all circumstances*. When young Nelson came home from a birds'-nesting expedition, his aunt chided him for being out so far into the night, and remarked, " I wonder fear did not make you come home." " Fear? " said Nelson, " I don't know him." That is a fitting speech for a believer when working for God. " Fear? I do not know it; what does it mean? " The Lord is on our side ; whom shall we fear? " If God be for us, who can be against us? " A minister stands trembling in the presence of a learned schoolmaster, who, with his twenty scholars, makes an important item in a village congregation ; but is that a consistent condition of heart for a prophet of the Lord? A preacher is all on a quiver because a person with a white cravat, under the gallery, looks like a minister, and probably is a London divine who is staying in the neighbourhood for his health ; is that trembling preacher a man? I say, a man! I will not ask, is he a man of God? If you have something of your own to say, my dear friend, do not try to say it when those learned people are present who can speak so much better than you can ; but if God has something to say through you, He knows which trumpet is most fit for Him to use ; and what matters it to you who may or may not be listening? Dare you play the coward in the presence of God? No. The conviction that you have a commission from God, and that the Spirit of the Lord is upon you, will make you very bold. Faith in God will cause us to honour our calling so much that we shall not dare to disgrace it by cowardice.

True faith in God will also make us *abundant in good works.* The eleventh of Hebrews is a chapter dedicated to the glorification of faith; but if I assert that it records the good works of the saints, can anybody contradict me? Is it not as much a record of works as of faith? Ay, verily, because where there is much faith, there shall surely ere long be abundant good works. I have no notion of that faith which does not produce good works, especially in the preacher. I question whether, as channels for damnation, Satan has upon earth more apt instruments for breeding infidelity, and for causing men to regard the gospel with contempt, than those who profess to believe it, and then act as though the belief were a matter of no consequence whatsoever.

Those philanthropists who are always telling us what ought to be done, and yet who do nothing,— what is their faith, and what is their philanthropy? To what shall I liken it? It reminds me of a shipwreck, off the Tuscan coast, some years ago. The Tuscan coastguard reported to his government that there had been a lamentable shipwreck on the coast, and he said, " Notwithstanding that I lent to the crew on board the ship every assistance possible *by means of my speaking-trumpet*, I regret to say that a number of bodies were washed upon the shore next morning, dead." Very wonderful, was it not? And yet this is the kind of assistance which many, who profess to have faith, have lent to the people. They have yielded them the assistance of rhetoric, flowers of speech, and poetical quotations, and yet men have

persisted in impenitence. There has been no real
care for souls. The sermon was preached, but the
people were not prayed for in secret, they were not
hunted for as men search for precious things. They
were not wept over; they were not in very deed cared
about. After all, it was the speaking-trumpet's help,
and nothing else.

But our faith makes us abundant in good works.
May I say to you, if you are doing all you possibly
can for Christ, endeavour to do yet more? I believe
a Christian man is generally right when he is doing
more than he can; and when he goes still further
beyond that point, he will be even more nearly right.
There are scarcely any bounds to the possibilities of
our service. Many a man, who now is doing little,
might, with the same exertion, do twice as much by
wise arrangement and courageous enterprise. For
instance, in our country towns, a sermon delivered on
the village green would, in all probability, be worth
twenty sermons preached in the chapel; and, in
London, a sermon delivered to a crowd in a public hall
or theatre may accomplish ten times as much good as
if it had fallen on the accustomed ears of our regular
auditors. We need, like the apostles, to launch out
into the deep, or our nets will never enclose a great
multitude of fishes. If we had but the pluck to come
out of our hiding-places, and face the foe, we should
soon achieve immense success. We need far more
faith in the Holy Ghost. He will bless us if we cast
ourselves entirely upon Him.

Faith in God enables many of you, I know right
well, *to bear much hardship, and exercise much self-
denial*, and yet to persevere in your ministry. My

heart rejoices over the many brethren here whom God has made to be winners of souls; and I may add that I am firmly persuaded, concerning many here present, that the privations they have undergone, and the zeal they have shown in the service of their Lord, though unrewarded by any outward success, are a sweet savour unto God. True faith makes a man feel that it is sweet to be a living sacrifice unto God. Only faith could keep us in the ministry, for ours is not a vocation which brings with it golden pay; it is not a calling which men would follow who desire honour and rank. We have all kinds of evils to endure, evils as numerous as those which Paul included in his famous catalogue of trials; and, I may add, we have one peril which he does not mention, namely, the perils of church-meetings, which are probably worse than perils of robbers. Underpaid and undervalued, without books and without congenial associates, many a rural preacher of the gospel would die of a broken heart, did not his faith gird him with strength from on high.

Well, brethren, to sum up a great many things in one, faith is to us *a great enlargement of our souls.* Men who are morbidly anxious to possess a self-consistent creed,—a creed which they can put together, and form into a square, like a Chinese puzzle,—are very apt to narrow their souls. Fancying that all truth can be comprehended in half-a-dozen formulæ, they reject as worthless every doctrinal statement which cannot be so comprehended. Those who will only believe what they can reconcile will necessarily disbelieve much of Divine revelation; they are, without knowing it, following the lead of the Rationalists.

Those who receive by faith anything which they find in the Bible will receive two things, twenty things, ay, or twenty thousand things, though they cannot construct a theory which harmonizes them all. That process of theory-making is an expensive folly, the invention of middle terms is a waste of ingenuity; it were far better to believe the truths, and leave the Lord to show their consistency.

Those who believe firmly are, moreover, the men who are *strong for service.* Have you ever seen the famous statue of the boy sitting down and picking a thorn out of his foot? I saw him twenty years ago, and I saw him again only the other day, and he was still extracting the little tormentor. I have known brethren of the same order in the ministry, they are always picking thorns out of their feet; they have a doubt about this, and a scruple about that; but the man who says, "I know whom I have believed, I know what I have experienced," he is the man who can run upon the Lord's errands.

Faith is also *our refreshment.* Our faith in God relieves us of our weariness. Even natural fatigue is sometimes overcome by faith. Certainly, faintness of spirit needs no better restorative than reliance upon God. Close to the Colosseum there stands the ruin of an ancient fountain and bath called the Meta Sudans. Here came the gladiators who escaped with life from the struggles of the amphitheatre; covered with blood, and begrimed with sweat and dust from the arena, they plunged into the bath, and felt delicious refreshment. Faith in God is just such a laver to our hearts.

III. My concluding question shall be, WHAT DOES OUR FAITH SAY TO US THIS MORNING?

First, *it claims to be well-founded*. I put it to you, brethren, in very simple words. Is the living God worth trusting? Does Omnipotence deserve that you should lean upon it? Does Omniscience warrant you in believing it? Does Immutability justify you in depending upon it? Why, if I were to bring here the best man of woman born whose name should be to you the synonym for virtue, and if I were to advise that you should trust him with your lives, I must speak with bated breath, for who shall trust in man? Ay, and if there stood here Gabriel, the angelic messenger of God, and he should tell us that he would zealously defend us, I might hesitate ere I said to you, " O sons of men, rest in angelic strength, and rely on seraphic zeal! " But when I speak of the Father, the Incarnate Son, the ever-blessed Spirit, who shall venture to hint a limit to our trust in God? What logician shall accuse us of folly in confiding in the Divine Trinity?

The older I grow, (and Mr. Rogers, who is much older, will agree with me, I am sure,) I feel more and more sure of the things which I believe, not merely (as some would insinuate) because I get into the habit of saying them, and therefore think I believe them, but because they tally with my soul's best experience. I read, occasionally, some of those productions of genius which are associated with the frothy religion of modern thought; but when my body is sick, or I am depressed in spirit, nothing suits my case but the gospel of our Lord and Saviour Jesus Christ, which was to our fathers the very truth of God; and I believe that the doctrine which a·man's innermost experience confirms to him in the day of trial, and in the day when he is nearest to God, is to him, at any rate, the very truth itself, and worthy of his credence.

I never feel, when I meet with intellectual men, who look down upon me as a mere preacher of platitudes, that they have any right to do so. To them I give place by subjection, no, not for an hour. I have rather to check a propensity to look down on them than to subdue any feeling of inferiority. To us, the truths of the gospel are absolute certainties for which we do not crave tolerance, but to which we demand submission. If any shall brand us with epithets, such as "bigot", "vulgar dogmatist", or "mere echo of departed Puritanism," (and all these have been used,) we will only reply, "You may apply to us what opprobrious titles you please, but we know that, if we were to express the truth about you, there is no adjective of contempt which you do not deserve ; and, therefore, because we know of no language sufficiently strong to set forth our abhorrence of your false doctrine, we will let you pass in silence."

My brethren, when you hear that a learned man has made a new discovery which contradicts the Scriptures, do not feel alarmed. Do not imagine that he is really a great man, but believe that he is just an educated idiot, or a self-conceited fool. If you find time to read the works of learned sceptics, you will soon see that their statements of fact are not reliable, their deductions are not logical, their inferences are monstrous, and their speculations are insane. I remember reading some statements of the great German, Oken, which to me sounded singularly like the babblings of Bethlehem Hospital. They reminded me of an incident which occurred when a prize was offered for verses of poetry, which were to be quite free from meaning. Two of the competitors were nearly equal, but in the poem of one of them there was the faintest glimmering of an idea, while the other had not even a trace of sense, and therefore gained the prize. I vote for the supremacy of the Neologians in that department, in sonorous nonsense, they excel. If I am thought to express myself too strongly, it must be so, for I believe I speak what God Himself would endorse; He applies no soft terms to boastful unbelievers. When He takes any notice of them at all, He calls them fools. You shall find that to be the expression which the Lord constantly uses concerning unbelievers in the Old Testament, and in the New, too: "Professing themselves to be wise, they became fools." And, brethren, when I hear my Heavenly Father say that a man is a fool, I dare not think him wise. Do not let us think otherwise than God does.

Though we may be confounded in argument, we cannot be confounded in experience, or driven from that which we have tasted and handled of the good Word of God. Neither are we confounded in our faith. We know that our faith is well-founded, and, therefore, we hear it say, "Do not treat me as if I were a dream. Do not deliver your message with bated breath. Tell it out boldly, for he who contradicts it is a liar!" If it be of God, it must be true. We are not adherents of an infallible church which founds its faith on its own authority, or of an infallible Pope who fancies himself to be the image of truth; if such were our boast, the world might well laugh us down; but, having learned God's truth by Divine revelation, we defy the world's sneer, and we do not

even say, "By your leave, gentlemen." No, but with
or without your leave, we will speak what God has
revealed to us.

Next, our faith asks us this question, "*Have I ever
deceived any one of you?*" I shall pass that enquiry
round. God put to His ancient people this question,
"Have I been a wilderness unto Israel?" And I
may ask you, Has the Lord ever failed you? Has He
turned His back upon you in the day of trouble; and,
when you have leaned upon His arm, has it proved
insufficient? If God has failed you, if His truth has
been a lie to any one of you, speak out now, and say
so; but if you could not, would not, must not, accuse
the Lord of unfaithfulness, but would loathe such a
thought because your experience would deny it, then,
brethren, go on to believe, and to believe more steadfastly; rest more implicitly on your ever-faithful God.

And so faith says, in the third place, "*Give me a
wider range. Trust your God far more.*" We have
only waded ankle-deep in faith as yet. We thought
the water very cold and chill when we timorously ventured in; but having tried it up to the ankles, we have
found it good and pleasant. Let us advance until
we are breast-deep, yea, and deeper. Blessed is that
man who gets his feet off the bottom, and swims in
the stream where he has no hope but his God, and no
confidence and no helper but the Invisible One who
sustaineth all things. Faith cries, "Trust me, my son,
to make you preach better. Have more enterprise.
Be more daring. Do not fight your own battle in the
church-meeting, leave it to your God; trust all with
Him. Do not be afraid to go and speak to that foul-
mouthed man; I will give you the right word to say to

him. Trust me, and go with prudence but with zeal into the darkest haunts of vice. Find out the worst of men, and seek their salvation. There is nothing you cannot do if you will but trust in God." Brother, your failure, if you fail, will begin in your faith. The air says to the eagle, "Trust me; spread thy broad wings; I will bear thee up to the sun. Only trust me. Take thy foot from off yon rock which thou canst feel beneath thee. Get away from it, and be buoyed up by the unseen element." My brethren, eaglets of Heaven, mount aloft, for God invites you. Mount! You have but to trust Him. An unknown glory rests upon Him, and the radiance thereof shall come upon you if you only know how to trust Him.

And then faith says, (and with that I shall close,) "*Feed me! Feed me!*" Faith has been everything to you; feed her upon the Bread of Heaven. Faith feeds on Christ. The other day, I saw a group of lovely ferns in a grotto from the roof of which continually distilled a cool, clear, crystal rain; those ferns were perpetually fresh and beautiful, because their leaves were constantly bathed in the refreshing drops. Although it was at a season when verdure was scant, those ferns were as verdant as possible. I observed to the friend who was with me that I would wish to live in the everlasting drip of grace, perpetually laved, and bathed, and baptized in the overflowing of Divine fellowship. This makes a man full of faith. You do not wonder if Moses had faith, for he had been forty days upon the mount with God; and if we have communed with God, it shall be a marvel if we doubt, and not that we believe. Feed faith with the truth of God, but especially with Him who is *the* Truth.

I pray the Lord to endow this College with faith. May we be both established and endowed,—established on a rock, and endowed with the blessings of the covenant of grace! Remember, brethren, that you and I are committed to faith now; it is too late for us to retire. We are in the condition of Bunyan's pilgrim; *we must go forward*. There are many perils before us, the Valley of the Shadow of Death lies on ahead; arrows will fly very thickly around us as we traverse its shades. 'Tis hard going on, but we cannot retrace our steps, for we have no armour for our backs. Suppose we should take to reasoning, suppose we should give up the fundamentals of our faith, what would remain to us? For my part, I should have nothing beneath the sun to do but to take the rope of Judas, and to end a miserable life, for only my faith makes it worth my while to live. If faith were gone, I would entreat permission to expire; to be extinct, were better than to live if these things be but a delusion after all. It must be onward with us, for in the case of brethren of this College, the most unsafe thing for us is to think of turning back. One or two of our former comrades have gone aside from us; I cannot judge their hearts, but I fear they have also gone aside from God. I will not say more of them than this,—they are the last men you would envy if you knew their whole history. If any men bear upon them, even in this life, the evident mark of God's disapprobation, it must be those who have known the truth, and defended it, and yet, for lucre's sake, or ambition's sake, have turned aside from it. If it were fitting, I could write narratives of apostate experiences which would harrow up your feelings, and they would relate to men into whose faces I have looked as I now look into yours, and who were familiar with me, but with whose names, once well-beloved, I am ashamed now to be associated. God have mercy upon them! It is all that I could say if I had to write their epitaphs, " God have mercy upon them! "

Well, brethren, you and I are committed to the onward course, we cannot go back; neither can we turn to the right hand or to the left. What shall we do, then? Shall we lie down, and fret? Shall we stand still, and be dismayed? No! In the Name of the Lord, let us again set up our banner, the royal standard of Jesus the Crucified. Let us sound the trumpets joyously, and let us march on, not with the trembling footsteps of those who know that they are bent upon an enterprise of evil, but with the gallant bearing of men whose cause is Divine, whose warfare is a crusade. Courage, my brethren; behold, the angels of God fly in our front, and, lo, the eternal God Himself leads our van. " The Lord of hosts is with us; the God of Jacob is our refuge." " Therefore will not we fear, though the earth be removed, and though the mountains be carried into the midst of the sea." Blessed faith! God grant us more of it, for Christ's sake! Amen.

"FORWARD!"

BRETHREN, the substance of my address, this morning, will be found in the words of God to His servant Moses, "*Speak unto the children of Israel, that they go forward*." "Forward" is the watchword of our Conference, let it ring through your ranks. Onward, ye elect of God! Victory is before you; your very safety lies in that direction. To retreat is to perish. You have most of you read the story of the boy, in an American village, who climbed the wall of the famous Natural Bridge, and cut his name in the rock above the initials of his fellows, and then became suddenly aware of the impossibility of descending. Voices shouted, "Do not look down, try and reach the top." His only hope was to go right up, up, up, till he landed on the top. Upward was terrible, but downward was destruction. Now, we, dear brethren, are all of us in a like condition. By the help of God, we have cut our way to positions of usefulness; and to descend is death. To us, forward means upward; and therefore forward and upward let us go. While we prayed, this morning, we committed ourselves beyond all recall. We did that most heartily when we first preached the gospel, and publicly declared, "I am my Lord's, and He is mine." We put our hand to the plough then; thank God, we have not looked back yet, and we must never do so.

The only course open to us is to plough right on to the end of the furrow, and never think of leaving the field till the Master shall call us home. But this morning you committed yourselves again to the Lord's work; you did not deliberate, or consult with flesh and blood; but you plunged right in, renouncing all for Jesus; and except ye be reprobates, ye have enlisted for life in His service. You are the branded servants of Christ, bearing in your bodies His mark. You have now no liberty to serve another, you are the sworn soldiers of the Crucified. Forward is your only way; you are shut up to it. You have no armour for your backs; and whatever dangers lie in front, there are ten thousand times as many behind. It is onward or nothing; nay, onward or dishonour; onward or death.

We were compared, last night, in the eloquent address of our friend Mr. Gange, to the little army of Sir Garnet Wolseley marching to Coomassie; and the parallel was very beautifully worked out in all respects. Fellow-soldiers, we are few, and we have a desperate fight in the bush before us, therefore it is needful that every man should be made the most of, and nerved to his highest point of strength. It is desirable that you should be the picked men of the Church, yea, of the entire universe, for such the age demands, therefore it is as to yourselves that I am most concerned that you should go forward. You must go forward in personal attainments, growing in gifts and in grace, in fitness for the work of God, and conformity to the image of Jesus. The points I shall speak upon begin at the bottom, and ascend.

I. First, dear brethren, I think it necessary to say

to myself and to you that we must GO FORWARD IN
OUR MENTAL ACQUIREMENTS.

It will never do for us to continually present ourselves to God at our worst. We are not worth His
having at our best; but, at any rate, let not the offering be maimed and blemished by our idleness. " Thou
shalt love the Lord thy God with all thy heart " is,
perhaps, more easy to comply with than to love Him
with all our mind; yet we must give Him our mind as
well as our affections, and that mind should be well
furnished, that we may not offer Him an empty casket.
Our ministry demands mind. I shall not insist upon
that phrase which is so frequently heard nowadays,
" the enlightenment of the age; " still, it is quite certain that there is a great educational advance among all
classes, and that there will be much more of it. The
time is past when ungrammatical speech sufficed for a
preacher. Even in a country village, where, according
to tradition, " nobody knows nothing," the schoolmaster is now abroad, and want of education will
hinder usefulness more than it once did; for, when
the speaker wishes his audience to remember the
gospel, they, on the other hand, will remember his ungrammatical expressions, and will repeat them as a
theme of jest, when we could have wished they had
rehearsed the gospel of Jesus Christ one to another in
solemn earnest.

Dear brethren, we must cultivate ourselves to the
highest possible point, and do this, first, by gathering
in knowledge that we may fill the barn; then, by
acquiring discrimination that we may winnow the
heap; and, lastly, by a firm retentiveness of mind,
which lays up the winnowed grain in the storehouse.

The three points may not be equally important, but they are necessary to a complete man.

We must, I say, first, *make great efforts to acquire information, especially of a Biblical kind*. We must not confine ourselves to one topic of study, or we shall not exercise our whole mental manhood. God made the world for man, and made man with a mind intended to occupy and use all the world; he is the tenant, and nature is for a while his house; why should he shut himself out of any of its rooms? Why refuse to taste any of the cleansed meats the great Father has put upon the table? Still, our main business is to study the Scriptures. The smith's main business is to shoe horses; let him see that he knows how to do it, for should he be able to belt an angel with a girdle of gold, he will fail as a smith if he cannot make and fix a horseshoe. It is a small matter that you should be able to write the most brilliant poetry,—as possibly you could,—unless you can preach a good and telling sermon, which will have the effect of comforting saints and convincing sinners. Study the Bible, dear brethren, through and through, with all helps that you can possibly obtain. Remember that the appliances now within the reach of ordinary Christians are much more extensive than they were in our father's days, and therefore you must be greater Biblical scholars if you would keep in front of your hearers. Intermeddle with all knowledge; but, above all things, meditate day and night in the law of the Lord.

Be well instructed in theology, and do not regard the sneers of those who rail at it because they are ignorant of it. Many preachers are not theologians, and hence the mistakes which they make. It cannot do any hurt to the most lively evangelist to be also a sound theologian, and it may often be the means of saving him from gross blunders. Nowadays, we hear men tear a single sentence of Scripture from its connection, and cry, " Eureka! Eureka! " as if they had found a new truth; and yet they have not discovered a diamond, but only a piece of broken glass. Had they been able to compare spiritual things with spiritual, had they understood the analogy of the faith, and had they been acquainted with the holy learning of the great Bible students of past ages, they would not have been quite so fast in vaunting their marvellous knowledge. Let us be thoroughly well acquainted with the great doctrines of the Word of God, and let us be mighty in expounding the Scriptures. I am sure that no preaching will last so long, or build up a church so well, as the expository. To renounce altogether the hortatory discourse for the expository, would be running to a preposterous extreme; but I cannot too earnestly assure you that, if your ministries are to be lastingly useful, you must be expositors. For this purpose, you must understand the Word yourselves, and be able so to comment upon it that the people may be built up by the Word. Be masters of your Bibles, brethren; whatever other works you have not searched, be at home with the writings of the prophets and apostles. " Let the Word of God dwell in you richly."

Having given that the precedence, neglect no field of knowledge. The presence of Jesus on the earth has sanctified the whole realm of nature; and what He has cleansed, call not you common. All that your Father has made is yours, and you should learn from it. You may read a naturalist's journal, or a traveller's narrative of his voyages, and find profit in it. Yes, and even an old herbal, or a manual of alchemy may, like Samson's dead lion, yield you honey. There are pearls in oyster shells, and sweet fruits on thorny boughs. The paths of true science, especially natural history and botany, drop fatness. Geology, so far as it is fact, and not fiction, is full of treasures. History —wonderful are the visions which it makes to pass before you,—is eminently instructive; indeed, every portion of God's dominion in nature teems with precious teachings. Intermeddle with all knowledge, according as you have the time, the opportunity, and the peculiar faculty; and do not hesitate to do so because of any apprehension that you will educate yourselves up to too high a point. When grace abounds, learning will not puff you up, or injure your simplicity in the gospel. Serve God with such education as you have, and thank Him for blowing through you if you are a ram's horn, but if there be a possibility of your becoming a silver trumpet, choose it rather.

I said that, next, we must *learn always to discriminate between things that differ;* and at this particular time, this point needs insisting on very emphatically. Many run after novelties, charmed with every new thing; learn to judge between truth and its counterfeits, and you will not be led astray. Others adhere to old teachings, like limpets stick to the rock; and yet these may only be ancient errors: wherefore, " prove all things," and " hold fast that which is good." The use of the sieve and the winnowing fan, is much to be commended. A man who has asked the Lord to give him clear eyes, by which he

shall see the truth, and discern its bearings, and who,
by reason of the constant exercise of his faculties, has
obtained an accurate judgment, is one fit to be a
leader of the Lord's host; but all ministers are not
thus qualified. It is painful to observe how many
embrace anything it if be but earnestly brought before
them. They swallow the medicine of every spiritual
quack who has enough of brazen assurance to appear
to be sincere. I say to you, as Paul wrote to the
Corinthians, " Brethren, be not children in understanding; " test everything that claims your faith.
Ask the Holy Spirit to give you the faculty of discern-
ing between good and evil, so shall you conduct your
flocks far from poisonous meadows, and lead them
into safe pasturage.

But then, if you have the power to acquire knowledge, and also to discriminate, seek next for *ability
to retain and hold firmly what you have learned.*
Alas! in these times, certain men glory in being
weathercocks; they hold fast nothing; they have, in
fact, nothing worth the holding. They believed yesterday, but not that which they believe to-day, nor
that which they will believe to-morrow; and he would
be a greater prophet than Isaiah who should be able
to tell what they will believe when next the moon
doth fill her horns, for they are constantly changing,
and seem to have been born under that said moon,
and to partake of her changing moods. These men
may be as honest as they claim to be, but of what use
are they? Like good trees oftentimes transplanted,
they may be of a noble nature, but they bring forth
nothing; their strength goes out in rooting and re-
rooting, they have no sap to spare for fruit. Be sure

you have the truth, and then be sure you hold it. Be
ready for fresh truth, if it be truth ; but be very chary
how you subscribe to the belief that a better light has
been found than that of the sun. Those who hawk new
truth about the street, as the boys do a new edition
of the evening paper, are usually no better than they
should be. The fair maid of truth does not paint her
cheeks and tire her head, like Jezebel, following every
new philosophic fashion ; she is content with her own
native beauty, and in her aspect she is the same yesterday, and to-day, and for ever.

When men change often, they generally need to be
changed in the most emphatic sense. Our "modern
thought" gentry are doing incalculable mischief to
the souls of men. Immortal souls are being damned,
yet these men are spinning theories. Hell gapes
wide, and with her open mouth swallows up myriads,
yet those who should spread the tidings of salvation
are "pursuing fresh lines of thought." Highly-cul-
tured soul-murderers will find their boasted "culture"
to be no excuse in the day of judgment. For God's
sake, let us know how men are to be saved, and get to
the work ; to be for ever deliberating as to the proper
mode of making bread while a nation dies of famine,
is detestable trifling. It is time we knew what to
teach, or else renounced our office. "Ever learning,
and never able to come to the knowledge of the
truth," is the motto of the worst rather than of the
best of men. Are they to be our model? "I shape
my creed every week," was the confession of one of
these divines to me. Whereunto shall I liken such
unsettled ones? Are they not like those birds which
frequent the Golden Horn, and are to be seen from

Constantinople, of which it is said that they are always on the wing, and never rest? No one ever saw them alight on the water or on the land, they are for ever poised in mid-air. The natives call them " lost souls " —seeking rest and finding none ; and, methinks, men who have no personal rest in the truth, if they are not themselves unsaved, are, at least, very unlikely to be the means of saving others. He who has no assured truth to tell must not wonder if his hearers set small store by what he says. We must know the truth, understand it, and hold it with firm grip, or we cannot be of service to the sons of men. Brethren, I charge you, seek to know, and, knowing, to discriminate ; having discriminated, I charge you to " hold fast that which is good." Keep in constant operation the three processes of filling the barn, winnowing the grain, and storing it in granaries, so shall you mentally " go forward."

II. We also need to GO FORWARD IN ORATORICAL QUALIFICATIONS.

I am beginning at the bottom, but all these matters are important, for it is a pity that even the feet of this image should be of clay. Nothing is trifling which can be of any service to our grand design. Only for want of a nail the horse lost its shoe, and so became unfit for the battle ; that shoe was only a trifling rim of iron which smote the ground, and yet the neck clothed with thunder was of no avail when the shoe was gone. A man may be irretrievably ruined for spiritual usefulness, not because he fails either in character or spirit, but because he breaks down mentally or oratorically ; and, therefore, I again remark that we must improve in utterance.

It is not every one of us who can speak as some can do, and even these men cannot speak up to their own ideal. If there be any brother here who thinks he can preach as well as he should, I would advise him to leave off altogether. If he did so, he would be acting as wisely as the great painter who broke his palette, and, turning to his wife, said, " My painting days are over, for I have satisfied myself, and therefore I am sure my power is gone." Whatever other perfection may be attainable, I am certain that he who thinks he has gained perfection in oratory mistakes volubility for eloquence, and verbiage for argument. Whatever you may know, you cannot be truly efficient ministers if you are not " apt to teach." You are probably all acquainted with ministers who have mistaken their calling, and evidently have no gifts for preaching ; make sure that none think the same of you. There are brethren in the ministry whose speech is intolerable ; either they dun you to death, or else they send you to sleep. No chloral can ever equal their discourse in sleep-giving properties. No human being, unless gifted with infinite patience, could long endure to listen to them, and nature does well to give the victim deliverance through sleep. I heard one say, the other day, that a certain preacher had no more gifts for the ministry than an oyster, and in my own judgment this was a slander on the oyster, for that worthy bivalve shows great discretion in his openings, and he also knows when to close. If some men were sentenced to hear their own sermons, it would be a righteous judgment upon them ; but they would soon cry out with Cain, " My punishment is greater than I can bear." Let us not fall under the same condemnation through any faults in our preaching which we can remedy.

Brethren, *we should cultivate a clear style.*   When a man does not make me understand what he means, it is because he does not himself know what he means. An average hearer, who is unable to follow the course of thought of the preacher, ought not to worry himself, but to blame the preacher, whose business it is to make the matter clear.   If you look down into a well, if it be empty, it will appear to be very deep ; but if there be water in it, you will see its brightness. I believe that many " deep " preachers are simply so because they are like dry wells with nothing whatever in them, except decaying leaves, a few stones, and perhaps a dead cat or two.   If there be living water in your preaching, it may be very deep, but the light of the truth will give clearness to it.   At any rate, labour to be plain, so that the truths you teach may be easily received by your hearers.

We must cultivate a *cogent* as well as a clear style ; we must be forceful.   Some imagine that this consists in speaking loudly, but I can assure them they are in error.   Nonsense does not improve by being bellowed. God does not require us to shout as if we were speaking to three millions when we are only addressing three hundred.   Let us be forcible by reason of the excellence of our matter, and the energy of spirit which we throw into the delivery of it.   In a word, let our speaking be *natural* and living.   I hope we have forsworn the tricks of professional orators, the strain after effect, the studied climax, the prearranged pause, the theatrical strut, the mouthing of words, and I know not what besides, which you may see in certain

pompous divines who still survive upon the face of the
earth. May such preachers become extinct animals
ere long, and may a living, natural, simple way of
talking out the gospel be learned by us all; for I am
persuaded that such a style is one which God is likely
to bless.

Among many other things, we must cultivate *persuasiveness*. Some of our brethren have great influence over men, and yet others with greater gifts are
devoid of it; these last do not appear to get near to
the people, they cannot grip them, and make them
feel. There are preachers who, in their sermons, seem
to take their hearers one by one by the buttonhole,
and drive the truth right into their souls, while others
generalize so much, and are withal so cold, that one
would think they were speaking to dwellers in some
remote planet, whose affairs did not much concern
them. Learn the art of pleading with men. You
will do this well if you often see the Lord. If I
remember rightly, the old classic story tells us that,
when a soldier was about to kill Darius, his son, who
had been dumb from his childhood, suddenly cried out
in surprise, " Know you not that he is the king? "
His silent tongue was unloosed by love to his father,
and well may ours also find earnest speech when the
Lord is seen by us crucified for sin. If there be any
speech in us, this will arouse it. The knowledge of
" the terror of the Lord " should also bestir us to persuade men. We cannot do other than plead with
them to be reconciled to God. Brethren, mark those
who woo sinners to Jesus, find out their secret, and
never rest till you obtain the same power. If you find
them very simple and homely, yet if you see them

really useful, say to yourself, " That method will do for me ; " but if, on the other hand, you listen to a preacher who is much admired, and on enquiry you find that no souls are savingly converted under his ministry, say to yourself, " This style is not the thing for me, for I am not seeking to be great, but to be really useful."

Let your oratory, therefore, constantly improve in clearness, cogency, naturalness, and persuasiveness. Try, dear brethren, to get such a style of speaking that you *suit yourselves to your audiences.* Much lies in that. The preacher, who should address an educated congregation in the language which he would use in speaking to a company of costermongers, would prove himself a fool ; and, on the other hand, he who goes down amongst miners and colliers, with technical theological terms and drawing-room phrases, acts like an idiot. The confusion of tongues at Babel was more thorough than we imagine. It did not merely give different languages to great nations, but it made the speech of each class to vary from that of others. A fellow of Billingsgate cannot understand a fellow of Brasenose. Now, as the costermonger cannot learn the language of the College, let the collegian learn the language of the costermonger. " We use the language of the market," said Whitefield, and this was much to his honour ; yet, when he stood in the drawing-room of the Countess of Huntingdon, and his speech entranced the infidel noblemen whom she brought to hear him, he adopted another style. His language was equally plain in each case, because it was equally familiar to his audience ; but he did not use the *ipsissima verba*, else his speech would have lost its plainness in the one case or the other, and would either have been slang to the nobility or Greek to the crowd. In our modes of speech, we should aim at being "all things to all men." He is the greatest master of oratory who is able to address any class of people in a manner suitable to their condition, and likely to touch their hearts.

Brethren, let none excel us in power of speech; let none surpass us in the mastery of our mother-tongue. Beloved fellow-soldiers, our tongues are the swords which God has given us to use for Him, even as it is said of our Lord, "Out of His mouth went a sharp twoedged sword." Let these swords be sharp. Cultivate your powers of speech, and be amongst the foremost in the land for utterance. I do not exhort you to this because you are remarkably deficient; far from it, for everybody says to me, "We know your College men by their plain, bold speech." This leads me to believe that you have the gift largely in you, and I beseech you to take pains to perfect it.

III. Brethren, we must be even more earnest to GO FORWARD IN MORAL QUALITIES.

Let the points I shall mention here come home to those who shall require them, but I assure you I have no special persons among you in my mind's eye. We desire to rise to the highest style of ministry; but even if we obtain the mental and oratorical qualifications I have mentioned, we shall fail, unless we also possess high moral qualities. There are evils which we must shake off, as Paul shook the viper from his hand, and there are virtues which we must gain at any cost. *Self-indulgence* has slain its thousands. Let us tremble lest we perish by the hands of this Delilah.

Let us have every passion and habit under due restraint; if we are not masters of ourselves, we are not fit to be leaders in the Church of Christ.

We must also put away all notion of *self-importance.* God will not bless the man who thinks himself great. To glory even in the work of God the Holy Spirit in yourself, is to tread dangerously near to *self-adulation.* "Let another man praise thee, and not thine own mouth," and be very glad when that other has sense enough to hold his tongue.

We must also *have our tempers well under restraint.* A vigorous temper is not altogether an evil. Men who are as easy as an old shoe are generally of as little worth. I would not say to you, "Dear brethren, have a temper;" but I do say, "If you have one, control it carefully." I thank God when I see a minister have temper enough to be indignant at wrong, and to be firm for the right; still, temper is an edged tool, and often cuts the man who handles it. "Gentle, and easy to be entreated," preferring to bear evil rather than inflict it, this is to be our spirit. If any brother here naturally boils over too soon, let him mind that, when he does do so, he scalds nobody but the devil, and then let him boil away as fast as he likes.

We must—some of us especially must—*conquer our tendency to levity.* A great distinction exists between holy cheerfulness, which is a virtue, and that general levity, which is a vice. There is a levity which has not enough heart to laugh, but trifles with everything; it is flippant, hollow, unreal. A hearty laugh is no more levity than a hearty cry. I speak of that religious veneering which is pretentious, but thin, superficial, insincere about the weightiest matters. Godliness is no jest, nor is it a mere form. Beware of being actors. Never give earnest men the impression that you do not mean what you say, and are mere professionals. To be burning at the lip, and freezing at the soul, is a mark of reprobation. God deliver us from being either superfine or superficial; may we never be the butterflies of the garden of God!

At the same time, we should *avoid everything like the ferocity of bigotry.* There are religious people about, who, I have no doubt, were born of a woman, but they appear to have been suckled by a wolf. I have done them no dishonour by that comparison, for were not Romulus and Remus, the founders of the city of Rome, nourished in that fashion? Some warlike men of this order have had power to found dynasties of thought; but human kindness and brotherly love consort better with the Kingdom of Christ. We are not to be always going about the world searching out heresies, like terrier dogs sniffing for rats, and to be always so confident of our own infallibility that we erect ecclesiastical stakes at which to roast all who differ from us, not, 'tis true, with faggots of wood, but with those coals of juniper, which consist of strong prejudice and cruel suspicion.

In addition to all this, there are mannerisms, and moods, and ways, which I cannot now describe, against which we must struggle, for little faults may often be the source of failure, and to get rid of them may be the secret of success. Count nothing little which makes you even a little more useful; cleanse out from the temple of your soul the seats of them that sell doves as well as the traffickers in sheep and oxen.

And, dear brethren, we must acquire certain moral faculties and habits, as well as put aside their opposites. He will never do much for God who has not *integrity of spirit*. If we be guided by policy, if there be any mode of action for us but that which is straightforward, we shall make shipwreck before long. Resolve, dear brethren, that you can be poor, that you can be despised, that you can lose life itself, but that you cannot do a crooked thing. For you, let the only policy be honesty.

May you also possess *the grand moral characteristic of courage!* By this, I do not mean impertinence, impudence, or self-conceit; but real courage to do and say calmly the right thing, and to go straight on at all hazards, though there should be none to give you a good word. I am astonished at the number of Christians who are afraid to speak the truth to their brethren. I thank God that I can say this,—there is no member of my church, no officer of the church, and no man in the world, to whom I am afraid to say before his face what I would say behind his back. Under God, I owe my position in my own church to the absence of all policy, and the habit of always saying what I mean. The plan of making things pleasant all round is a perilous as well as a wicked one. If you say one thing to one man, and another to another, they will one day compare notes, and find you out, and then you will be despised. The man of two faces will sooner or later be the object of contempt, and justly so. Now, above all things, avoid that. If you have anything that you feel you ought to say about a man, let the measure of what you say be this, " How much dare I say to his face?" We must not allow ourselves a word more than that in censure of any man living. If that be your rule, your courage will save you from a thousand difficulties, and win you lasting respect.

Having the integrity and the courage, dear brethren, may you be gifted with *an unconquerable zeal!* Zeal, —what is it? How shall I describe it? Possess it, and you will know what it is. Be consumed with love for Christ, and let the flame burn continuously; not flaming up at public meetings, and dying out in the routine work of every day. We need indomitable perseverance, dogged zeal, and a combination of sacred obstinacy, self-denial, holy gentleness, and invincible courage.

Excel also in one power, which is both mental and moral, namely, *the power of concentrating all your forces upon the work to which you are called*. Collect your thoughts, rally all your faculties, mass your energies, focus your capacities. Turn all the springs of your soul into one channel, causing it to flow onward in an undivided stream. Some men lack this quality. They scatter themselves, and therefore fail. Mass your battalions, and hurl them upon the enemy. Do not try to be great at this, and great at that,—to be " everything by starts, and nothing long; " but suffer your entire nature to be led in captivity by Jesus Christ, and lay everything at His dear feet who bled and died for you.

IV. Above all these things, we need to GO FORWARD IN SPIRITUAL QUALIFICATIONS, the graces which must be wrought in us by the Holy Spirit Himself. This is the main matter, I am sure. Other things are precious, but this is priceless.

We need, first, *to know ourselves.* The preacher should be well acquainted with the science of the heart, the philosophy of inward experience. There are two schools of experience, and neither is content to learn from the other; let us be willing, however, to learn from both. The one school speaks of the child of God as one who knows the deep depravity of his heart, who understands the loathsomeness of his nature, and daily feels that in his flesh there dwelleth no good thing. "That man has not the life of God in his soul," say the men of this school, "who does not know and feel this, and feel it by bitter and painful experience from day to day." It is in vain to talk to them about liberty, and joy in the Holy Ghost; they will not have it. Yet let us learn from these one-sided brethren. They know much that should be known, and woe to that minister who ignores their set of truths! Martin Luther used to say that temptation is the best teacher for a minister. There is truth on that side of the question.

Believers of another school dwell much—and rightly and blessedly so—upon the glorious work of the Spirit of God. They believe in the Spirit of God as a cleansing power, sweeping the Augean stable of the soul, and making it into a temple for God. But frequently they talk as if they had ceased to sin, or to be annoyed by temptation; they glory as if the battle were already fought, and the victory won. Yet let us also learn what we can from these brethren. All the truth they can teach us, let us know. Let us become familiar with the hilltops of salvation, and the glory that shines thereon,—the Hermons and the Tabors, where we may be transfigured with our Lord. Do not

be afraid of ever growing too holy, or of being too full
of the Holy Spirit.

I would have you wise on all sides, and able to deal
with man both in his conflicts and in his joys, as one
who is familiar with both experiences. Know where
Adam left you; know where the Spirit of God has
placed you. Do not know either of these things so
exclusively as to forget the other. I believe that, if
any men are likely to cry, "O wretched man that I
am! who shall deliver me from the body of this
death?" it will always be the ministers of the gospel,
because we need to be tempted in all points, so that
we may be able to comfort others. In a railway carriage, last week, I saw a poor man with his leg placed
upon the seat. An official happening to see him in
that posture, remarked, "Those cushions were not
made for you to put your dirty boots on." As soon
as the guard was gone, the man put up his leg again,
and said to me, "He never broke his leg in two places,
I am sure, or he would not be so sharp with me."
When I have heard brethren, who have lived at ease,
enjoying good incomes, condemning others who are
much tried, because they could not rejoice in their
fashion, I have felt that they knew nothing of the
broken bones which others have to carry throughout
the whole of their pilgrimage.

Brethren, *know man, in Christ, and out of Christ.*
Study him at his best, and study him at his worst;
know his anatomy, his secrets, and his passions. You
cannot gain this knowledge from books; you must
have personal acquaintance with men if you are to
help them in their varied spiritual experience. God
alone can give you that wisdom which you will need

in dealing wisely with them, but He will give it to you in answer to believing prayer.

Among spiritual acquirements, it is beyond all other things needful *to know Him who is the sure remedy for all human diseases.* Know Jesus. Sit at His feet. Consider His nature, His work, His sufferings, His glory. Rejoice in His presence; commune with Him from day to day. To know Christ, is to understand the most excellent of all sciences. You cannot fail to be wise if you commune with Incarnate Wisdom; you cannot lack strength if you have constant fellowship with God. Let this be your desire,—

> "I would commune with Thee, my God;
> E'en to Thy seat I come;
> I leave my joys, I leave my sins,
> And seek in Thee my home."

Dwell in God, brethren; not sometimes go to Him, but abide in Him. They say in Italy that, where the sun does not enter, the physician must. Where Jesus does not shine, the soul is sick. Bask in His beams, and you shall be vigorous in the service of your Lord.

Last Sunday night, I had a text which mastered me: "No man knoweth the Son, but the Father." I told the people that poor sinners, who had gone to Jesus, and trusted Him, thought they knew Him, but that they knew only a little of Him. Saints of sixty years' experience, who have walked with Him every day, think they know Him; but they are only beginning to know Him yet. The perfect spirits before the throne, who have been for five thousand years perpetually adoring Him, perhaps think they know Him, but they do not to the full. "No man knoweth the Son, but the Father." He is so glorious, that only the infinite God has full knowledge of Him, therefore there will be no limit to our study, or narrowness in our line of thought, if we make our Lord the great object of all our thoughts and researches.

So, brethren, as the outcome of this knowledge, if we are to be strong men, we must be *conformed to our Lord*. Oh, to be like Him! Blessed be that cross on which we shall suffer, if we suffer for being made like unto the Lord Jesus. If we obtain conformity to Christ, we shall have a wondrous unction upon our ministry; and without that, what is a ministry worth? In a word, we must labour for holiness of character. What is holiness? Is it not wholeness of character? A balanced condition in which there is neither lack nor redundance. It is not morality, that is a cold, lifeless statue; holiness is life. You must have holiness; and, dear brethren, if you should fail in mental qualifications (though I hope you will not), and if you should have a slender measure of the oratorical faculty (though I trust you will not), yet, depend upon it, a holy life is, in itself, a wonderful power, and will make up for many deficiencies; it is, in fact, the best sermon the best man can ever deliver. Let us resolve that all the purity which can be had we will have, that all the sanctity which can be reached we will obtain, and that all the likeness to Christ that is possible in this world of sin shall certainly be in us through the effectual working of the Spirit of God. The Lord lift us all, as a College, right up to a higher platform, and He shall have the glory!

V. I have not finished my message, for I have further to say, GO FORWARD IN ACTUAL WORK.

After all, we shall be known by what we have done, more than by what we have said. Like the apostles, I hope our memorial will be our *acts*. There are good brethren in the world who are impractical. The grand doctrine of the Second Advent makes them stand with open mouths, peering into the skies, so that I am ready to say, " Ye men of Plymouth, why stand ye here gazing up into Heaven ? " The fact that Jesus Christ is to come again, is not a reason for star-gazing, but for working in the power of the Holy Ghost. Be not so taken up with speculations as to prefer a Bible-reading over an obscure passage in the Revelation to teaching in a Ragged-school or discoursing to the poor concerning Jesus. We must have done with day-dreams, and get to work. I believe in eggs, but we must get chickens out of them. I do not mind how big your egg is, it may be an ostrich's egg if you like ; but if there is nothing in it, pray clear away the shell. If something comes of your speculations, God bless them ; and even if you should go a little further than I think it wise to venture in that direction, still, if you are thereby made more useful, God be praised for it !

We want facts,—deeds done, souls saved. It is all very well to write essays, but what souls have you been the means of saving from going down to hell? Your excellent management of your school interests me, but how many children have been brought into the church by it? We are glad to hear of those special meetings, but how many have really been born to God in them? Are saints edified? Are sinners converted? To swing to and fro on a five-. barred gate, is not progress; yet some seem to think that it is. I see them in a kind of perpetual Elysium, humming over to themselves and their friends, " We are very comfortable." God save us from living in comfort while sinners are sinking into hell! In travelling along the mountain roads in Switzerland, you will continually see marks of the boring-rod; and in every minister's life there should be traces of stern labour. Brethren, do something; *do something;* DO SOMETHING. While Committees waste their time over resolutions, do something. While Societies and Unions are making constitutions, let us win souls. Too often we discuss, and discuss, and discuss, while Satan only laughs in his sleeve. It is time we had done planning, and sought something to plan. I pray you, be men of action all of you. Get to work, and quit yourselves like men. Old Suwarrow's idea of war is mine: " Forward and strike! No theory! Attack! Form column! Fix bayonets, and charge right into the very centre of the enemy." Our one aim is to save sinners, and this we are not merely to talk about, but to effect in the power of God.

VI. Lastly, and here I am going to deliver a message which weighs upon me, GO FORWARD IN THE MATTER OF THE CHOICE OF YOUR SPHERE OF ACTION.

I plead this day for those who cannot plead for themselves, namely, the great outlying masses of the heathen world. Our existing pulpits are tolerably well supplied, but we need men who will build on new foundations. Who will do this? Are we, as a company of faithful men, clear in our consciences about the heathen? Millions have never heard the Name of Jesus. Hundreds of millions have seen a missionary only once in their lives, and know nothing of

our King. Shall we let them perish? Can we go to
our beds and sleep, while China, India, Japan, and
other nations are being damned? Are we clear of
their blood? Have they no claim upon us? We
ought to put it on this footing,—not, "Can I prove
that I *ought* to go?" but, "Can I prove that I *ought
not* to go?" When a man can honestly prove that
he ought not to go, then he is clear, but not else.
What answer do you give, my brethren? I put it to
you man by man. I am not raising a question among
you which I have not honestly put to myself. I have
felt that, if some of our leading ministers would go
forth, it would have a grand effect in stimulating the
churches, and I have honestly asked myself whether I
ought to go. After balancing the whole thing, I feel
bound to keep my place, and I think the judgment of
most Christians would confirm my decision; but I
hope I would readily, and willingly, and cheerfully, go
abroad if I did not feel that I ought to remain at
home. Brethren, put yourselves through the same
process. We must have the heathen converted; God
has myriads of His elect among them, we must go and
search for them somehow or other. Many difficulties
are now removed, all lands are open to us, and distance is almost annihilated. True, we have not the
Pentecostal gift of tongues; but languages are now
readily acquired, while the art of printing is a full
equivalent for the lost gift. The dangers incident to
missions ought not to keep any true man back, even
if they were very great, but they are now reduced to
a minimum. There are hundreds of places where the
cross of Christ is unknown, to which we can go without risk. Who will go?

The men who ought to go are young brethren of good abilities who have not yet taken upon themselves family cares. Each student entering the College should consider this matter, and surrender himself to the work unless there are conclusive reasons for his not doing so. It is a fact that, even for the Colonies, it is very difficult to find men, for I have had openings in Australia which I have been obliged to decline. It ought not to be so. Surely there is some self-sacrifice among us yet, and some among us who are willing to be exiled for Jesus. The Mission languishes for want of men. If the men were forthcoming, the liberality of the Church would supply their needs; and, in fact, the liberality of the Church has provided the supply, and yet there are not the men to go. I shall never feel, brethren, that we, as a band of men, have done our duty until we see our comrades fighting for Jesus in every land in the van of the conflict. I believe that, if God moves you to go, you will be among the best of missionaries, because you will make the preaching of the gospel the great feature of your work, and that is God's sure way of power.

I wish that our churches would imitate that of Pastor Harms, in Germany, where every member was consecrated to God in deed and of a truth. The farmers gave the produce of their lands, the working-men their labour; one gave a large house to be used as a missionary college, and Pastor Harms obtained money for a ship which he fitted out, to make voyages to Africa, and then he sent missionaries, and little companies of his people with them, to form Christian communities among the Bushmen. When will our churches be equally self-denying and energetic?

Look at the Moravians, how every man or woman becomes a missionary, and how much they do for the Lord in consequence. Let us catch their spirit. Is it a right spirit? Then it is right for us to have it. It is not enough for us to say, " Those Moravians are very wonderful people." We ought to be wonderful people, too. Christ did not purchase the Moravians any more completely than He purchased us; they are under no more obligation to make sacrifices than we are. Why then this backwardness? When we read of heroic men who gave up all for Jesus, we are not merely to admire, but to imitate them. Who will imitate them now? Come to the point? Are there not some among you willing to consecrate yourselves to the Lord? " Forward " is the watchword to-day! Are there no bold spirits to lead the van? Pray all of you that, during this Pentecost, the Spirit may say, " Separate Me Barnabas and Saul for the work whereunto I have called them."

Brethren, on wings of love mount upward, and fly forward. **Amen.**

INDIVIDUALITY, AND ITS OPPOSITE.

WHEN the late excellent Field-Marshal, Sir John Burgoyne, took the chair at the Tabernacle, at a lecture by Mr. Henry Vincent, he discharged his duty as chairman briefly, but admirably, by saying that, as chairman, he looked upon himself as merely called upon to ring the bell to announce the starting of the train. That is somewhat my position with regard to this Conference, only it rises to a higher degree of responsibility, because your President has not only to start the train of good thoughts and words for this week, but to a large measure he will give a tone for better or worse to all that shall follow. I am, therefore, more like the pitch-pipe of the olden times, which gave the key-note to the singers in the gallery, and through them to the whole congregation, and I feel inexpressibly anxious that the key-note should be a right one. Brethren, a measure of the sense of responsibility is helpful, and in many ways qualifies a man for saying the right thing; but it may be pushed too far, it may go beyond humbling the mind, and reach to the crushing of the spirit; it may so overwhelm you with the feeling of what is to be done as utterly to disqualify you for the doing of it. I am somewhat in that condition as to my part in this Conference to-day. I pine to inspire and not to repress your zeal, I long to lead you into the highest spiritual condition, and not to divert your attention to lower matters, and these strong desires master me ; my heart conquers my head, and disturbs the equanimity so needful for the creation and utterance of thought. However, I shall do my best, and leave myself in the hands of our great Illuminator, the Holy Spirit, that He may speak through me as He wills.

Our subject is a duplicate, and involves the advocacy of personality, or say,—

INDIVIDUALITY, AND ITS OPPOSITE,—

for which I cannot find the exact word,—either in the English or Latin tongue. I want to show that each one of us is a man by himself, and then that no one is alone by himself. Our individuality and our fellowship, our personality and our union with the Lord, our separate existence and our absorption into Christ ;— these are the themes upon which I am going to dilate.

Perhaps my one thought will come better if I give you a text from the 1st of Corinthians, the 15th chapter, and 10th verse : " *I laboured more abundantly than they all : yet not I.*" " I, yet not I ;"—I to the very full, every bit of me : Paul, once the Pharisee, the blasphemer, the persecutor, called now to be an apostle, who finds it cause of joy that this grace is given unto me to preach among the Gentiles the unsearchable riches of Christ ; I, not a whit behind the very chief of the apostles : and yet not I, for I feel myself to be nothing, yea, and less than nothing, and Christ is all and in all. So it is I, yet not I.

I. Commencing, then, let me speak of OUR INDIVIDUALITY. Dear brethren, may we, every one of us, be as far removed as possible from anything like egotism, which is hateful to the last degree! It is to be hoped that vanity is rare in ministers, for vanity is the vice of novices, and may be sooner excused in young students than in actual teachers of the Word. Experience, if it be worth having, exterminates a man's vanity; but so bad is our nature, that it may increase his pride if it be an experience sweetened with success. It were hard to say which is the greater sin, vanity or pride; but we know which is the more foolish and ridiculous. A proud man may have some weight, but a vain man is light as air, and influences no one. From both these egotisms may we be kept, for they are both injurious to ourselves and hateful to God. Too frequent an intrusion of self is another form of egotism to be avoided. I hope our sermons will never be of the same order as those which were set up in a certain printing office, and the chief compositor had to request the manager to send for an extra supply of capital I's. The letter " I " is a noble vowel, but it may be sounded too loudly. Great " I " is very apt to become prominent with us all; even those who labour after humility can barely escape. When self is killed in one form, it rises in another; and, alas! there is such a thing as being proud of being humble, and boasting of being now cleansed from everything like boasting.

Brethren, I hope that, however useful God may have made us in our several spheres, we do not conceive ourselves to be vastly important, for indeed we are no such thing. The cock was of opinion that the sun rose early every morning on purpose to hear him crow; but we know that Sol did nothing of the kind. The world does not revolve, the sun does not blaze, the moon does not wax and wane, the stars do not shine, entirely for the especial benefit of any one brother here, however admirable he may be in his own place ; neither does Christendom exist for the purpose of finding us pulpits, nor our own particular church that it may furnish us with a congregation and an income ; nay, nor does even so much as one believer exist that he may lay himself out for our sole comfort and honour. We are too insignificant to be of any great importance in God's vast universe ; He can do either with us or without us, and our presence or absence will not disarrange His plans.

Yet, for all that, our subject is individuality, and we hope that each man will recognize and honourably maintain his personality. The proper recognition of the EGO is a theme worthy of our attention. I will make a word if I may : let *egotism* stand for proud, vainglorious, intrusive selfhood, and let *egoism* stand for the humble, responsible, and honest selfhood which, finding itself in being, resolves to be at the Divine bidding, and to be at its best, to the glory of God. In this age, when crowds follow their leaders, and bold men easily command a following ; when the flocks cannot move without their bell-wethers, and rough independence is rarely to be found, it is well for us to be self-contained, whole men, and not merely limbs of a body, maintaining ourselves in the integrity of personal thought, conscience, manner, and action. Nowadays, monopolizers almost push the individual trader out of the market : the members of one party cry up " wood " as the only material for building the house of the Lord, and those who belong to another sect with equal zeal extol their own " hay and stubble." We shall not, by all their efforts, be induced to cease from building with the few "precious stones" which the Lord has entrusted to us; nor shall even our brethren, who so admirably pile up the "gold and silver," persuade us to hide away our agates and carbuncles. We must each build with such material as we have; if the work be true and honest, we ought neither to censure others nor to condemn ourselves because our labour is after its own kind.

Upon this matter of individuality, note first, *the necessity of an earnest sense of our individual interest in the gospel which we preach.* Brethren, we shall never preach the Saviour of sinners better than when we feel ourselves to be the sinners whom He came to save. A penitent mourning for sin fits us to preach repentance. "I preached," says John Bunyan, "sometimes, as a man in chains to men in chains, hearing the clanking of my own fetters while I preached to those who were bound in affliction and iron." Sermons wrung out of broken hearts are often the means of consolation to despairing souls. It is well to go to the pulpit, at times, with "God be merciful to me a sinner" as our uppermost prayer. Some mourners will never be cheered till they see the preacher smite upon his own breast, and hear him confess his personal sense of unworthiness.

It would not be right, however, for us to stay upon such low ground, for we preach the gospel, and not the law; we are bound, therefore, to rejoice because we feel the power of the blood of Jesus upon our own consciences, giving us peace and pardon in Him. Our joy will give life to our message. We have also tasted of the honey of communion with Jesus: we have not, perhaps, feasted upon handfuls of it, as some of our Samsons have done; but we have at least, like Jonathan, dipped the end of our rod into it, and our eyes have been enlightened, so that our hearers can see them sparkle with joy while we tell them how precious Jesus is. This gives emphasis to our testimony. When we speak as ministers and not as men, as preachers instead of penitents, as theologians instead of disciples, we fail; when we lean our head too much upon the Commentary, and too little upon the Saviour's bosom; when we eat too largely of the tree of knowledge, and too little of the tree of life, we lose the power of our ministry. I am myself a sinner, a sinner washed in the blood, and delivered from the wrath to come by the merit of my Lord and Master; —all this must be fresh upon our mind. Personal godliness must never grow scanty with us. Our own personal justification in the righteousness of Christ, our personal sanctification by the indwelling power of the Holy Spirit, our vital union with Christ, and expectancy of glory in Him, yea, our own advancement in grace, or our own declension; all these we must well know and consider.

We must never preach to others with a counterfeit voice, narrating an experience which we have not ourselves enjoyed; but if we feel that we have backslidden to any degree, we must either rally to the mark, or penitently speak from the standpoint we actually occupy. On the other hand, if we have grown in grace, it is wicked to conceal what we have tasted and handled, and affect a mock humility; in fact, we dare not do so, we cannot but speak what

Christ has taught us. We must speak out of the
God-given fulness within, and not borrow from another; better far to be silent than to do that. We
must be true to our personal condition before God, for
perhaps the Lord allows the state of heart of His
ministers to vary on purpose that their roving paths
may lead to the discovery of His wandering sheep. I
have sometimes traversed a portion of the pilgrim
path by no means to be desired, and I have groaned
in my soul, " Lord, why and wherefore is it thus with
me?" And I have preached in a way which made
me lie in the dust, fearing that the Lord had not
spoken by me, and all the while He was leading me
by the hand in a way that I knew not, for the good of
His own. There have come forward, ere long, one or
two who have been just the people God intended to
bless, and they were reached by the very sermon which
cost me so much, and grew out of an experience so
exceedingly bitter.

The prophet Ezekiel said, " The hand of the Lord
was upon me, and carried me out in the Spirit of the
Lord, and set me down in the midst of the valley
which was full of bones;" and such carryings, so often
as they occur, are matters for praise. Not so much
for our own good or edification, as for the benefit of
our fellow-men, are we borne into valleys of dry bones
and chambers of imagery. We must watch these
phases of soul, and be true to Divine impulses. I
would not myself preach upon the joy of the Lord
when I felt broken-hearted, neither would I enlarge
upon a deep sense of indwelling sin while rejoicing in
a full sense of cleansing by the Word. We must pray
the Holy Spirit to elevate and keep up our individual

life in its connection with our ministry. We must ever remember that we are not preaching doctrine which is good for others merely, but precious truth which has been proved to be good for ourselves. We may not be butchers at the block chopping off for hungry ones the meat of which we do not partake; but we must ourselves feed upon it, and must show in our very faces what fattening food it is which we present to the starving sons of men.

Brethren, this personality of life in Christ being well kept in our minds, it will be well for us never to forget *our personal commission to preach the gospel*, for I hope you have each of you received such a personal commission, and know it; or else why are you here? Leave the ministry, brethren, if you have not received it of the Lord. I preach—I dare to say it—because I can do no otherwise; I cannot refrain myself; a fire burns within my bones which will consume me if I hold my peace. Every God-sent Christian minister is as much called to preach the gospel as was that apostle to whom Ananias spoke concerning "the Lord, even Jesus, that appeared unto thee in the way." This makes our preaching a solemn business. Suppose that, this morning, in going down the stairs of this College alone, an angel should meet you, and lay his hand upon you, and say, "The Lord God Almighty hath sent me to commission you to preach the gospel henceforth." Brother, you would feel a burden laid upon you, and yet you would feel renewed confidence and ardour. But no mere angel's hand has touched thee, brother; the Lord Jesus Christ Himself, who redeemed thee with His most precious blood, has laid this "necessity" upon thee. The

pierced hand, which gave thee healing, has appointed
thee to thy Lord's service, and made thee a chosen
vessel to bear His Name. Hear afresh from His lips
the commands, "Feed My sheep" and "Feed My
lambs," even as Peter did by the Sea of Galilee.

Keep that matter of your commission always clearly
before you. Who shall stand to oppose your preaching if the Lord has bidden you preach? Who shall
dictate your message, or drive you to change it, if the
Incarnate Wisdom has taught you what to say? You
are well equipped for preaching the gospel if you can
truly say, with Paul, "For I neither received it of man,
neither was I taught it, but by the revelation of
Jesus Christ." Dear brothers, we must feel just that ;
I believe you do, and I want you to keep the feeling
fresh and warm. Kings, you know, claim to reign by
the grace of God. It may be so. God is very gracious to allow some of them to reign. But of this
thing I am sure ; every true minister is a defender
of the faith, "*Dei gratia.*" "By the grace of God I
am what I am" both as a minister and as a believer.
There may be a question about the legitimacy of
monarchs, and a tribunal of judges is too often needed
to test the election of senators ; but if we have the
witness of the Holy Spirit within us, our kingdom
cannot be moved, our election cannot be disproved.

Brethren, in connection with our individuality, we
ought to feel a great respect for *our own sphere of
labour.* You who are pastors are not only set to be
watchmen for souls, but to be watchmen for the souls
in particular places. You brethren, as a whole, are to
go into all the world to preach the gospel, but each
one of you must feed that flock of Christ over which

the Holy Ghost has made you an overseer. There your principal labours must be expended, for there your principal responsibilities lie. I would have every brother think very highly of the position in which God has placed him. If I am a sentinel, set to guard the army at a certain point, I know that every post in the whole cordon is important; but I am not to dream that mine is not so. If so, I may be inclined to sleep, and the foe may surprise the camp at the point which I ought to have guarded. I am to feel as if the whole safety of the entire camp depended upon me;—at least, I ought to be as zealous and as watchful as if it were so. You see the links of that chain; each one of them has a certain strain upon it. Suppose that one of them should say, " I may rust through; it does not matter, for many other links are strong." No, my friend, the chain depends upon each link; and so, for the completeness of church work, and for the perfect edification of the body of Christ, a great weight of responsibility lies *upon you.* I am very responsible; I admit it, but you have each one your measure of responsibility, which you cannot shift to another's shoulders. If all the rest of the world should be blest, and the hamlet to which you minister should be un-visited, the general revival would be no joy to you if your negligence had made your little vineyard a mournful exception to the rule. You might rejoice in the increase of blessing elsewhere, but the deeper would be your regret that you had none of it at home.

Let each man stick to his own work. If I felt that I had a call to be an evangelist, and to go everywhere preaching the Word, I would not retain my pastorate, because it would be unjust to the people who call me

their Pastor. I rejoice when I see very useful
brethren travelling far and wide, but I lament when I
find their churches left to be starved and scattered.
That is a sad confession of the spouse in the Canticles,
" They made me the keeper of the vineyards ; but
mine own vineyard have I not kept." If we cannot
do the two things, we had better not try. I am not
for a moment wishing to discourage the most ex-
tended labours on the part of any of our brethren ; —
the farther you can go, the better, for all the world is
your parish ; —but this must not be done at the expense of the work to which you have pledged yourselves by accepting pastorates.

A dear brother said to me, " I wish you would go
abroad, and preach the Word ; " and he urged as a
reason that my people would appreciate me better if
they had less of me. I replied that I did not want
my people to appreciate me any more, for they go
already as far in that direction as would be safe, and
I assured him that I should stop at home for fear they
should appreciate me more. I might have rambled all
the world over, and done great good, if that had been
my calling ; but the day will declare whether I have
not been more in the path of duty and real usefulness
by fostering Institutions at home, and scattering the
Word by my printed sermons far more widely than
I could have done with my voice. Be it so or not,
brethren, when you know which part of the Lord's
work He has committed to you, give your whole soul
to it. Going through the famous factory at Sèvres,
the other day, I noticed an artist painting a very
beautiful vase. I looked at him, but he did not look
at me ; his eyes were better engaged than in staring

at a stranger. There were several persons at my heels, and they all looked at him, and made various observations, yet the worker's eye never moved from his work. He had to paint the picture upon that vase, and what benefit would he get from noticing us, or from our noticing him? He kept to his work. We would fain see such abstraction and concentration in every man who has the Lord's work to do. "This one thing I do." Some frown, some smile, but "this one thing I do." Some think they could do it better, but "this one thing I do." How they could do it, may be their business; but it certainly is not mine.

Remember, dear brother, if you give your whole soul to the charge committed to you, it does not matter much about its appearing to be a somewhat small and insignificant affair, for as much skill may be displayed in the manufacture of a very tiny watch as in the construction of the town clock; in fact, a minute article may become the object of greater wonder than another of larger dimensions. Quality is a far more precious thing than quantity. Have you ever seen the famous picture at the Hague, called "Paul Potter's Bull"? It is one of the world's immortal paintings. What is it? Well, it is only a bull; and there are, besides, a man, and a tree, and a frog, and a few weeds. It is only a bull; ah, but there is not upon canvas another bull in the world to equal it! Many a man has attempted to depict a marvellous piece of natural scenery in the Alps or in Cumberland, or he has tried his pencil upon a magnificent sea-piece, with a fleet of yachts dancing on the waves, and he has not succeeded. The subjects were superior, but the art was poor. We must never think, because the particular work we have in hand seems to be insignificant, that therefore we cannot do it, or should not do it, thoroughly well. We need Divine help to preach aright to a congregation of one. If a thing is worth doing at all, it is worth doing well. If you had to sweep a crossing, it were well to sweep it better than anybody else. If you only preach in Little Peddlington, let Little Peddlington know that you are doing your best, and seeking its good. Many a minister has achieved fame, and, what is far better, has brought glory to God, in a congregation which could be counted by units, while another has presided over a large church, and though at first there was a great blast of trumpets, it has ended in the silence and sadness of utter failure. Know your work, and bend over it, throwing your heart and soul into it; for, be it great or small, you will have to praise God to all eternity if you are found faithful in it.

Come fair or come foul, my comrades, hold ye the fort. Some men attempt to excuse their own negligence by blaming the times. What have you and I to do with the times, except to serve our God in them? The times are always evil to those who are of morbid temperament. A scholar tells us that he once read a passage from a book to a worthy gentleman of the desponding school; it described " these days of blasphemy and rebuke,"—I think that is the correct expression,—and lamented the failure of the faithful from among men. " Ah, how true! " said the worthy man, " it is the precise picture of the times." " What times? " exclaimed the scholar. " These times, of course," was the reply. " Pardon me," said the scholar, " the sentiment was delivered about four hundred years ago; examine for yourself the date of the volume." The benefit of railing at the times it would be hard to discover, for railing does not mend them. What have you to do with the times? Do your own work. Charles the Twelfth of Sweden had his secretary sitting by his side writing from dictation, when a bombshell fell through the roof into the next room. The secretary, in alarm, dropped his pen, upon which the king exclaimed, "What are you doing?" The poor man faltered, "Ah, sire, the bomb!" The king's answer was, "What has the bomb to do with what I am telling you?" You will say that the secretary's life was in danger. Yes, but you are safe in any case, for you are side by side with Jesus in holy service, and no evil can befall you. Watch on, and work on, even to the crack of doom. Leave the times and the seasons with God, and go on with your work. Carlyle speaks somewhere of the house-cricket chirping on while the trump of the archangel is sounding;—who blames it for so doing? If God had made you a house-cricket, and bidden you chirp, you could not do better than fulfil His will. As He has made you a preacher, you must abide in your vocation. Even if the earth should be removed, and the mountains should be cast into the midst of the sea, would that alter our duty? I trow not. Christ has sent us to preach the gospel; and if our life-work is not yet finished, (and it is not,) let us continue delivering our message under all circumstances till death shall silence us.

We should consider, in the fourth place, *our personal adaptation*, desiring to keep it ever in the best possible condition. There is not only a work ordained

for each man, but each man is fitted for his work.
Men are not cast in moulds by the thousand; we are
each one distinct from his fellow. When each of us
was made, the mould was broken;—a very satisfactory circumstance in the case of some men, and I
greatly question whether it is not an advantage in
the case of us all. If we are, however, vessels for the
Master's use, we ought to have no choice about what
vessel we may be. There was a cup which stood
upon the communion table when our Lord ate that
passover which He had so desired to eat with His disciples before He suffered; and, assuredly, that cup
was honoured when it was put to His lips, and then
passed to the apostles. Who would not be like that
cup? But there was a basin also which the Master
took, into which He poured water, and washed the
disciples' feet. I protest that I have no choice
whether to be the chalice or the basin. Fain would
I be whichever the Lord wills so long as He will but
use me. But this is plain,—the cup would have made
a very insufficient basin, and the basin would have
been a very improper cup for the communion feast.
So you, my brother, may be the cup, and I will be the
basin; but let the cup be a cup, and the basin a basin,
and each one of us just what he is fitted to be. Be
yourself, dear brother, for, if you are not yourself, you
cannot be anybody else; and so, you see, you must be
nobody. The very worst notes in music are those
which are untrue; each true sound has its own music.
In my aviary are many birds, and they sing very
sweetly; but there are among them three grass paro-
quets, which do not sing, but imitate the other birds,
and very effectually spoil the concert. Their imitation

seems to drown the natural music of the rest.   Do not
be a mere copyist, a borrower and spoiler of other
men's notes.   Say what God has said to you, and say
it in your own way ; and when it is so said, plead personally for the Lord's blessing upon it.

Keep your adaptation for your work up to the
highest pitch.   Be not in so much hurry *to do* that
you forget *to be*,—so anxious to give out that you
never take in.   This is the haste which makes no
speed.   Old Nat had a large wood pile before him,
and he sawed very hard to make that pile smaller.
His saw wanted sharpening and re-setting, and it was
dreadful work to make it go at all.   An honest neighbour stepped up to him, and said, " Nat, why don't
you get that saw sharpened ?   You want to get that
put to rights, and then you could do a deal more than
you are now doing."   " Now then," replied Nat, " don't
you come bothering here.   I have quite enough to do
to saw that pile of wood, without stopping to sharpen
my saw."   It is unnecessary to point the moral of that
anecdote ; take note of it, and act accordingly in
future.   It is a waste of time, not an economy of it, to
dispense with study, private prayer, and due preparation for your work.

Keep your adaptation right, especially in a spiritual
sense.   We have more cause to pray and read our
Bibles than any other people in the world.   It was a
very wet day the last time I was at Cologne, and I
occupied a room in the hotel, which presented me
with a highly-picturesque view of a public pump.
There was nothing else to see, and it rained so hard
that I could not shift my quarters, so I sat and wrote
letters, and glanced at the old pump.   People came

with pails for water, and one came with a barrel on his back, and filled it. In the course of an hour, that individual came several times ; indeed, he came almost as often as all other comers put together, and always filled up his vessel. He was coming, and coming, and coming all the while ; and I rightly concluded that he was a seller of water, and supplied other people ; hence he came oftener than anybody else, and had a larger vessel. And that is precisely our condition. Having to carry the living water to others, we must go oftener to the well, and we must go with more capacious vessels than the general run of Christians. Look, then, to the vigour of your personal piety, and pray to be " filled with all the fulness of God."

Once more, remember *our personal responsibility.* I shall not trust myself to go very deeply into this question, but every brother should remember that, however well or ill another man may do his work, it can have no effect whatever upon our own personal responsibility before God. Some blame others with a kind of silently-implied belief that they are thereby praising themselves ; for, if we censure the methods adopted by other workers, we tacitly suggest that our own modes are—or, if we had any, would be—superior to theirs. Well, brother, it may be so. It may be that others are not wise, are scarcely sound, are fanatical, erratic, and the like ; but what hast thou to do with them? To their own Master they shall stand or fall, and God's grace is able to make them stand ; but your supposed wisdom, which leads you to criticize them, may prove a snare to you, and make you fall. You have yet to bring your work before God, to be tried by fire. Souls are entrusted to you, and for these you must give account. God does not mean to bless those souls by anybody else, they are to be converted through you; so, are you acting, living, and preaching in such a way that God is likely to convert them through you? That is the question for each one of us to answer.

We ought to feel our personal responsibility now, or it may one day come home to us in a way both forceful and painful. If you are smitten with sickness, and lie hour after hour tossing upon your bed in the silent watches of the night, if you have a little respite from pain, or even if you have not, you will, in all probability, occupy your mind mainly with the overhauling of the work which you have hitherto done or left undone. Believe me, brethren, this overhauling does not minister to one's gratification. There are portions of your work over which you linger with joy, and you say, " Glory be to God, this work was done, at any rate, with a pure heart, and to His glory, and He blessed it;" and you feel ready to sing over it; but you have hardly time to finish the song before you have to weep over a piece of work that was slurred and blotted, and you cannot help wishing that you could do it all over again. O brethren, we shall soon have to die! We look each other in the face to-day in health, but there will come a day when others will look down upon our pallid countenances as we lie in our coffins, and we shall not be able to return their glances. It will matter little to us who shall gaze upon us then, but it will matter eternally how we have discharged our work during our lifetime. " Thou art weighed in the balances, and art found wanting,"—will that be the verdict on any one of us

when we shall stand before the Lord God Almighty,
who trieth the hearts and searcheth the reins of the
children of men? His fire is in Zion, and His furnace
is in Jerusalem. His jealousy is most fierce against
those who come nearest to Him; He will not tolerate
sin in His choicest servants, for He slew Nadab and
Abihu because they offered strange fire upon His
altar, and He made the false apostle to be an eternal
monument of scorn. May we be kept faithful by grace
almighty, or the responsibility which rests upon us
will grind us to powder!

I feel that this matter of personality may be pressed
very earnestly upon you, my brethren, in all five of its
points; and in all it will be useful. If our individual
responsibility be rightly felt, we shall refrain from
judging others. We are all too ready to ascend the
judgment-seat. One man judges his fellow, and condemns him because he has had so few additions to his
church. I should myself be sorry if I saw few conversions, and I should severely censure myself; but
I should be very, very wrong if I were to utter an
indiscriminate censure upon others. Our brother's
congregation may be smaller than ours; the people's
hearts may have been long steeled by a cold, dead,
stereotyped ministry, and it may be that there is a
good deal of work to be done before they will become
interested in the gospel, much less affected by it.
Possibly it may happen that the preacher, who has
one convert, might say as the lioness did about her
one cub, when the fox boasted that she had so many,
" One, *but that one is a lion!* " The minister, whose
whole year's work ended with one convert, and that
one was Robert Moffat, did not reap a scanty harvest.

On the other hand, I have noticed—and I think rather more frequently—that brethren who have few converts judge those who have many. Now, that also would come to an end if each man knew his own place, and had joy in his own work, and was not envious of another. You say, "Oh, but these numerous conversions cannot all be genuine!" Why not? Why should their number create suspicion? I have very few sovereigns in my purse, and there are heaps at the Bank of England; yet I guess that, in the multitudes of golden coins which pass into the Bank of England, there is not so much probability of there being a counterfeit as in the few which reach my pocket or yours. Quantity need not deteriorate quality. I have an idea sometimes,—I do not know whether it is correct,—that where there are very few converts added to the church, there may be some unbelief. When I came along the Corniche Railway, from Genoa, it was broken in several places; and in one spot the embankment was not quite destroyed, but it was weakened, and therefore they passed the carriages over it one by one. They were afraid of the road, and so did not allow too many upon it at one time. I may not judge, but I sometimes think that, when brethren bring the converts in so very slowly, they have a little trembling about the power of saving grace to bear so many. It would not be difficult to be censorious on either side, but we shall not be so if we look well to the charge committed to us, and feel our own need of Divine help.

Our individuality will preserve us, by God's grace, from envying others. This vice is loathsome, and eats as doth a canker. "Wrath is cruel, and anger is outrageous; but who is able to stand before envy?" I have known persons utter sentiments which condemned themselves merely with the view of injuring others. They cared not if they perished, like Samson, so long as they pulled the house down upon others. An ancient story tells us that a king invited to his palace two men, one of whom he knew to be the slave of envy. "Now," said he, "I will give you whatever you please, upon the condition that this man shall choose first, and his companion shall have twice as much as he." The first man was envious: he desired great wealth, but he could not endure that the other man should have double. He therefore thought that he would reduce what he asked for, but this also left his companion his superior; and as the fable goes,— for peradventure it was only a fable,—his envy so prevailed that he chose to have one of his eyes torn out that the other man might be rendered totally blind. Somewhat similar is the spirit of those who oppose others upon principles fatal to their own work. Brother, do not so. If thy neighbour be honoured of God, thank God for it; if thou art not so honoured, be humbled, and pray more earnestly. If the blessing comes not to thee, still rejoice that it gladdens thy comrade. In any case, do not envy others.

On the other hand, dear brethren, this sense of individuality ought to prevent our despising others. The question sometimes comes to the lip concerning a very weak and scantily-gifted brother, "Lord, and what shall this man do?" The answer of the Lord is, "What is that to thee? Follow thou Me." There are much better ways of spending our time than in deriding or despising our brethren. A nobler work by far is to help those who are weak, and to encourage those who are cast down.

Dear brethren, I have said enough upon this first point, and I shall not be so long upon the other lest I should weary you. I wish, however, that what I have said may abide in the hearts of us all.

II. Come we now to THE OPPOSITE OF INDI-VIDUALITY. I shall not imitate the old logicians, who could "confute, change sides, and then confute," for what I have to say is not in opposition, but in apposition; it is not the reverse, but the converse. I cannot find the word with which to head it. Our language is still imperfect; it does not contain the converse of individuality. I looked in Roget's *Thesaurus;* I did more, I consulted a living dictionary now among you; but I could not find the word, and there is not such a word, though there ought to be. Will anybody here, who is a word-maker, be so kind as to coin me a word to stand in opposition or apposition to the word indi-viduality? Till that is done, I must dispense with a catchword, and proceed.

Let us all feel, dear brethren, that, though we have each one a work to do, and are personally fitted to do it, *we are not the only workers in the world.* Brother, you are not the only lamp to enlighten earth's dark-ness, you are not the only sower to sow the field of the world with the good seed, you are not the only trumpet through which God proclaims His jubilee, yours is not the only hand by which He feeds the multitudes. You are only one member of the mystic body, one soldier of the grand army. This thought should encourage you, and relieve the despondency engendered by loneliness. When God sent the flies,

and locusts, and caterpillars to conquer Egypt,
Pharaoh might have ridiculed any one of those insignificant warriors, and said, " What can this caterpillar do? I defy the Lord and His caterpillars."
But the caterpillar might have answered, " Beware, O
king, for there are ten thousand times ten thousand
of us! We come in mighty armies, and will cover all
the land. Weak as we are one by one, the Lord will
evidence His omnipotence by the multiplication of
our numbers." Thus was it in the early days of
Christianity. Christians came into Rome,—a few
poor Jews they were, and they dwelt in the Ghetto,
in obscurity; by-and-by, there were more. Meanwhile, a few had passed over into Spain; soon there
were more. A few had reached Britain; soon there
were more. The nations, angry at this invasion, set
to work to destroy those pests of society, which turned
the world upside down. They tormented, burned,
and destroyed them; but they continued to come in
shoals and swarms, and though they were slain without mercy, there were always more to follow. The
foes of God could not possibly stand against the vast
host that pressed forward. " The Lord gave the
Word : great was the company of those that published
it." Even so it is at this day. You are not alone in
sounding the praises of Christ, your voice is but one
of a mighty orchestra. The whole world is full of the
praises of God : "their line is gone out through all
the earth; and their words to the end of the world."

Nor do we think only of the church militant; we
lift our eyes beyond the firmament, and see a still
more glorious band; for the Master's honour and
glory are not left in the hands of workers here below,

toilworn and weary. His glory is sounded forth from
harps that never clash, struck by hands that are
never defiled. As a College, we have our comrades in
yonder host whose memories are yet green. I will
not mention many names; but I can never forget our
early brother, Alfred Searle, in character beautiful as
a choice flower; and Paterson, in perseverance indomitable, who wore himself out in self-denying
labour. Never can we fail to remember our apostolic
brother Sargeant, worthy of a monument of precious
stones; and Benjamin Davies, unwearied in his
Master's cause. It would only awaken mournful re-
flections if I were to continue the right noble list of
those who have gone up higher; may we prove as
faithful as they were! But it is not merely with them
that we have fellowship; we are one with all the
faithful. Luther, and Calvin, and Wycliffe, and
Latimer, and Whitefield, and Wesley, are our comrades, and all the saints who have preached Jesus
Christ. They are not preachers now, it is true; but
they are still glorifying God, and that after the noblest
fashion. It refreshes my heart to think of those whose
battle is fought and won for ever. We are told that
the Venetian women, when their husbands are out
upon the Adriatic fishing, go down to the verge of the
sea on the sweet summer evenings, when all is calm
and bright, and begin to sing a hymn. They sing the
first stanza in the shrill silvery notes of woman's voice,
and then they wait. They cannot see a single boat
upon the sea, the blue Adriatic is not dotted with a
sail; but, presently, mysteriously wafted across the
waters, comes the second stanza. Their husbands are
out of sight, but they are not out of hearing; and they

have taken up the second part of the hymn. Even thus, at this moment, our friends on the shores of Heaven are chanting to us. Hearken, I pray you! This is the strain,—

> "All we who dwell above,
> In realms of endless love,
>   Praise Jesu's Name;
> To Him ascribèd be,
> Honour and majesty,
> Through all eternity,
>   Worthy the Lamb!"

Did you not hear that canticle? Shall we reply? Come, my brethren, let us answer them! Let us rapturously sing,—

> "While you, around the throne,
> Cheerfully join in one,
>   Praising His Name;
> We who have felt His blood
> Sealing our peace with God,
> Sound His dear fame abroad;
>   Worthy the Lamb!"

Brethren, we are not alone. Legions of angels are all around us. Hosts of glorified spirits look down upon us. We are surrounded with a mighty band of helpers. We are compassed about with a great cloud of witnesses; wherefore, "let us lay aside every weight, and the sin which doth so easily beset us, and let us run with patience the race that is set before us, looking unto Jesus."

It is well for us to remember, in addition to this, that, although we are individuals, and must keep up our personality, *we are only instruments for the accomplishment of the Divine purposes.* We are nothing at all apart from God; and, blessed be God, we are not apart from Him. It is well to fall back, every now and then, in sheer weariness, upon the great truth of Divine predestination. It is a bed for some men's idleness; to us, it should be a couch for our refreshment. After all, God's will is done. His deep, eternal, immutable purposes are accomplished. The rage of hell and the enmity of men are neither of them able to stay the course of the eternal decrees. God doeth as He wills, not only among the armies of Heaven, but among the inhabitants of this lower world. He maketh the wrath of man to praise Him, and out of evil He bringeth forth good.

It is very blessed to feel that God is behind you, that God is in you, and that He is working with you. Mr. Oncken, in the early days of his preaching at Hamburg, was brought up before the burgomaster many times, and imprisoned. This magistrate one day said to him, in very bitter terms, " Mr. Oncken, do you see that little finger? " " Yes, sir." " As long as that little finger can be held up, sir, I will put you down." " Ah! " said Mr. Oncken, " I do not suppose that you see what I see, for I discern not merely a little finger, but a great arm, and that is the arm of God, and as long as that arm can move, you will never put me down." The opposition which is waged against the true minister of Christ does not, after all, amount to more than the burgomaster's little finger, while the power which is with us is that eternal and omnipotent arm whose forces sustain the heavens and the earth. We need not, therefore, fear. God's presence makes us bold. Let the Uhlan in the late war be our example. Picture him, a solitary man, brave and cool, riding upon a fleet horse. He is going along

one of those interminable French roads which have no
variety, except that now and then one poplar may be
half an inch taller than another; he rides hard and
fearlessly, though there are foes on all sides. That
one man passes through a hamlet, and frightens everybody. He enters a town. Is he not foolhardy? All
alone he has ridden up to the Town Hall, and demanded beds and stores. Why is he so bold? They
are all afraid of him, evidently. Ask the man why he
is so daring, and he replies, "There is an army behind
me, and therefore I am not afraid." So must you,
dear brother, be one of the Uhlans of the Lord God
Almighty, and never be afraid, for the eternal God
will be your rearward. "All power is given unto Me
in Heaven and in earth," says our Commander; "go
ye therefore, and teach all nations, baptizing them in
the Name of the Father, and of the Son, and of the
Holy Ghost." I feel as if He were here, this very
morning, looking on you as His soldiers, and saying,
"Conquer in My Name." Go, then, my brethren, ride
to those villages, and arouse them. Go to those
towns, and summon them to surrender. Go to the
great cities, and say to the people in them, "Christ
demands that you yield your hearts to Him." Do
this, and He will make your word effectual.

It is well for us to feel, in association with this
matter of individuality, that *we have the Spirit of God
in us.* I am what I am; but I am much more than I
am, for there is resident within me the Holy One of
Israel. "Know ye not that ye are the temple of God,
and that the Spirit of God dwelleth in you?" Not
the country residence, the mountain chalet of a travelling personage who will tarry there for a little while,—

your bodies are the *temple* of the Holy Ghost. This ought to make us respect ourselves ;—understand me, and do not misconstrue the expression. You should feel that what you do, under the influence of the Divine Spirit, is not such a feeble work as otherwise it would be. Where the Spirit of God is, there is power for the accomplishment of the Divine purposes. It would be far better to speak six words by the Spirit than to speak six thousand without him. A sermon is not to be judged according to its words, a certain inner force is its soul and life ; and God's judgment of the discourse will be according to how much there was of the real flower and fruit of the indwelling Spirit underlying the leaves of the sermon. Dear brethren, I have known a person say, " I heard So-and-so preach, and there really was nothing in it ; but still a great many were impressed." Just so ; God does not need a painted temple ; stained glass, and all manner of adornments and outward array, He cares not for. The man who thinks so is Popish, whether he thinks so concerning the temples made with hands, or the temples of our manhood. Is there not a Popery of intellect, and a Popery of elocution, in consequence of which we suppose that God is not resident in the un-educated or hesitating speaker, but only dwells with fluency and elegance ?

Where God chooses to dwell, there is a palace ; His presence glorifies the place of His abode. Is there anything very wonderful· in the architecture of Shakespeare's house at Stratford-on-Avon ? Yet, from the utmost ends of the earth, admirers of the world's great poet will come, because Shakespeare once lived there. Suppose Shakespeare were there now! What would his admirers do then? Now, this day, brethren, our poor humble constitutions and frames and bodies,—be they what they may,—are the temples of the Holy Ghost. It is not only that He *was* there;—that fact makes us respect the very ashes of the saints, but He *is* there now. May we never have to lament His absence! You may often see a fine house, of which the owner is dead, only the picture of him hangs on the wall; but our delight is that the living Christ is in us now by the power of His Spirit. I went to the monastery which adjoins the church of St. Onofrio, in Rome, some years ago, and they showed me there the rooms in which Tasso lived, and they had so skilfully drawn his likeness on the wall, that it looked for all the world as if Tasso were there. There were also his bed, and his pen, and his inkstand, and some of the paper on which he wrote; but there were no fresh stanzas of " Jerusalem Delivered " to be heard. Even so, we may have the likeness of Christ in our theological knowledge of Him, in our power of speaking for Him, we may have the pen with which He used to write, and we may have the paper on which He was accustomed to write in hearts that were interested in the gospel; but no " Jerusalem Delivered " will be produced, unless Jesus Himself is there. Brethren, we must have Christ in us, the hope of glory; the Spirit dwelling in us, the pure, the everflowing life, or our lives will be failures. O Lord, abide with us, and abide in us!

I must conclude with the remark that it is a very delightful thing to feel that *all the work we are doing is Jesus Christ's work.* All the sheep we have to shepherd are His sheep; the souls

we have to bring to Him were bought with His blood ;
the spiritual house that is to be built is for His habita-
tion. It is all His. I delight in working for my Lord
and Master, because I feel a blessed community of
interest with Him. That is not *my* Sunday-school, it
is my Lord's ; and He says, " Feed *My* lambs." It is
not *my* church, but His ; and He cries, " Feed *My*
sheep." Mine are His, and His are mine ; yea, all are
His. In the days when servants used to be servants,
and were attached to their masters, one of our nobility
had with him an old butler who had lived with his
father, and was getting grey. The nobleman was
often much amused with the way in which the good
old man considered everything that was his master's
to be his own. I was not only pleased with the story,
but it touched my heart when I heard it. His lordship once said to him, " John, whose waggon is that
which has just come up loaded with goods ? " " Oh ! "
said he, " that is ours. Those are goods from our
town house." His lordship smiled, and as a carriage
came up the drive, he said, " John, whose coach is
that coming into the park ? " " Oh ! " said he, " that
is our carriage." " But," said the master, " there are
some children in it, John ; are they *our* children ? "
" Yes, my lord, they are our children, bless them, I will
run, and bring them in." My Lord Jesus, how dare
I have the impertinence to claim anything which is
Thine ? And yet, when I gaze upon Thy Church, I
am so completely Thy servant, and so wholly absorbed in Thee, that I look upon it as mine as well as
Thine, and I go to wait upon Thy beloved ones. Yea,
Lord, and all these my brethren are going, too. Come
with us, Lord, for Thy love's sake ! Amen.

HOW TO MEET THE EVILS OF THE AGE.

———

BELOVED friends, allow me to welcome you all most heartily. I have already received a blessing in the prayers which have been offered; and we have all, I think, enjoyed the earnest of a Divine refreshing during the first hallowed hour of our meeting. Let us continue in the believing confidence that He, who has already deigned to visit us, will tarry with us until the time shall come for us all to say, "Let us go hence."

I can hardly indicate in a few words the run of my address; you will discover its subject or range of subjects as we go along, but if one line could contain it, it would be—

HOW TO MEET THE EVILS OF THE AGE.

So far as I remember, every year has been an exceedingly critical period; and so far as I can see in history, almost every six months some fervid spirit or another has written about "the present solemn crisis." There are persons who always believe in the imminent peril of the universe in general and of the Church of God in particular, and a sort of popularity is sure to be gained by always crying "Woe! Woe!" Prophets who will spiritually imitate Solomon Eagle, who went about the streets of London in the time of the plague, naked, with a pan of coals on his head, crying "Woe!

Woe!" are thought to be faithful, though they are
probably dyspeptic. We are not of that order: we
dare not shut our eyes to the evils that surround us,
but we are able to see the Divine power above us, and
to feel it with us, working out its purposes of grace.
We say to each of you what the Lord said to Joshua
in the chapter we have just read, "Be not afraid,
neither be thou dismayed: for the Lord thy God is
with thee whithersoever thou goest." Our trust is in
the living God, who will bring ultimate victory to His
own cause.

Still, it is a wise thing to admit that these days
have their own peculiar perils and trials. The
kaleidoscope shifts, the scenes presented to our gaze
are changed, whether for good or evil; good has
infinite varieties, and so has evil. We are not troubled,
as our Puritan forefathers were, by persecution and
oppression such as would take from us our civil rights
and our liberty to worship God. Evil has assumed quite
another form with us, and we must meet it as we find
it. The battle-front is altered, but do not imagine
that the conflict will be less severe. I look for a
sterner struggle than we have ever yet engaged in,
and we must be prepared for it. During the progress
of a battle, the Duke of Wellington was observed
riding along the lines to a certain part of the field,
and a soldier said to his fellow, "There goes the
Duke, and there's sure to be warm work." Brethren,
we have evidence that the Lord Jesus is with us, let
us therefore set the battle in array. He is not a
general who rides about for mere parade, He means
fighting wherever He comes, and we may expect
warm work. When He girds His sword upon His

thigh, and rides forth on His white horse, you may rest assured that His sword will smite heavily, and His arrows will fly thick and fast, while on the other hand His enemies will furiously rage,

First among the evils of the age, we must notice *the return of superstition.* Ritualism has sprung up among us, and spread as most ill weeds do. It is, I suppose, distinguishable from Romanism by omniscience, but it is also probable that omniscience sees more of its likeness to Romanism than we do. It is sadly spreading,—spreading everywhere. It suits our Evangelical brethren in the Church of England to speak of "a noisy minority practising Ritualism," and to remind us that each denomination has its difficulties; but to us, who are impartial onlookers, it seems that the most vital and vigorous part of the Anglican Church is that which is tainted with this error. The difference in the two parties is most marked, for the Ritualists are brave as lions, and the Evangelicals are timid as hares. You have only to go into the churches immediately around us, or into those of large towns, such as Brighton, to see the strength, the force, the determination, in a word, the detestable vitality of Ritualism. Every doctrine of Romanism is preached by these men except the infallibility of the Pope, and perhaps the celibacy of the clergy;— the presence of certain rosy-cheeked boys and girls in the rectory garden proving many Anglicans to be soundly Protestant upon that point. I am persuaded that there are many priests in the Church of Rome who preach more gospel, and understand it better, than do these pretended priests in the Church of England.

The worst of it is, that the growth of sacramental-
ism in the Established Church is not like that of the
mistletoe or a fungus upon an oak, it is a real and
legitimate branch of the parent stem.   There is no
man living, and there never was a man, and never can
be one, who believes the whole of the Book of
Common Prayer in its natural signification.   The only
way in which it can be done is by some such device
as that of the two nuns who had borrowed a mule
which would not go without being sworn at.   As
neither of them could be so profane as to swear, one
good sister pronounced the first syllable of the French
word *sacré*, and the other finished it, and thus between
the two the mule was made to go.   So must it be
with belief in the Prayer-book, no one man can believe
it all ; possibly High Church, Low Church, and Broad
Church can manage it between them.   But if I were
driven, at the point of the bayonet, to certify that one
of the parties was a grain or two more consistent with
the Prayer-book than the others, I must declare in
favour of the High Church party.   It is true that
the Articles are against them, but what are the
Articles ?   They are only read over perhaps once in a
lifetime.   The mischief is in the Catechism and the
service book which are in constant use.   We have not
to deal with a parasitical evil, but with a natural off-
shoot of the national vine, which will remain as long
as the Book of Common Prayer is unrevised ; and
when will it be revised?

Then, too, this mischief is carried on by men who
mean it.   They are in downright earnest.   I believe
there is among them a remnant who, despite their
ceremonialism and their mummeries, are true believers

in the Lord Jesus Christ. With them, there is a host of mere believers in postures, masquerading, and drapery, and all that kind of rubbish; but there is, nevertheless, a gracious company, whose sweet spirit breathes in holy hymns, and in devout, Herbert-like utterances concerning our Lord, which we should be sorry to have missed. As a party, they are earnest, they compass sea and land to make one proselyte, and great are the sacrifices which they make for the cause which they have espoused. This system, my brethren, is well entrenched, and you have to dislodge it.

This superstition, too, is in harmony with the innate idolatry of the human heart; it offers gratification to the eye and to the taste, it sets up a visible priest and outward symbols, and these man's fallen heart craves after. It offers to save men the necessity of thought by offering an outward service, and furnishing a priest to do their religion for them; but, alas! it takes man off from the real and spiritual, it consoles him without true regeneration, and buoys him up with hope though he has not submitted himself to the righteousness of Christ.

A second, and what I regard as an equally terrible evil, is *abounding unbelief*. I am not speaking now of that coarse kind of infidelity which rails at the Scriptures, and blasphemes the Name of the Lord our God. There is not much mischief in such a devil as that; he is too black, too plainly a fiend of hell! There is a more dangerous spirit now abroad, entering into Nonconformist churches, climbing into their pulpits, and notably perverting the testimony of some who count themselves somewhat, and are regarded as leaders by those who reckon themselves to be men of culture and intellect. Macaulay rightly said that theology is immutable ; but these men are continually contradicting that opinion in the most practical manner, for their theology is fickle as the winds. Landmarks are laughed at, and fixed teaching is despised. "Progress" is their watchword, and we hear it repeated *ad nauseam.* Very far are we from denying that men ought to make progress in the knowledge of the truth, for we are aiming at that ourselves ; and by daily experience, by study, and by the teaching of the Holy Ghost, we trust that, in some humble measure we are gaining it. But words need interpreting,—what is intended by "progress" in this case? Which way does it go?

It is too often progress *from the truth,* which, being interpreted, is progressing backwards. They talk of higher thought, but it is an ascending downwards. I must use their terms, and talk of progress ; but their progress is a going from, and not a going to, the place of our desires. Evidently, it is progress *from usefulness.* They invite us to follow them in their advance towards a barren Socinianism, for thither the new theology tends, or to something worse. Now, we know, at the present time, certain ancient chapels shut up, with grass growing in the front of them, and over the door of them is the name *Unitarian Baptist Chapel.* Although it has been said that he is a benefactor of his race who makes two blades of grass grow where only one grew before, we have no desire to empty our pews in order to grow more grass. We have in our eye certain other chapels, not yet arrived at that consummation, where the spiders are dwelling in delightful quietude, in which the pews are more numerous than the people, and although an endowment keeps the minister's mouth open, there are but few open ears for him to address.

It is pretty certain that Christ is not lifted up there, for He does not draw all men unto Him. There is no attractive force, no power, no influence for good; it is a frost-bound religion, and we are not at all desirous of making an excursion to that sea of ancient ice. "Sir," we say to the preacher, "you are immensely clever; we often wonder how one small head can carry all you know; but, for all your cleverness, we cannot give up the old, old gospel, for the results of your preaching do not fascinate us. Where are your converts? Where are your hearers? Where will your members soon be found?" Handel, on one occasion, played the organ in a country church; and, at the close of the service, he gave a voluntary of such a sort that all the people lingered to hear it. The old organist was indignant, and said, "Now, let that organ alone, *you* can't play the people out; let *me* do it." These progressive gentlemen certainly can play the people out. Their gifts of dispersion are amazing. Put them down in any warm-hearted Christian community, and see if they will not scatter and divide it; place them in any town you may select, and though they may be at first attractive (for some people are attracted by any novelty, however erroneous), yet, after a short time, there being no life, there will be no power to retain the people. We remember the experiment of Daventry, under that eminently godly man, Dr. Doddridge, and we are not inclined to try the like under any circumstances. That worthy man did not dogmatize to "the dear young men" who came to his College, but adopted the plan of letting them hear the argument upon each side, that they might select for themselves. The result was as disastrous as if error had been taught, for nothing is worse than lukewarmness as to truth. Dissent became enervated with a faint-hearted liberalism, and we had a generation of Socinians, under whom Nonconformity almost expired. Both General and Particular Baptists have had enough of this evil leaven, and we are not inclined to put it again into the people's bread.

Besides, we are invited to follow the guidance of men who are not qualified to be leaders. I have waited, with a good deal of interest, to see whether modern thought would be capable of producing *a man*, a man of mark, of profound mind, and philosophic genius ; but where is he? Where is the man who will found a school, and sway his fellows ; a man for the orthodox to tremble at, a great Goliath, head and shoulders above his fellows? Truly, there are some who think they have power, and so they have amongst those young gentlemen whose moustachios are on the point of developing ; but they have no influence over those who read their Bibles, have had experience, and are accustomed to " try the spirits."

The great lights are the literary men who produce articles in certain Reviews which are the oracles of the *élite*, or of those who think themselves so. I wonder how many of these precious Reviews are sold ; but that, of course, is of small consequence, because the *quality* of their readers is so high! See what airs a man gives himself because he reads a Review! Are these things so very clever? I am unable to see it. I used to hear that Evangelical writers produced platitudes; I believe they did, but surely they never wrote more watery trash than is published in the present day in opposition to the orthodox faith; but then, you see, it is given out in such a Latinized jargon that its obscurity is mistaken for profundity. If you have the time and patience to read a little of what is written by the modern-thought gentlemen, you will not be long before you are weary of their word-spinning, their tinkering of old heresies into original thought, and their general mystifying of plain things. It only needs a man of power to smash them up like potters' vessels, but then the result would only be pieces of broken pottery. " Show us a man worth following," say we, " and when you do, we will not follow him, but fight with him; at the present, we are not likely to leave Calvin, and Paul, and Augustine, to follow you."

We are invited, brethren, most earnestly to go away from the old-fashioned belief of our forefathers because of the supposed discoveries of *science.* What is science? The method by which man tries to conceal his ignorance. It should not be so, but so it is. You are not to be dogmatical in theology, my brethren, it is wicked; but for scientific men, it is the correct thing. You are never to assert anything very strongly; but scientists may boldly assert what they cannot prove, and may demand a faith far more credulous than any we possess. Forsooth, you and I are to take our Bibles, and shape and mould our belief according to the ever-shifting teachings of so-called scientific men. What folly is this! Why, the march of science, falsely so-called, through the world, may be traced by exploded fallacies and abandoned theories. Former explorers, once adored, are now ridiculed; the continual exposure of false hypotheses is a matter of universal notoriety. You may tell where the learned have encamped by the *débris* left behind of suppositions and theories as plentiful as broken bottles. As the quacks, who ruled the world of medicine in one age, are the scorn of the next, so has it been, and so will it be, with your atheistical *savants* and pretenders to science. But they remind us of *facts*. Are they not yet ashamed to use the word? Wonderful *facts*, made to order, and twisted to their will to overthrow the actual facts which the pen of God Himself has recorded! Let me quote from " Is the Book Wrong? " by Mr. Hely Smith, a pamphlet worthy of an extensive reading : —

" For example, deep down in the alluvial deposits in the delta of the Nile were found certain fragments of pottery. Pottery, of course, implies potters; but these deposits of mud, Sir Charles Lyell decreed, must have taken 18,000 years to accumulate, therefore there must have been men carrying on the occupations of civilized life at least 7,000 years before the creation of man as recorded in Scripture. What clearer proof could be wanted that the Book was wrong? For who would presume to suspect Sir C. Lyell of making a mistake in his work? A mistake, however, he had made, for, in the same deposits of mud, at the same depth in which this 'pre-Adamite pottery' was discovered, there also turned up a brick bearing the stamp of Mahomet Ali! [Yet we were bound to shift the Bible to suit that 'fact'—muddy fact!] Again, some curiously-shaped pieces of flint were discovered

in 1858 in what has been called 'the famous cavern
at Brixham.' It was at once decided that the flints
showed signs of human workmanship, and as they
were found in company with the bones of extinct
animals, it was also at once considered proved that
man must have existed in immensely remote ages,
and the evidence was said to have 'revolutionized the
whole of Western Europe on the question of man's
antiquity.' The history of these flints is remarkable.
For fourteen years, they were kept under lock and
key in the rooms of the Geological Society; but
public curiosity was gratified by plaster casts shown
at the cavern, and by illustrated descriptions published
in an imposing volume. According to the evidence
thus afforded to the public, there seemed no doubt left
but that these flints bore the marks of the mind and
hand of man, thus associating man with a pre-Adamite
race of animals. The cause of truth owes a debt of
gratitude to Mr. Nicholas Whitley, Honorary Secretary of the Royal Institution of Cornwall, for the
acuteness which led him to suspect that there was
something wrong, the perseverance with which he followed up his suspicions, and the boldness with which
he made public the result, which was simple, but sug-
gestive. The plaster casts, the drawings and descriptions, *were not the casts, drawings, or descriptions of
the real flints found in the cavern!* The originals
were, with one or two exceptions, evidently purely
natural specimens of flints; and persons who have
seen the landscape stones, and the marvellous likeness
of human faces on inaccessible rocks, will not be dis-
posed to overthrow the whole of Revelation because
of one or two curiously-shaped stones found in com-

pany with the remains of extinct animals. If the cause had not been so weak, what was the necessity for trying to strengthen and supplement it by presenting the public with false statements? With regard to all these supposed flint implements and spears and arrow-heads, found in various places, it may be as well to mention here the frank confession of Dr. Carpenter. He has told us from the presidential chair of the Royal Academy that no 'logical proof can be adduced that the peculiar shapes of these flints were given them by human hands.' "

So the bubbles go on bursting, and meanwhile more are being blown, and we are expected to believe in whatever comes, and wait with open mouth to see what comes next. But we shall not just yet fall down and worship the image of human wisdom, notwithstanding all the flutes, harps, sackbuts, psalteries, dulcimers, weekly papers, quarterly reviews, and boastful professors. *Show us a man of science worthy of the name*, and then we will not follow him if he dares to oppose revealed truth ; but show us one in whom the next generation will believe ; at present, there is not one alive worthy to be compared with Newton and other master-minds reverent to the Scriptures, compared with whom these men are mere pretenders. See, my brethren, we have unbelief, scientific and otherwise, to contend with, and we must meet it in the Name of the Lord.

Another manifest evil of this our time is not so serious, but it is exceedingly annoying ; I refer to *the spirit of disintegration* which infects portions of the Church of God, and causes much heartburn and discord in certain quarters. Years ago, when a man was converted, he used, as a matter of course, to unite with that church with which he most nearly agreed, and work for the Lord in connection with it; but now, a brother does not like to go to the place where most of the Christians in the town or village assemble, but he prefers to hold a meeting in his own room, in order to show that he dislikes sectarianism, and believes in Christian unity. Not caring to work with any recognized organization, because it is denominational, he feels bound to form a little denomination of his own. We would not, in an angry spirit, forbid these brethren because they follow not with us; but we cannot conceal the fact that, by thus working alone, they are injuring themselves, weakening our churches, and robbing us of those who ought to be our most efficient helpers. I fear that some are bitten with the notion that work outside the church is more useful than regular efforts; but a little experience will, I hope, teach many of them better. Christian labours, disconnected from the church, are like sowing and reaping without having any barn in which to store the fruits of the harvest; they are useful, but incomplete. I trust the evil of Ishmaelitish enterprise will gradually cure itself, but meanwhile it goes on, and loving, earnest people are decoyed away from our fellowship. On the other hand, it is a good thing for some brethren, who "count themselves something though they be nothing," to have the opportunity of finding a sphere of activity, where they will probably be less troublesome to us than they would have been nearer home. Some persons, distinguished by a kind of piety which might be called *mag*-piety, are happiest where they can talk most. They are fond of hearing

themselves speak, and can sing, "How charming is
the sound!" Such people are best accommodated in
assemblies of their own convening. We have this to
deal with, and to some brethren it is a cause of heart-
break, and has bowed them down with grief of soul.
Many an earnest pastor can testify to this.

The fourth evil is one to which I call your very
earnest attention, *the growth of wickedness in the
land*, especially in two forms, which we ought not to
overlook. One is, *the growing worldliness among
professing Christians*. They are indulging in extravagance in many ways; in luxurious habits, dress,
equipages, feastings, and so on, and wasting the substance of which they are stewards. When a man is
giving liberally to the cause of God, I count it very
foolish to forbid his spending liberally in other ways,
for men usually spend by scale. It would be absurd
to hold up a wretched miser, who gives nothing either
to God or man, as an example to a liberal spender;
but there is too much of ostentatious extravagance
abroad, which wastes the Master's money in worldly
pleasures and doubtful amusements, yea, and amusements worse than doubtful. Some, who are called
ministers of Christ, have in these days even defended
amusements which moralists have felt bound to
abandon, but let us hope that such ministers will not
repeat the mistake. We must be careful, wise, and
yet decided in our dealings with this growing evil, or
we shall lose all spirituality from the churches.

But, beside this, have you not noticed with horror
the increase of *the national sin of drunkenness*
throughout the land? Only look at the bill for intoxicating drinks! That amount cannot be expended

annually without producing a terrible record of drunkenness, crime, disease, and death. Ten years ago, it is pretty certain that men drank quite enough; to what must we impute this ever-growing consumption? The evil is positively appalling. I look upon the law permitting the sale of wines and spirits at the grocers' as one of the most mischievous pieces of modern legislation. To my grievous knowledge, the sin of intoxication among women has been suggested in some instances, and promoted in others, by this easy and respectable method of obtaining strong drink. For women to drink, is loathsome even to men who can freely indulge in it themselves. Is it really more shameful that women should be drunken than men? It has that appearance, and the frequency of the evil among them proves that the drink cancer is getting nearer to the heart of the body politic.

I was in France, at the Carnival at Mentone, and I remarked again and again that I saw no sign of intoxication. All day long, the peasants and townspeople amused themselves with masks, and music, and confetti,—amusements fit for little children; but I saw no drunkenness, and do not think there was any. Yet France is a Popish country: do we not blush to think that it should excel us in so ordinary a virtue as sobriety? One of my friends said to me, "If this Carnival had been held in England, these people would all have been drunk before they started the procession." Several years ago, when staying on the island of Heligoland, I noticed with regret a regulation that no more than four English sailors should come ashore at one time, and then each one must be attended by a soldier till he returned to the boat. I saw hale and hearty sailors come to the little town, and walk up the street; but how differently they reeled back, and how difficult it seemed to get them safely away! Are our fellow-countrymen to become the scorn of mankind for their drunkenness? The world will begin to cry shame upon the Christian Church unless something is done in this matter. Consider the suffering and poverty which arise out of the waste of money involved in this vice, and the crime which is its inevitable result. The whole land reeks before the Lord, and is corrupt with this sin. If Christians do not labour to stay this evil, who will do it? If ministers do not seek to the utmost of their ability to apply a remedy, the world will think that their outcry against unbelief and other evils is not very sincere. He who does not cry out against the wolf cannot surely be at enmity with the lion.

These are the mischiefs. Now for THE REMEDY. What are we to do to meet this superstition, and this unbelief, and this disintegration, and this growing worldliness and drunkenness? I have only one remedy to prescribe, and that is, that we do preach the gospel of our Lord and Saviour, Jesus Christ, in all its length and breadth of doctrine, precept, spirit, example, and power. To give but one remedy for many diseases of the body, is the part of an empiric; but it is not so in the affairs of the soul, for the gospel is so divinely compounded as to meet all the evils of humanity, however they may differ from one another. We have only to preach the living gospel, and the whole of it, to meet the whole of the evils of the times.

The gospel, if it were fully received through the whole earth, would purge away all slavery and all war, and put down all drunkenness and all social evils; in fact, you cannot conceive a moral curse which it would not remove; and even physical evils, since many of them arise incidentally from sin, would be greatly mitigated, and some of them for ever abolished. The spirit of the gospel, causing attention to be given to all that concerns our neighbour's welfare, would promote sanitary and social reforms, and so the leaves of the tree which are for the healing of the nations would work their beneficial purpose. Keep to the gospel, brethren, and you will keep to the one universal, never-failing remedy. You have read of sieges, in which the poor inhabitants have been reduced to skeletons; and fevers and diseases, scarcely known at other times, have abounded: when the city has at last surrendered, if you wished to give the people what would meet all their wants, you would begin by giving them food. Hunger lies at the bottom of the fever, hunger has caused the other diseases, gaunt and grim; and when the constitution is again built up by food, it will throw off most of the other ills. Give the bread of life to the multitude, and the maladies and diseases of fallen humanity will be divinely removed; I am sure it is so.

It is evident enough that the gospel meets *superstition*. In the Revelation we read, " Babylon is fallen, is fallen," and we see her cast like a millstone in the flood. But was it not because, as we read a little before, " I saw another angel fly in the midst of Heaven, having the everlasting gospel to preach unto them that dwell on the earth "? Between the flight of the angel and the fall of Babylon there was an intimate connection. If you were to enter a ruin, and could not bear the hooting of the owls and the presence of the bats, and wanted to disperse them, if you could let the blessed light shine into the deserted halls, the bats and owls would soon find their wings. Let the flambeaux blaze in every corner, and the creatures of darkness will quit the scene. Do you wish to put an end to baptismal regeneration, the lie of lies? Proclaim spiritual regeneration by the Holy Ghost, and exalt the work of the Spirit of the Lord. Would you make men see through the sham of Romish and Anglican priesthood? Proclaim the everlasting priesthood of our great Melchisedec. If you would end belief in sacraments, proclaim the substance, of which ordinances can never be more than the shadow. You will find men turn away from the husks when you set before them solid food, God by His Spirit being with you to give them the wisdom to discern between things that differ.

As to the *unbelieving* business, my brethren, I bear my witness that the preaching of the gospel confronts it well. I was speaking to a brother-minister concerning the number of young men who fall into one form or another of false doctrine. When I told him that I was very little troubled in that way, he replied, " I don't suppose you are. Calvinism drives them away, it does not allow them enough scope. A man of that kind would not come to hear you many times." Now I am bold to say that, in some preaching, dovecots are provided for the birds of doubt, and I am not surprised that they fly in clouds, and as doves to their windows. Preach the doctrines of grace, dear brethren, and those who like not your Lord will either be changed themselves or change their minister. Preach the gospel very decidedly and firmly, no matter what people may say of you, and God will be with you. Some would like us to treat the Bible as if it were a peal of bells, sounding forth from a church steeple, which we can make to say whatever we please; rather let us sound forth Scriptural truth like a trumpet, giving a certain sound, that people may know that there is a meaning in it, and may learn at the same time what that meaning is.

I give the progressive gentlemen a motto to be engraved on their escutcheon, for which I hope they will be very grateful; it is this,—" *Ever learning.*" It is their boast that they are ever learning. Accept it, gentlemen, but take the whole of it : " ever learning, and never able to come to the knowledge of the truth." (2 Tim. iii. 7.) They themselves confess that they do not come to definite knowledge, for they are always telling us that what they teach to-day they may repudiate to-morrow, for a process of development is going on, so that, having commenced with the oyster of Calvinism, they may yet reach the superlative manhood of atheism, for where else will it stop? Preach the truth with all your hearts as God teaches it to you, and this plague will be stayed.

As to *disintegration*, I know of no way of keeping God's people together like giving them plenty of spiritual meat. The simple shepherd said that he tied his sheep by their teeth, for he gave them such good food that they could not find better, and so they stayed with him. Be this our custom as the Holy Spirit shall help us. Let us also labour, by our preaching, to make church-fellowship a great deal more real. Have we not many times heard the remark, perhaps a pardonable one, " I will never go to another church-meeting "? Why should it be so? An old story furnishes me with an illustration. A clergyman was burying a corpse, and not knowing whether to use the word " brother " or " sister " in the service, he turned to one of the mourners, and asked, " Is it a brother or a sister? " " No relation at all, sir," was the prompt reply, " only an acquaintance." We are always talking about beloved brethren and sisters; but, on examination, how much of real brotherhood is there in most churches? Does it not amount to this,—" No relation at all, only an acquaintance "? Do you wonder that people start a little meeting of their own, where they hope that there will be a little more communion? Try to make church-fellowship full of life and love by preaching and living the gospel of love and brotherhood. Be to your people like a father among his children, or an elder brother among his brethren, that you may be the means of blessing to them, and at the same time meet the evil of disintegration.

As to that terrible matter of *drunkenness*, I believe there are many palliations for the disease, but I am equally certain that there is no complete and universally applicable cure for it except the gospel. The best way to make a man sober is to bring him to the foot of the cross. It is a practical question, well worth your pondering, whether, in order to bring him there, it may not be necessary to get him sober first, for we cannot hope to see men converted when they are drunk. You may find it wise to use with vigour all the appliances which the temperance movement has so amply provided; but whether you personally agree to do so or not, if you see others earnestly warring with the demon of drink, even though they use weapons which you do not admire, do not despise them, nor treat them otherwise than as allies. Let your own personal habits be such as shall tend to overthrow the evil, and to encourage those who are labouring to that end. Let the current and tone of your conversation be always friendly to the man who fights this foe, even if he does not come upon your platform, for the enemy is so strong and so all-devouring that no honest helper may be scorned. But, after all, the gospel is the needle-gun of the conflict. If you could make every man in England sign the pledge of total abstinence, you could not secure sobriety for any length of time, since pledges are too often broken; but if men's hearts are changed, and they become believers in the Lord Jesus Christ, then the stamina of principle will, by Divine grace, be given to the mental constitution, promises will be kept, and vices will be forsaken.

So far you have followed me in *the general truth*, I will now give you a few practical exhortations. The old, old gospel is to be *preached;* it is not to be ground out, like tunes from a barrel organ; but to be preached in the very best way; and, by God's blessing, we are so to work up the church that both ourselves and our fellow-members shall confirm the witness of the gospel, and be hearty and unanimous in spreading it.

To begin with, *we must have more knowledge of the gospel*. It is not every minister who understands

the gospel; many ministers, who understand its
elements, have never attempted to grasp and to preach
the whole of it, and even he who knows most of it
needs to understand it better. You must preach the
whole of the gospel. The omission of a doctrine, or
an ordinance, or a precept, may prove highly injurious. Even points which others think trivial must not
be trivial to the man who would make full proof of his
ministry.

Do not, for instance, fail to be faithful upon believers' baptism; for if that part of your testimony
be left out, an ingredient essential to meet superstition
will be wanting. Though it may seem, at first sight,
as if you might very well leave out a minor doctrine
without mischief, do not so; for, since the God who
put it into the Word is supremely wise, he is not a
wise man who would leave it out. Fulfil the whole
of your commission: "teaching them," says your
Lord, "to observe all things whatsoever I have commanded you." Preach the gospel North, South, East,
and West; but be sure that you preach the whole
gospel as far as God has taught it to you, and preach
nothing else.

To accomplish this, we are bound to search and
study in order to know more and more of the inspired
Word. Have you not found that the precious gospel
is like a cavern into which you must enter bearing
the torch of the Holy Spirit, who alone can show you
all things? Were you not astonished as you stood
in the first chamber, and saw its clear soft silver light?
What treasures were all around you, for all its walls
were slabs of silver, and the roof was hung with
filagree of the precious metal! "I have found it! I

have found it!" you cried, for very joy. But, just then, one of the shining ones touched you on the shoulder, and said, "Come hither, and I will show thee greater things than these." You passed through a portal hitherto unobserved, and, lo! there opened up another chamber, more lofty and more spacious than the last. The floor, the roof, and the pendant stalactites were all of gold,—pure gold, like unto transparent glass; and then you said, "Now have I entered the innermost shrine of truth." Yet was there more to be seen, for again the shining one touched you, another secret door flew open, and you were in a vast hall, where every form of precious stone flashed forth upon you; rubies, and jaspers, and emeralds, and amethysts emulated each other's beauties, while all in a blaze of light the terrible crystal and all manner of choice gems made the cavern to shine like a thousand firmaments crowded with stars. Then you marvelled indeed. And now, perhaps, having seen such treasures, you are of opinion that nothing more remains; but no mortal hath fully seen God's glory as yet, and the Divine Spirit waits to lead you by study and prayer to a yet clearer vision of the deep things of God.

In order to preach the gospel well, we must have such a knowledge of it that we are *practically conversant with it.* We must have it in our hearts, and also, as the common saying has it, at our fingers' ends. We must be rich that we may scatter treasures. We must be scribes well instructed that we may be apt to teach. Let us see well to this, dear brethren; and if any of you have at all slurred your private studies, and your communion with God, and your deep search-

ing of the Word, I pray you do not so; for you may
get on a little while with the stores you have on hand,
but they will soon be spent, or become mouldy.
Gather fresh manna every morning; gather it fresh
from Heaven. Manna is all very well out of a
brother's omer if I cannot go where it falls, but God's
rule is for each man to fill his own omer. Borrow
from books if you will; but do not preach books, but
the living Word. Get much inward knowledge, and
then deal it out to your people.

Secondly, *we must seek after a deeper and more
experimental acquaintance with the gospel.* The
word "experimental" is one which theology has
manufactured; but it is not correct, for true religion
is no experiment. Surely it is a well-ascertained fact,
a force the result of which may safely be predicted,
for no cause more certainly ensures its effect. But
we mean "experiential"—that which groweth out of
experience,—pardon the uncomely coinage. Does a
man know any gospel truth aright till he knows it by
experience? Is not this the reason why God's servants are made to pass through so many trials, that they
may really learn many truths not otherwise to be
apprehended? Do we learn much in sunny weather?
Do we not profit most in stormy times? Have you
not found it so—that your sick-bed—your bereave-
ment—your depression of spirit, has instructed you
in many matters which tranquillity and delight have
never whispered to you? I suppose we ought to
learn as much by joy as by sorrow, and I hope that
many of my Lord's better servants do so; but, alas!
others of us do not; affliction has to be called in to
whip the lesson into us.

Brethren, a minister who handles the Word of God as one who has tried and proved it, is known at once by his congregation. Even the unconverted recognize the touch of the practised surgeon of souls. If a woman, who had never nursed anybody before, were to come to your bedside to attend to you during an illness, you would find it out without being told. But mark the skilled nurse. Note the wonderful way in which she makes up your pillow! What an art she has in putting on the bandages! How downy are her fingers when she touches the wounded flesh! And if she has ever been afflicted as you now are, how pleasantly she says, " Ah, I know how you suffer! I understand that feeling; for I have felt the same." Why, you feel that nurse to be the very one you needed. There is a way of talking about the gospel, and its privileges and duties, in a style which does not come home to the heart at all. I once read the following criticism upon a certain preacher. I do not think it was at all just as applied to him, so I shall not mention his name ; but the remarks were as follows :—" He preaches as if you had no father or mother, no sister or brother, no wife or child, no human struggles and hopes; as if the great object of preaching was to fill you with Biblical pedantry, and not to make you a better, wiser, stronger man than before. Perhaps it may be, because this is the case, that the church is so thronged. You need not tremble lest your heart be touched, and your darling sin withered up by the indignant denunciations of the preacher. He is far away in Genesis or in Revelation, telling you what the first man did, or the last man will do ; giving you, it may be, a creed that is Scriptural and correct, but that does not interest you, for it has neither life, nor love, nor power; it is as well adapted to empty space as to this gigantic Babel of competition, and crime, and wrong, in which we live and move."

Such a criticism would justly apply to many preachers. They do not treat the gospel as a practical thing, or as a matter of fact which immediately concerns the people before them. If the gospel referred only to certain unclothed humanities in the bush of Australia, they could not themselves appear to be less interested in it. A pleading experimental sermon from them we could not expect, nor even the simple gospel, except so far as they may occasionally condescend to men of low estate by abasing themselves from the serenities in which their highnesses exist in order to consider a few of the depravities of the lower classes! This will never do. No; we must have personal experience of the things of God. As to our own depravity, we must feel it, and mourn it; and as to the glorious power of the grace of God, and the wondrous riches of Christ, we must go on to realize these in our own souls more and more, if we are to preach with power, and meet the evils of the times.

I have to say, thirdly, that *we must keep to the gospel more continually.* I do not know any audience to whom there is less need to say this than to the present; but, still, let me " stir up your pure minds by way of remembrance." It is worth while stirring up that which is pure; the impure will be best let alone. Seeing that ye have these things, let me excite you to have them more abundantly. Often, very often,

ought we to teach the simple rudiments of the gospel.
It is astonishing, after all the preaching that there has
been in England, how little the gospel is understood
by the mass of men. They are still children, and
have need to be told the A B C of the gospel of
Christ. Keep most to those themes, brethren, which
are most soul-saving,—to those which are practically
useful to the people. Keep close to the cross of
Christ. Point continually to the atoning sacrifice, and
to the doctrine of justification by faith, which, when
preached aright, are never preached without the
Divine approbation. Every truth is important, let it
have its due place; but do not suffer any secondary
truth to take you away from the first. Aristotle, in
his wonderfully unnatural natural history, tells us that,
in Sicily, the herbs in the woods and fields smell so
exceedingly sweet that the dogs lose all scent of their
prey, and so are unable to hunt. Let us beware of
such herbs. There is to our minds—to mine, I know,
—a great fascination in poetry, in true science, in
metaphysics, and the like; but you, I trust, dear
brethren, will prove to be dogs of so keen a scent
that the perfume of none of these shall prevent your
following closely after the souls of men, for whom you
hunt at your Master's bidding. No doubt many are
drawn off from the main pursuit, and think, when they
have taken to frivolous philosophizings, that they
have outgrown their fellow-Christians; but be not ye
of their mind.

A woman was once very busy in fetching out of her
burning house her pictures and her choicest pieces of
furniture. She had worked a long while, toiling
hard to save her little treasures; when, on a sudden,

it came to her mind that one of her children was missing. The child had been left in the burning house; and when the mother rushed back again, that chamber had long ago been consumed, and the child had, doubtless, perished. Then did she wring her hands, and bitterly bewail her folly. She seemed to curse every bit of furniture that she had saved, and wished that she had not saved it, because, by looking after such poor stuff, she had lost her child. Even so, every little piece of curious learning, and quaint proverb, and deep doctrine, that you manage to save from the fire, will only accuse your conscience if you let men's souls perish. We *must* have them saved; and it is infinitely better that fifty of those admirable discourses upon a difficult point should lie by till we are dead than that we should bring them out, and waste fifty Sundays when precious souls are waiting for the good news of mercy.

I have often wondered why certain sermons were ever preached, what design the preacher had in concocting them. I would not suspect the preachers of wishing to display themselves; yet what else they were doing, I do not know. Caligula marched his legions, with the beating of drums, and sounding of trumpets, and display of eagles and banners, down to the sea-shore, *to gather cockles!* And there are sermons of that sort: beating drums, and sounding trumpets, and flaunting flags, *and cockles!* A beautiful story is told of the famous Bernard. He preached one day to a congregation with marvellous eloquence and poetic diction; he charmed them all; but when the sermon was done, Bernard was observed to walk away disquieted. He wandered into the wilderness, and spent the night alone, fasting because of his sadness. The next day, at the time for preaching, he was ready, and delivered himself of a commonplace discourse, of which the great gentlemen who had listened to him the day before thought nothing ; but the poor of the people understood his words, and drank them in ; and though he heard the censures of the critics, he was observed to walk away with a smile upon his face, and to eat his bread with a merry heart. When one asked him the reason, he said, " *Heri Bernardum ; hodie Jesum Christum.*" " Yesterday, I preached Bernard ; but to-day, Jesus Christ." You, my brethren, will feel happy when you have preached unto them Jesus ; and, whoever frowns, your sleep will be sweet to you, for your Master will have accepted you.

Keep to the gospel, then, more and more and more. Give the people Christ, and nothing but Christ. Satiate them, even though some of them should say that you also nauseate them with the gospel. At every meal, set out the salt without prescribing how much. If they do not like it (and there are creatures that cannot endure salt), give them all the more of it, for this is according to your Lord's mind.

I would add that, in our preaching, *we must become more and more earnest and practical*. That paragraph, which I read to you just now concerning a certain divine, must never be true concerning us. We must preach as men *to* men, not as divines *before* the clergy and nobility. Preach straight *at* them. It is of no use to fire your rifle into the sky when your object is to pierce men's hearts. To flourish your sabre finely is a thing which has been done so often that you need not repeat it. Your work is to charge home at the heart and conscience. Fire into the very centre of the foe. Aim at effect. "Oh! oh!" say you, "I thought we ought never to do that." No, not in the perverted acceptation of the term; but, in the right sense, *aim at effect,*—effect upon the conscience and upon the heart.

Some preachers remind me of the famous Chinese jugglers, who not long ago were everywhere advertised. One of these stood against a wall. and the other threw knives at him. One knife would be driven into the board just above his head, and another close by his ear, while under his armpit and between his fingers quite a number of deadly weapons were bristling. Wonderful art to be able to throw to a hair's breadth and never strike! How many among us have a marvellous skill in missing! "Be not afraid," says the preacher, "I am never personal. I never give home-thrusts." Stand quite still, my friend! Open your arms! Spread out your fingers! Your minister has practised a very long while. and he knows how to avoid troubling you in the least with truth too severely personal. Brethren, cultivate that art if you desire to be damned, and wish your hearers also to be lost; but if you want to be the means of saving both yourselves and them that hear you, cry to your Lord for faithfulness,, practicalness, real heart-moving power. Never play at preaching. nor beat about the bush; get at it, and always mean business. Plutarch tells us of two men at Athens who were nominated for a public office. One of them was famous for his oratory; and to gain the election, he gave a description of what he could and would do if the citizens would choose him. He would have charmed them with his fine promises, but they knew him too well. His rival was a man of few words, and simply said, " All that this gentleman has *said*, I mean to *do*." Now, be ye of that kind, not speakers of the Word only, but doers also.

Have you not heard scores of sermons about the gospel, and about what the gospel is to do? Is it not a grand thing, at a public meeting, to give a glorious description of what the gospel has accomplished, and what it will accomplish, though you have contributed nothing to the grand result? But of what avail is it to preach *about* the gospel? Let us *preach the gospel itself.* Hope not to alarm the foe by a description of a Krupp-gun; but wheel up your artillery, and open fire. Do not be content with describing conviction of sin; but labour, in the power of the Spirit, to produce conviction at once. Do not satisfy yourself by picturing the peace which follows upon believing; but preach the truth which men are to believe, so that they may actually obtain the peace which you describe. We want more of what I call the " doing " preaching, and less of the " talking " preaching. Set yourselves steadily to labour with men even to an agony. Show them their sin; set it out before them, and say, " Sinners, is not this sin? Are you so blind that you cannot see it? If you cannot see it, I will mourn your blindness, and pray the ever-blessed Spirit to open your eyes. And, sinners, do you not see Christ? I have seen Him! It was the most blessed sight I ever beheld, for His wounds are my healing, and His death is my life. I have nothing to show you but Christ my Master; but a look at Him will save you.

I will pray the Holy Spirit to illuminate you; but if you do not understand, it shall be the fault of *your* mind, and not of *my* language." We have heard sermons preached, in which the minister prayed God to save souls; but, unless He had departed from His usual laws of procedure, it was not possible even for the Almighty God to use such discourses for any such purpose, for they have consisted of mere trifling with words, or an exposition of some minute point of opinion, or a philosophizing away of the mind of the Spirit. Pray the Lord to save your hearers, and then drive at them as though you could save them yourself. Trust in God, and then employ such logical arguments as may convince the judgment, and such pathetic appeals as may touch the heart, so that, if effects depend upon causes, you may see them produced, God's hand being with you.

I need scarcely add to you, brethren, that *we must be more and more simple and clear in the preaching of the gospel.* I think we are pretty clear and plain already; but, sometimes, young men are fascinated by some famous preacher whose style is grandiose, sublime, or involved. They see the thing done very splendidly, and as they look on, they marvel, and by degrees they think they will try that style, too; and so they put on the seven-league boots, large enough for them to live in, and the result is ridiculous, nay, worse than that, it is spiritually useless. When a man tries to do the magnificent, with elaborate sentences, and pompous diction, and grandeur of manner, it must and will come to nought. There is also a tendency, among some young gentlemen, to go off into excessive quotation of poetry. There are superfine young men who probably were born with a rose between their lips, and with a nightingale singing above their bed when first their infant cries were heard, and they seem to be consecrated to the sublime and beautiful. Every breeze wafts to them from the mountains of Araby the sweet odours of poetic thought. It was concerning a man of this school that Samuel Butler wrote,—

> "For rhetoric, he could not ope
> His mouth, but out there flew a trope."

That style of speaking is very fine, brethren; but do not you be beguiled by it. As much as ever you can, avoid all artificial oratory, or what simpletons nowadays mistake for eloquence. The word is shamefully misused; but, in the common acceptation of the term, the most detestable thing is eloquence. Speak from your heart, and never mind about eloquence. Do not speak after the manner of the orator; speak as a lover of souls, and then you will have real eloquence. The oratory which allies itself with the dancing-master, and practises before a looking-glass, and is fond of classical quotations, and obscure verses from unknown poets, is for ever to be abhorred by you. Perishing sinners do not want your poetry, they want Christ. If you are poetical, ride on the back of your poetry, but do not let it ride you. What you have to do is to be the means of saving souls, and look you well to that. If soldiers can win a battle and sing sweetly at the same time, by all means let them sing; but if it so happens that, while regarding the harmonies, they miss a cut at their enemies, let the singing come to an end at once. There, young warrior, give over your crochets

and quavers, and vault into your saddle! Regard
your pulpit as your steed, and dash into the battle
like Khaled of old, smiting right and left with daunt-
less valour; and when you come back, you will have
more honour from your Master than he will who
stayed at home to arrange the plumes of his helmet,
and then at length rode out bedizened to admiration,
only to come home like that inglorious hero of whom
the poet sings,—

> " The King of France, with forty thousand men,
> Went up a hill, and so came down agen."

I must hasten on to notice that, if we are to make
the gospel meet the evils of the time, *we must be quite
sure to exemplify it in our lives when out of the
pulpit*. I thank God I know, in the case of numbers
of brethren here, that the gospel which they preach is
illustrated in their lives by their self-denials and self-
sacrifices. It charms me when I hear a brother say,
" I left my position to go to one where my income
would be twenty pounds a year less, for I felt that
there was a wider sphere of usefulness before me, and
that I should not be building on another man's
foundation, but conquering new territory for Christ."
I glory in God's grace as shown in many of you,
because of your zeal, your endurance of poverty, and
your faith in God. The Lord will bless you. It
delights my soul to think that the spirit of the apostles
and martyrs is in many of you. You make sacrifices
for Christ, and say nothing about them, content to do
grandly though none proclaim it. Go on, my brethren,
in the Name of the Lord. I hope you will not have
to suffer more than needs be; but where there is a

needs be, take you the suffering joyfully. If we cannot conquer without the loss of a few men, do not let us hesitate for a moment. If we cannot take this Malakoff without filling the trench with dead bodies, let us leap in. Let us never shrink from poverty, rebuke, or hard labour; but determine that the old flag shall be carried to the top of the fortress, and, in the Name of the Lord Jesus Christ, error shall be trodden under foot as straw is trodden for the dunghill. It is a cause worthy of your utmost zeal; if you could spill your blood in a thousand martyrdoms a day, the cause deserves it. It is the cause of God, the cause of Christ, the cause of humanity. Preach the gospel, brethren, preach it all, and preach it with the Holy Ghost sent down from Heaven, and you shall yet be the means of helping to save this perishing world; but may God give you grace to live in the spirit of the gospel, or else you will surely fail.

I am afraid that there are some ministers who get into a pulpit, intending to stick there. There is no moving *them*, and they never move the people. It is sometimes remarked to me, " Some of your men move about a good deal." " Yes," I reply, " many shall run to and fro, and knowledge shall be increased." I like the self-sacrifice of a man who feels that he can move, and will move when he can do more good elsewhere. Never move or stay for selfish reasons, but hold yourself at your great Captain's beck and call. An old Scotch minister, as he was riding along, saw, according to his own description, something coming which greatly alarmed him. It was a gipsy riding aloft upon an ass which he had loaded high with faggots. The beast, which the minister was riding, was alarmed as

well as its rider, set its feet down very firmly, and put
its ears back, after the manner of amiable horses!
" And," said the minister in describing it, " I prepared
myself for a fall, so that I fell somewhat more easily."
" But," said a friend, " I should have got off." That
idea had never crossed the worthy man's mind. So it
is with some ministers, they prepare themselves to be
dismissed by their people, but never propose to
remove of their own will. It is within my knowledge
that a brother, not of our Conference, said to his
people, when they were in a most earnest manner endeavouring to get rid of him, " It was the Spirit of
God that brought me here, and I shall never go till
the Spirit of God leads me to go away, *and that
will be a very long while.*" The last sentence cast
suspicion on all that preceded it, for, surely, he could
not foretell what the mind of the Spirit might be.
Stay or move, brethren ; go to Africa, or America, or
Australia, or flit from John o' Groat's house to the
Land's End, only do accomplish your mission, and
glorify God. Be holy, be gracious, be prayerful, be
disinterested, be like the Lord Jesus ; thus only will
your lives be consistent with the gospel you are called
to preach.

. One thing more, and it is this. Let us, dear
brethren, try to *get saturated with the gospel.* I
always find that I can preach best when I can manage
to lie a-soak in my text. I like to get a text, and find
out its meaning and bearings, and so on ; and then,
after I have bathed in it, I delight to lie down in it,
and let it soak into me. It softens me, or hardens me,
or does whatever it ought to do to me, and then I can
talk about it. You need not be very particular about

the words and phrases if the spirit of the text has filled you; thoughts will leap out, and find raiment for themselves. Become saturated with spices, and you will smell of them; a sweet perfume will distil from you, and spread itself in every direction;—we call it *unction*. Do you not love to listen to a brother who abides in fellowship with the Lord Jesus? Even a few minutes with such a man is refreshing, for, like his Master, his paths drop fatness. Dwell in the truth, and let the truth dwell in you. Be baptized into its spirit and influence, that you may impart thereof to others. If you do not believe the gospel, do not preach it, for you lack an essential qualification; but even if you do believe it, do not preach it until you have taken it up into yourself as the wick takes up the oil. So only can you be a burning and a shining light. Personally, to me, the gospel is something more than a matter of faith; it has so mingled with my being as to be a part of my consciousness, an integral part of my mind, never to be removed from me. Faith in the old orthodox creed is not a matter of choice with me now. I am frequently told that I ought to examine at length the various new views which are so continually presented. I decline the invitation; I can smell them, and that satisfies me. I perceive in them nothing which glorifies God or magnifies Christ, but much that puffs up human nature, and I protest that the smell is enough for me.

> "Should all the forms that men devise
>   Assault my faith with treacherous art,
> I'd call them vanity and lies,
>   And bind the gospel to my heart."

I hope the truths of the gospel have become our life;

experience has incorporated them with our being. Be laid low with pain, and nothing will then suffice you but gracious realities. Bind philosophy around an aching heart, and see if it will relieve the agony. Take a draught of modern thought, and see if it will cure despair. Go to death-beds, where men are looking into eternity, and see if the principles of the sceptical school can help the sick to die in triumph.

Brothers, I beseech you keep to the old gospel, and let your souls be filled with it, and then *may you be set on fire with it!* When the wick is saturated, let the flame be applied. Fire from Heaven is still the necessity of the age. They call it " go ", and there is nothing which goes like it; for when fire once starts upon a vast prairie or forest, all that is dry and withered must disappear before its terrible advance. May God Himself, who is a consuming fire, ever burn in you as in the bush at Horeb! All other things being equal, that man will do most who has most of the Divine fire. That subtle, mysterious element called fire,—who knoweth what it is? It is a force inconceivably mighty. Perhaps it is the motive force of all the forces, for light and heat from the sun are the soul of power. Certainly fire, as it is in God, and comes upon His servants, is power omnipotent. The consecrated flame will, perhaps, consume *you*, burning up the bodily health with too great ardour of soul, even as a sharp sword wears away the scabbard; but what of that? The zeal of God's house ate up our Master, and it is but a small matter that it should also consume His servants. If, by excessive labour, we die before reaching the average age of man, worn out in the Master's service, then, glory be to God, we shall have so much less of earth and so much more of Heaven! And suppose we should be abused, misrepresented, and slandered for Christ's sake, then glory be to God that we had a reputation to lose for His sake, and blessed be our Lord who counted us worthy to lose it! Be on fire within yourselves with perfect consecration to God, and then you will blaze in the pulpit.

There are the evils, brethren. I have tried to set them forth; you will not forget them. But we have only one remedy for them; preach Jesus Christ, and let us do it more and more. By the roadside, in the little room, in the theatre, anywhere, everywhere, let us preach Christ. Write books if you like, and do anything else within your power; but whatever else you cannot do, *preach Christ*. If you do not always visit your people (though I pray God you may not be blameworthy there), yet be sure to preach the gospel. The devil cannot endure gospel preaching; nothing worries him so much as preaching. The Pope cannot bear it; nothing makes him so ill as preaching. Preaching is our great weapon, so use it perpetually. Preaching is the Lord's battering-ram, wherewith the walls of old Babylon are being shaken to their foundations. Work on with it, brothers, work on. Preach, preach, preach, preach, preach, preach, till you can preach no more, and then go above to sing the praises of God in Heaven, and to make known to the angels the wonders of redeeming love.

"A NEW DEPARTURE."

BELOVED fellow-servants of Christ, our work requires us to be in the best possible condition of heart. When we are at our best, we are feeble enough; we would not, therefore, fall below our highest point. As instruments, we owe all our power for usefulness to the Divine hand; but, since tools should always be kept in order, we would have our spirit free from rust, and our mind sharp of point and keen of edge to answer at once to the Master's will. It is because I fear we do not always keep up to the mark that the subject for this morning's address shall be "*A New Departure*," or, in other words, a renewal, a revival, a starting afresh, a return to our first love, even the love of our espousals, when first our soul was wedded to our Redeemer's work.

The subject is exceedingly needful to us all, because *the process of running down is such a very easy one*. Upon that topic, let me speak for a few minutes. To run down, requires no care or effort: it can be accomplished without a wish; it can come to pass, in a measure, in opposition to our wish; we can decline and decay without so much as being conscious of it, and all the more easily because we fancy that we are rich and increased in goods. By a law which asks no help from us, we gravitate to a lower level. Do not wind up the weights, and the wheels will soon cease to move, and the old clock on the stairs will remain motionless, useless, silent, dead, like a coffin set on end. To keep a farm in good order, needs constant labour and watchfulness ; but to let the land get out of heart till it would starve a lark, is a very simple matter, which can be accomplished by any sluggard ; simply let it alone, or take crop after crop from it, and give it neither manure nor rest, and you will change fruitful fields into barrenness, and turn a garden into a desert. It is just so with ourselves. Only do not wind up your soul with daily prayer, and you will soon run down ; only neglect the culture of the heart, and thorns and briers will grow uninvited. Neglect your inner life, and your whole being will deteriorate.

I do not know, my brethren, that we can expect to see energy continuous at its full in any one of us. I suspect that he who burns like a seraph knows moments in which the flame somewhat abates. As the sun itself is not at all times alike powerful, so the man who, like the shining light, shineth more and more unto the perfect day, is not uniformly bright, nor always at his noon. Nature does not hold the sea for ever at flood ; ebbs intervene, and the ocean pauses a while ere it returns again to the fulness of its strength. The vegetable world has its winter, and enjoys a long sleep beneath its bed of snow. It is not wasted time, that ebb or that winter ; flood and summer owe much to ebb and frost. I suspect that, because we are in affinity with nature, we, too, shall have our changes, and shall not abide at one elevation. No man's life is all climax. Let us not despond if, just now, our spirit is at a low ebb ; the tide of life will roll up as before, and even reach a higher point. When we stand leafless and apparently lifeless, our soul having become like a tree in winter, let us not dream that the axe will cut us down, for our substance is in us though we have lost our leaves, and before long the time of the singing of birds will come, we shall feel the genial warmth of returning spring, and our lives shall again be covered with blossoms, and laden with fruit.

It will not be wonderful if there should be lulls and pauses in our spiritual work, for we see the like in the affairs of men. The most eager after worldly objects, who can by no means be accused of a want of earnestness in their endeavours, are yet conscious that, by a sort of law, dull times will come, wherein business necessarily flags. It is not the tradesman's fault that, sometimes, trade must be pushed, and that after pushing it remains as dull as ever. It seems to be the rule that there should be years of great prosperity, and then years of decline; the lean kine still devour the fat kine. If men were not what they are, there might be a perpetuity of equable progress, but it is evident that we have not reached that point yet.

In religious affairs, history shows us that churches have their palmy days, and then again their times of drought. The Universal Church has been thus circumstanced; it has had its Pentecosts, its Reformations, its revivals; and between these there have been sorrowful pauses, in which there was much more cause for lamentation than for rejoicing, and the *Miserere* was more suitable than the *Hallelujah.* I should not, therefore, wish any brother to condemn himself if he is not conscious just now of possessing all the vivacity of his youth,—he may find it return before

our meetings close. I would have the husbandman
long for spring, and yet not despair because of the
present cold; so would I have a man lament every
degree of decline, and yet not despond. If any man
walk in darkness, and see no light, let him trust in
God, and look to Him for brighter days.

Still, taking all this into account, and allowing all
margin and discount, I fear that many of us do not
maintain our proper elevation, but sink below par.
Many things tend that way, and it may do us good to
think of them. A degree of running down in spirit
may be purely physical, and arise out of *the evapora-
tion of our youthful vigour.* Some of you enjoy all
the force of your early manhood; you are fleet of foot
as the roes of the field, and swift of movement as birds
on the wing; but others of us wear a tinge of grey in
our locks, and middle life has sobered us. Our eye
has not yet waxed dim, nor has our natural force
abated; but yet the flash and flame of our youth have
departed, and from the style of our speech and the
manner of our action men miss that morning dew
which was the glory of life's young hours. Older men
are apt to ridicule young fellows for being too
zealous; let them not retaliate, but cautiously abstain
from ever charging the elder brethren with excess of
fervour. Surely, malice itself would not dare to invent
such a libel.

For my own part, I would have remained a young
man if I could, for I fear I am by no means improved
by keeping. Oh, that I could again possess the elas-
ticity of spirit, the dash, the courage, the hopefulness
of days gone by! My days of flying are changed to
those of running, and my running is toning down to a

yet steadier pace. It is somewhat cheering that the Scriptures seem to indicate that this is progress, for such is the order which it prescribes for saints : " They shall mount up with wings as eagles ; " away they go, out of sight. In your first sermons,—how you mounted up! Your first evangelistic efforts,—what flights they were! After that, you slackened and yet improved your pace ; but it grew more steady, and perhaps more slow, as it is written : " They shall run, and not be weary ; and they shall walk, and not faint." God grant that we may not faint ; and if our running days are over, may we walk with God as Enoch did, till the Lord shall take us home!

Another cause which frequently conduces to the abatement of vigour is *the possible cessation of early success.* I do not mean that it is always so ; but, usually, when a man goes to a new field, there are many unreaped portions, and he gathers a large harvest, which he does not find afterwards because there is less to reap. If you have a narrow pond, you cannot keep on catching as many fish as you did at first, because there are not so many fish remaining. In London, we are, as it were, in an ocean, and we may spread our nets as often as we please ; but in a small town or village, a man may soon have done all his direct converting work if the Lord greatly blesses him ; and if, after a time, more souls are not saved, it may be because few unconverted persons attend his ministry. God may have given the brother all those whom He intended to bless by him in that place, and it may be wise for him to fish in other waters. I have read of a lighthouse-keeper who puts a rope round the lighthouse, and then to this cord he attaches a number

of lines and hooks. These are all under water at high
tide, and at favourable times the fish bite, and when
the tide goes down, the lighthouse is festooned with
fish of all kinds; there they hang, and the successful
fisherman has nothing to do but to gather the spoils.
Thus it was with us at first; we baited our hooks, and
we drew in the fish without stint. But perhaps, later on,
the lighthouse-keeper peers out from his tower, and he
cannot see, for the fog is dense, the storm-cloud has
settled down around his light, and the wind rages
furiously; he is obliged to keep every door and
window closed, or he could not live, and then he
thinks it hard to be a lighthouse-keeper, and wishes
himself ashore. We also are, at times, in a similar
condition. We are asked, " Watchman! what of the
night?" And the answer is, " No morning cometh,
but the night thickens, and the darkness grows
denser." We do not every day draw the net to land
full of great fishes, but we experience dreary intervals
of fruitless toil, and then it is no wonder that a man's
spirit faints within him.

The natural wear and tear of an active life also
tend to our running down. Some of our people think
that we have little or nothing to do but to stand in the
pulpit, and pour out a flood of words two or three
times a week; but they ought to know that, if we did
not spend much time in diligent study, they would get
poverty-stricken sermons. I have heard of a brother
who trusts in the Lord, and does not study; but I
have also heard that his people do not trust *in
him;* in fact, I am informed that they wish him to go
elsewhere with his inspired discourses, for they say
that, when he did study, his talk was poor enough, but

now that he gives them that which comes first to his
lips, it is altogether unbearable. If any man will
preach as he should preach, his work will take more
out of him than any other labour under heaven. If
you and I attend to our work and calling, even among
a few people, it will certainly produce a friction of soul
and a wear of heart which will tell upon the strongest.
I speak as one who knows by experience what it is to
be utterly exhausted in the Master's service. No
matter how willing we may be in spirit, the flesh is
weak; and He who made a tender apology for His
sleeping servants in the garden knows our frame, and
remembers that we are dust. We need that the
Master should say to us, every now and then, "Come
ye yourselves apart into a desert place, and rest a
while;" and He does say so, for He is not a hard task-
master, and whoever may use the lash, and cause the
weary steed to die in harness, our gentle Lord doth
not so.

Besides this, we are very apt to run down *through
our duty becoming routine work*, by reason of its
monotony. Unless we are careful, we shall be likely
to say to ourselves, "Monday evening here again, I
must give an address at the prayer-meeting. Thursday evening, and I have to preach, although I have
not yet a topic! Sunday morning, Sunday evening;
I have to preach again! Yes, preach again! Then
there are all those extra engagements; it is for ever
preach, preach, preach! I am always preaching.
What a weariness it is!" Preaching ought to be a joy,
and yet it may become a task. Constant preaching
should be constant enjoyment, and yet, when the
brain is tired, pleasure flies. Like the sick boy in the

prophet's day, we are ready to cry, "My head! my head!" We ask, "How can we keep up our freshness?" It is hard to produce so much with such scant leisure for reading; it is almost as bad as making bricks without straw. Nothing can maintain us in the freshness of our beginnings but the daily anointing of the Spirit.

I do not wonder that some brethren run down *through want of association with others of warm heart and of kindred spirit.* I will give you another lighthouse illustration; a gentleman, who called to see the keepers of a lone light, said to one of them, "I suppose, after all, you fellows are quite happy in this tower?" "We might be happy," replied the man, "if we had a chat with one another; but my mate and I have not exchanged a word with each other for a month." If you are banished to a country place, where you have no superior or even equal mind to converse with, no intellectual or spiritual friend near at hand, I can feel for you. "Iron sharpeneth iron; so a man sharpeneth the countenance of his friend," and when that sharpening is missed, it is no marvel that the mind grows dull. We cannot live alone, brethren, and yet a dreadful solitude as to our higher cares is one of our sorest trials. Oh, for a twin spirit to converse with! The worst of it is that, if we have few to refresh us with their conversation, we have many to vex us with their chatter; and when we would fain be uplifted to noble themes, we find ourselves dragged down by the dreary gossip of a hamlet. What wonder if, with such surroundings, we lose force, and run down!

Yet, dear brethren, none of these things furnish us

with an excuse for falling into a low state, and *it may possibly be true that our mental decline is the result of our weak spiritual condition.* It may be that we have left our first love, that we have wandered away from the simplicity of our faith, that we have backslidden in heart, and grieved the Holy Spirit, so that our God walks contrary to us because we walk contrary to Him. Perhaps the rain is withheld because prayer has been restrained, and the heavenly wind has ceased to blow because we have been too indolent to spread the sail. Has there been no unbelief to hinder the blessing? We often talk of unbelief as if it were an affliction to be pitied instead of a crime to be condemned. For us to give the lie to Him who has unveiled the secrets of His heart to us, and almost, I was about to say, gone out of His way to bless us in an extraordinary and unusual manner, must pain the great Father's heart. Perhaps we feel less love to Jesus than we once did, less zeal in doing His work, and less anguish for the souls of others; if so, it is no wonder that we enjoy less of the presence of God, and are soon cast down. If the root is not strong, how can the branches flourish?

May not self-indulgence have mixed with unbelief? Have we made provision for the flesh? Have we lost the intimacy with Jesus which we once enjoyed? Have we violated the consecration with which we started? If so, the blue mould will settle on the unsound place. Selfishness will mar our strength, and destroy our usefulness. I will not suppose that this is the case with any of you; or, at least, I will only suppose it, and let it remain a supposition.

It is a dreadful fact that, *sometimes, these runnings*

down end in a catastrophe. After secret backsliding comes a sin which is publicly reported, and men cry, " Shame ! " Yet it is not that one sin, but the general state of the man's heart which is the saddest part of it. No man becomes bad all at once. True, the single lightning flash slew its victim, but the bolt had not fallen if there had been no previous gathering of the elements into the condition of storm. The overt scandal is only the development of what was in the man,—the root of the evil lies deeper still. When we hear of a man who has ruined his character by a sur- prising act of folly, we may surmise, as a rule, that this mischief was but one sulphurous jet from a soil charged with volcanic fire ; or, to change the figure, one roaring lion from a den of wild beasts. As you would, on your bended knees, cry day and night that no moral catastrophe may occur to you, beware of the sin which leads to it, beware of the backsliding which culminates in it ; for if we have not the cause, the effect will not follow. The Lord will preserve us if, day by day, we cry unto Him to cleanse our way.

There is an evil under the sun which is as terrible as an open catastrophe,—indeed, it works greater ill to the church in the long run,—and that is, *when a man's ministry is eaten through and through with spiritual dry rot.*

I heard an old Indian describe the way in which furniture may be devoured by the white ants. The ants will come into the house, and eat up everything ; and yet, to all appearance, nothing is touched. The bookcases stand just where they did, and the trunks and everything else remain exactly as they were ; at least, it is so to the eye ; but directly they are touched, they all crumble to pieces, for the ants have eaten the substance out of them. In the same way, some men still remain in the ministry, and yet the soul of their ministry has gone. They have a name to live, yet they are dead : what can be worse than this condition? One might almost sooner have an explosion, and have done with it, than see men continuing to maintain the form of religion after vital godliness has gone, scattering death all around them, and yet maintaining what is called a respectable position. God save us from this last as much as from that first! If I am a rotten bough, let me be cut off ; but to hang upon the tree, all verdant with parasitical lichen and moss, is deplorable. A respectable ministry, devoid of spiritual life, is little better than respectable damnation, from which may God deliver us!

When men drift into this condition, they *generally adopt some expedient to hide it.* Conscience suggests that there is something or other wrong, and the deceitful heart labours to conceal or palliate this fact. Some do this *by amusing themselves with hobbies instead of preaching the gospel.* They cannot do the Lord's work, so they try to do their own. They have not honesty enough to confess that they have lost gospel power, so they ride a hobby ; and it is a very mild form of evil when they raise some side issue, which has no other fault about it than that it diverts them from the main point. Many are these playthings ; I have no time to mention more than one.

I have known *certain brethren give themselves solely to expound prophecy.* Now, a man full of the life of God may expound prophecy as much as he likes; but there are some who, having lost their love of the gospel, try to win back what little popularity they once had by taking up with guesses at the future. They may be quite sure that, if they cannot profit men by bringing them to the manger and the cross, they will make a complete failure of it if they handle the seals and the vials. Did you ever notice, in Calvin's *Commentaries*, that there is no exposition of the Book of Revelation? Why not? He said, " I have not expounded that Book because I do not understand it." When I hear a man say, " I have found much in Matthew which does not belong to the Church, l have outgrown much of the Romans and Galatians, and I cannot enjoy the Psalms, for they do not rise to the perfection of my experience; I want something more elevated and spiritual, more abstruse and wonderful;" I conclude that this brother is spinning his last hank, and spending his last pennyworth of sense.

I have been amused by observing the manner in which speculators have been taken in when they have left the old ship of the gospel to become prophets. The beast of the Revelation was reported to be Napoleon I., and then the creature suddenly reappeared in his nephew, Napoleon III. By-and-by, the deadly wound was healed, and the Prince Imperial wore the dreadful honours of the prophetic book; but the prince is now dead, and it will be needful for the seers to invent a new theory. There is no fear but what they will do it before long; and, meanwhile, " our Israelitish origin" will do to fill up the time. In the story of Sindbad the Sailor, it is said that, as they sailed along, they saw an island, and at the sight thereof they greatly rejoiced. The crew left the ship, and feasted on the island, and were going to take possession of it in the name of the king, when suddenly it began to quiver and to plunge, and finally it went down altogether, for it was a whale's back, and not an island at all! I have known brethren disport themselves upon the back of some novel speculation, when suddenly the facts of history have gone against them, and the whole thing has gone down very like a whale. I have mentioned one of the more harmless hobbies, but some have taken to fancies which have bred greater mischief. Speculation is an index of the spiritual poverty of the man who surrenders himself to it. His flour has all been used, so he tries plaster of Paris; he has no more gold or silver, so he coins the baser metals. He cannot prophesy after the measure of faith, so he exercises his immeasurable imagination. His own experience does not serve him with topics for his ministry, and therefore he takes airy flights into regions of which he knows nothing.

Far worse is it when a man so runs down in heart and spirit that *he has no principles left*, and believes nothing at all. He is a Baptist, but he would very cheerfully minister to a Pædo-baptist church. He is a Calvinist, but he is not narrow, and will promise to offend no one. He holds certain views, but " a view to the pastorate " is the chief of them, and in that view the salary is the charm. He boasts of possessing large-heartedness, and receptivity of spirit, and all that sort of thing. He has dry rot in his soul! That is the truth of the case, and he tries to cover it up with this nonsense! Such persons remind me of an advertisement of a school in France; its concluding paragraph was to this effect: "The pupils will be taught any religion which may be selected by their parents." It is abominable when ministers as good as say that any religion will be taught which may be selected by the deacons. "Pray inform me whether the church likes a high-toned Calvinism, or prefers Arminianism." It is with such as it was with the showman who exhibited the battle of Waterloo, and in answer to the question, "Which is Wellington, and which is Napoleon?" replied, "Whichever you please, my little dears; you pays your money, and you takes your choice." These broad-churchmen are prepared to supply any article for which there is a demand. This is a terrible condition of things, but men do not generally rest there; in the lowest depth, there is still a lower deep.

When the heart has got out of order, and the spiritual life has run down, *men soon fall into actual doctrinal error*, not so much because their head is wrong, for many of them have not erred very much there, but because their heart is in an ill condition. We should never have known that some men had brains at all if they had not addled them. Such departers from the faith usually fall by little and little. They begin by saying very little concerning grace. They serve out homœopathic doses of gospel: it is marvellous what a very small globule of the gospel will save a soul, and it is a great mercy that it is so, or few would be saved. These snatches of gospel, and the preacher who gives them, remind us of the famous dog of the Nile, of whom the ancients said that he was so afraid of the crocodiles that he drank of the river in a great hurry, and was away from it directly. These intellectual gentry are so afraid of the critical croco- diles that the moment they touch the living water of the gospel they are away again. Their doubts are stronger than their beliefs. The worst of it is that they not only give us very little gospel, but they give us much that is not the gospel. In this they are like mosquitoes, of whom I have often said that I do not mind their taking a little of my blood, but it is the poison which they put into me which is my great cause of quarrel with them. That a man should rob me of the gospel, is bad enough; but that he should impregnate me with his poisonous doctrine, is in- tolerable.

When men lose all love to the gospel, they try to make up for the loss of its attractions by sparkling inventions of their own. They imitate life by the artificial flash of culture, reminding me of the saline crystals which cover the salt deserts. There is a life- less plain, in the heart of Persia, so sterile and accursed that even saline plants do not thrive; " but the salt itself, as if in bitter mockery, fashions its crystals in the form of stems and stalks, and covers the steppe with a carpet of unique vegetation, glittering and glistening like an enchanted prairie in the dazzling light of the Eastern sun." Woe be unto the poor congregations who behold this substitute for life, this saline efflorescence of dainty errors and fascinat- ing inventions! Alas, whatever a man may now pro- pound, he will find learned personages to support him in it! Fontenelle used to say that, if he could only get six philosophers to write in its favour, people could be made to believe that the sun is *not* the source of

light and heat; and I think there is a great deal of
truth in the remark. We are told, " Well, he is a very
learned man, he is a Fellow of Brazenface College,
and he has written a book in which he upsets the old
dogmas." If a learned man writes any nonsense, of
course it will have a run; and there is no opinion so insane but, if it has the patronage of so-called scientific
men, it will be believed in certain quarters. I have
myself watched the labours of novelists in theology,
and have tried to get what I could out of their books,
but I have been struck with the remarkably poor
results of their lucubrations. I have stood by the
shore at Mentone, and seen fishermen with miles of
line, and a vast net buoyed up by great tubs, visible
far out at sea. A dozen men are hauling at one rope,
and as many more are pulling in another, drawing this
great net to land. Pull away! Ahoy! Pull away at
the ropes, and bring the fish to land. I believe that,
on one occasion, I did see them produce a fish not so
long as my little finger, but that was a rather successful occasion! Our German friends have diligently
made vast nets with which they have enclosed the sea
of thought; and upon drawing them out, what a noise
there has been, and what a sensation, and what a
trembling and a fainting among the old ladies of
Christendom; but when we have seen their mighty
catch, it has not been the tenth part of a sardine!
The next philosopher who came along, has fitted on
his spectacles with due gravity, after wiping them most
solemnly, and then he has put his critical fork into
this small fish, and, holding it up to be admired of all,
he has discoursed upon its species, till another philosopher equally wise has declared that it was rotten,

and pitched it back into the deeps. This kind of game is continually going on, and many young ministers have been fools enough to give up the apostolic fishery to join in this stupid waste of mental effort. What have they ever done, these doubters, since the world began? What will they do? What can they do? All that they can do now is to wriggle into our churches, and hiss from pulpits which were once filled by the orthodox. They cannot build places of worship of their own,—they could not build a mousetrap; as a rule, there is not power enough in their teaching to gather a congregation, or to keep one when it is gathered. All the vitality, force, and energy they possess are spent, cuckoo-like, in laying their eggs in the nests which we take the trouble to fashion, for they cannot build their own.

God forbid that we should ever try to cover our decline of heart by the invention of our self-conceit! I hope that, when our ministry begins to lose power, we shall be driven to our knees, and to our God, that He may quicken us again by His good Spirit.

Perhaps I have spoken at too great length upon the former part of my subject; I now propose to dwell upon *the necessity of renewing grace.* If any of us have come down from the heights, it is time that we returned to them again. If we have fallen from our first love, it is most needful that we should at once renew the ardour of our youth. If we have gone down even in a small degree, it behoves us to ask for help to get back what we have lost.

This is necessary on account of *our own happiness;* for I appeal to any brother who declines in heart, and grows weak in faith, and doubtful in spirit, whether he is not unhappy. Do you not derive the purest joy and the most solid satisfaction from walking with God? Indeed, those who are "called to be saints" are doomed to be unhappy apart from Christ. It is a doom which destiny has fixed upon you that, if you depart from Christ, you must depart into hell; for it is hell for you to depart from Christ. If, therefore, in any measure, you have roamed away from Christ, mind that you fly home again to Him at once. Last year, when sojourning in the South of France, I went for a mountain ride to the foot of Castiglione, an old, half-deserted town. It was clear and bright at the time, and while the friends who were with me went up the hill to survey the place, I remained a little lower down. I soon observed that the clouds were coming from the other side of the mountains, and in a few minutes I was in a fog, chilled to the bone. I could just see Mentone under the bottom of the clouds, and I said to my man-servant, "Get the horses in, for I must get down again into the sun at once." Soon, the fog was all round me, and I hastened to descend until I reached the sunlight again. You must feel like that, my brethren; if you are caught in a mist, and a chill is upon you, you must hurry back to Christ. You may joyfully repose in Him, and find every blessing and comfort surrounding you; but if you have climbed into high notions, and entered upon the cold regions of speculation, you must hasten down again. You must say of the old gospel, "I can see the blessed spot of my repose, and I will get back to it at once." This is wise advice for those who are conscious of lost comfort through leaving the good old way.

We cannot afford, I am sure, to be in a state of running down, for *we were never too much alive.* Our shortcomings, at our best, are quite sufficient to warn us against what we should be if we were worse. I can imagine some men losing a part of their courage, and yet remaining brave; but if any of mine were to evaporate, I should be a coward indeed. There would have been power in Calvin even if half the steadfastness of his mind had gone, for he was a man of mighty faith; but if I were to lose any measure of my faith, I should be a sorry unbeliever, for I have not a grain of faith to spare.

Dear brethren, have we ever reached our right condition as compared with *our early ideal of what we hoped to be?* Do you recollect when you first entered the College or the ministry? Do you remember what a high standard you set up for yourself? You did well to fix the mark high; for, if you aim at the moon, you will shoot higher than if you fired at a bush. You did well to have a high standard, but you do not well to fall short of it; and, yet, who does not fall short even of his own ideal? Do you not wish to hide your head when you contrast yourself with your Lord? He saved others, and therefore could not save Himself; but we are keen to guard ourselves and our reputations, and often act as if we thought self-preservation the highest law of nature. Our Lord endured great contradiction of sinners against Himself, while we are provoked if we are thwarted in any degree. He loved His sheep, and followed them when they went astray; but we have far too little pity even upon those who gather at our call. We are far, far, far below the true glory of the Well-beloved, and even fall short of our poor ideal of Him. Neither in private in His prayers, nor in public in His life, or His ministry, or His teaching, do we approximate to Him so nearly as we should; and yet, to fall short of likeness to Him, ought to make us blush and weep. We cannot afford, therefore, to run down.

Indeed, if we do not compare ourselves with our Master, but only with our brother-ministers (for certain of them have done right noble work for Jesus), we shall come to the same conclusion. Some of our brethren have held on under fearful discouragements, serving the Lord faithfully; others have won souls for Christ, to whom the winning of one soul has cost more self-denial than the winning of hundreds has cost certain of us. I could sit with delight at the feet of such consecrated brethren as I am now thinking of, and look up to them, and glorify God in them. Such have been found among men of inferior abilities, slender powers, and small attainments; but how they have worked, and how they have prayed, and how God has blessed them! It may be that, with ten times their ability and opportunity, we have not done anything like as much as they have. Do we not mourn over this? Can we afford to decline?

Beloved brethren, we cannot afford to remain in any state lower than the very best; for, if so, *our work will not be well done.* Time was when we preached with all our might. When we began to preach, what preaching it was for zeal and life! In looking back, it must increase our self-humiliation if we perceive that, in our younger days, we were more real and intense than we are now. We preach much better, so the critics say; and we know that there is more thought and more accuracy in our sermons, and that we use better elocution than we did in our young days; but where are the tears of our early ministry? Where is the heart-break of those first sermons in our first sphere? Where is the passion, where is the self-annihilation that we often felt when we poured out our very life with every syllable we spoke? Now, sometimes, we go into the pulpit resolved that we will do as we did then, just as Samson went out to shake himself as he had done aforetime. He had snapped the cords and bands before, and he was going to do the same again; but the Lord had departed from him, and he was weak as another man. Brethren, what if the Lord should depart from us? Alas for us, and for our work!

Nothing can be done if the Holy Spirit be withdrawn; indeed, nothing truly good will be attempted. I have marvelled at the way in which certain persons avoid preaching the gospel when they profess to be doing it. They get a text which you think must cut into the conscience, and they contrive to speak so as neither to arouse the careless nor distress the self-confident. They play with the sword of the Spirit as if they were mountebanks at a show, instead of thrusting the two-edged sword into the hearts of men, as soldiers do in actual combat. The Emperor Gallienus, when a man hurled a javelin many times at a bull without hitting him, and the people hissed him, called the performer to his seat, and placed a wreath on his head, saying, " You are most clever to be able to miss so large a mark so many times." What shall we twine into a crown for those ministers who never strike the heart, never convince men of sin, never drive a Pharisee out of his own righteousness, never influence the guilty so that he casts himself as a lost sinner at the feet of Jesus? He may expect one day to be crowned with shame for such a crime. Meanwhile, twine the deadly nightshade about his brows. Be it ours to be like the left-handed men of Benjamin who "could sling stones at an hair breadth, and not miss." We cannot reach to this unless the life of God be in us and abound.

A man ought to take care of himself, merely as a man, for the sake of himself and his household; but much more should a man, who is a minister, take care of himself *for the sake of those who are committed to his charge.* A captain, in the South Seas, was observed to go beyond the usual point for turning into the harbour, taking a longer but a safer course. On someone remarking to him that he was too careful, he replied, "I have so many souls on board, I cannot afford to run any risk." How many souls there are on board of some of our vessels! How many souls— ay, notwithstanding that the doctrine is unfashionable, I repeat it,—how many souls, not of creatures which will die out like cats and dogs, but of priceless, immortal beings, are committed to our charge! Since, upon our ministry, under God, hang everlasting things,—life and death, Heaven and hell,—what manner of persons ought we to be? How careful we ought to be as to our inner health! How anxious to be always at our very best! If I were a surgeon, and I had to operate upon a patient, I should not like to touch either the knife or his flesh if I felt bilious, or if my hand was quivering; I would not like to be in any but the calmest, coolest, most forceful condition, at the moment in which the difference of a hair's breadth might touch a vital chord, and end a precious life! God help all soul-physicians to be always at their best!

I believe *the headway of God's cause in the world depends upon our being in prime condition.* We are come to the kingdom for such a time as this. As much as ever Simon Menno was raised up to preach believers' baptism in Holland, and keep the lamp burning for God there, and as surely as ever, in our own land, such men as Hansard Knollys, and Kiffin, and Keach, and the like, were bold to stand the brunt of the battle for the Lord, so I believe that you are intended to be in lineal succession defenders of the purest form of gospel truth. We have it in charge to pass on to the next age the everlasting gospel which our venerable sires have handed down to us. As Neander said, there is a future for the Baptists. There is a future for any church which has faithfully kept the ordinances of God, and is resolved in all things to be obedient to its covenant Head. We have neither prestige, nor wealth, nor the State at our back; but we have something better than all these.

When a Spartan was asked what were the boundaries of his country, he replied, " The limits of Sparta are marked by the points of our spears." The limit of our church is also determined by the points of our spears; but our weapons are not carnal. Wherever we go, we preach Christ crucified, and His word of solemn proclamation, " He that believeth and is baptized shall be saved." The enquirer turned, and said to the Spartan, " You have no walls to Sparta." " No," he replied, " the walls of Sparta are the breasts of her

sons." We have no defences for our churches, either
in Acts of Parliament or enforced creeds; but the
regenerated hearts and consecrated spirits of men,
who resolve to live and die in the service of King
Jesus, have hitherto sufficed, in the hands of the
Spirit, to preserve us from grievous heresy. I see no
beginning to this business, this battle of truth commenced so long ago; and I see no end to it, except
the coming of the Master and the eternal victory.
Yet some trembling persons say we ought to stop, and
let the young men already in College learn a trade,
and forego the ministry, lest England should become
over-ministered; and they add that there is no use
in preparing men for the foreign fields, for the Missionary Society is in debt, and its expenses must be
curtailed. God bless the Missionary Society! But
the condition of a Society is not the limit of our personal endeavour; besides, the Society will soon throw
off its burden. If you, my brethren, are worthy of
your calling, you will be bravely independent, and not
hang too much upon the help of others. Sparta could
not have been defended by a race of timid creatures
armed with pointless spears, neither can young men
of timorous spirit do great things for God. You must
be braced to heroism, brethren, if you are to meet the
demands of the hour. May God make the feeblest
among you as David, and the house of David as God!
(Zech. xii. 8.)

I have a proposal to make before I come to my
conclusion, and it is this: *let this be the time of
renewal to each one of us.* Let us each seek for a
personal revival by the Divine Spirit.

We shall see that it is a fit time if we *take an out-look upon our own nation.*   Politically, we have come back to a condition in which there will be a respect for righteousness, justice, and truth, rather than for self-assertion, and national gain, and conquest.   We shall, I trust, no longer be steered by a false idea of British interests, and the policy which comes of it ; but by the great principles of right, justice, and humanity.   This is all I want to see : parties, as such, are nothing to us; nor individual statesmen, except so far as they represent right principles.   We are for those who are on the side of justice, peace, and love. And now, instead of lying still year after year, and making no progress,—no laws amended, no home legislation attended to, but time wasted upon glittering foreign adventures,—something will be done that is worth doing.

At this period, also, our schools are educating the people, and I thank God for that.   Though education will not save men, it may be a means to that end ; for when all our peasants can read their Bibles, we may surely hope that God will bless His own Word.   It will be a grand thing for all our agricultural labourers, by going to the New Testament for themselves, to escape from receiving their religion at second-hand. Godly people must take care to supply them with good books, and so feed the new appetite with healthy food.   All light is good, and we, who most of all prize the light of revelation, are on the side of all kinds of true light.   God is raising up the people, and I think our time is come to avail ourselves of their advance ; and as our one business is to preach Jesus Christ, the more we keep to our work the better, for true religion is the strength of a nation, and the foundation of all right government.

Whatsoever things are honest, true, kind, humane, and moral, may reckon on our aid. We are on the side of temperance, and therefore on the side of the limitation of the abominable traffic which is ruining our country; and we are opposed to all that licenses vice among men, or allows cruelty to animals. We are up to the hilt advocates of peace, and we earnestly war against war. I wish that Christian men would insist more and more on the unrighteousness of war, believing that Christianity means no sword, no cannon, no bloodshed, and that, if a nation is driven to fight in its own defence, Christianity stands by to weep and to intervene as soon as possible, and not to join in the cruel shouts which celebrate an enemy's slaughter. Let us always be on the side of right. To-day, then, my brethren, I beg you to join with me in seeking renewal. Now is the time for a man to buckle on his harness, and bestir himself.

Surely our holy fellowship at this happy hour should help us all to rise to a higher level. The sight of many of our brethren is cheering and stimulating. When I remember concerning some their holiness, their depth of piety, their perseverance, I feel comforted in the belief that, if the Lord has strengthened others, He has yet a blessing in reserve for us also. Let this Feast of Tabernacles be the time for renewing our vows of consecration unto the Lord our God.

Let us begin it with *repentance for all our mistakes and shortcomings*. Let each one do this for himself. You remember how the ancient giant fought with Hercules, and the hero could not overcome him, because every time he fell he touched his mother earth, and received new strength. Let us, too, fall upon our faces, that we may rise invigorated; let us go back to our first simple faith, and recover our lost strength. Men who have been sore sick have cried, "Take me back to my native air, and I shall soon be well. Among the buttercups and daisies of the meadows, in which I used to play when I was a child, and near the brook where I caught the minnows, I shall soon revive." Ah! it does our soul good to get back to our days of child-like faith, when we sang,—

> "Just as I am,—without one plea
> But that Thy blood was shed for me,
> And that Thou bidd'st me come to Thee,
>   O Lamb of God, I come."

This will help you to renew your youth: it seems an easy way, but it is the only way.

Next, *let us renew our consecration.* I do not invite any of you literally to stain the door-post of the College with your blood, but I ask you to think upon that Israelitish slave whose time had run out, but who chose to remain in service because he loved his master and his master's children, and therefore he put his ear against the post of the door, and they bored it through with an awl. May the Lord bore the ear of each of us, that we may be His servants for ever! We love our Master, do we not, brethren? We love our Master's work; and we love our Master's servants and His children, and for His sake we will serve them all, for better or worse, till death doth part us from this lower service. Oh, to get back to the old moorings! I would like for us to *preach our old sermons;*

I do not mean the same sermons, but with the same force as when we began to—

"Tell to sinners round,
What a dear Saviour we had found."

People said, " That dear young man does not know very much, but he loves Jesus Christ, and he talks about nothing else." I would like to preach again as I did at first, only a great deal better. I intensely believed and meant every word I spoke ; I do so now, but doubts will arise now which never vexed me then. I would like to be a child again before the Lord, and to keep so, for I am sure that questions and doubts are a sad loss to any man.

Return, my brethren, to *your earliest Bible-readings*, when you were wont to let the promise lie under your tongue as a dainty morsel. Ah! this Book, as I turn it over, wakes up many a memory ; its pages glow with a light which I cannot describe, for they are set with stars which in my many hours of gloom have been the light of my soul. I did not then read this divine volume to find a text, but to hear my Lord speak to my own heart ; I was not then as Martha, cumbered with much serving, but as Lazarus, who sat at the table with Jesus.

God grant us also a revival of *the first aims of our spiritual career!* Then, we thought nothing of pleasing men, but only aimed at pleasing God and winning souls ; we were rash enough to care for nothing but the fulfilment of our mission ; is it so now? We *can* preach now, can we not? We feel that we are proficient in our art. It might be better if we did not feel quite so well equipped. I find it better to go to the pulpit in prayerful weakness than in self-reliant strength. When I groan out, " What a fool I am!" and come down, after the sermon, ashamed of my poor attempt, I am sure it is better with me than when I am pleased with my performance. Are any of us such babies as to feel like that? What a sense of responsibility we had in our first services; do we retain that solemnity of spirit? We then prayed about the choice of every hymn, and the manner of reading the Scriptures; we did nothing carelessly, for a heavy anxiety pressed upon us. I always read the Scripture carefully at home, and tried to understand it before I read it to the people, and I thus formed a habit from which I have never swerved; but it is not so with all. Some say, " I have been about all the day, and I have to preach to-night, but I can manage." Yes, but it will not please God for us to offer Him that which costs us nothing. Others have a stock of sermons, and I have heard that, just before the time for entering the pulpit, they turn over their precious manuscripts, pick out a likely one, and without further preparation read it as God's message to the people. The Lord deliver us from a state of mind in which we dare to put on the table of shewbread the first loaf which comes to hand! No; let us serve the Lord with growing carefulness and reverence.

It would be well for many *to get back to their first prayers and watchfulness,* and all else that is good.

Can it be done? Brother, it can be done. You can have all the life you had, and more, by the blessing of the Holy Spirit. You can be as intense as you ever were. I have seen old horses turned out to

grass, and come back fresh and vigorous. I know a
pasture wherein, if a worn-out steed doth graze, it
shall come back to be harnessed to the gospel chariot
with strength renewed. Let us remember those hallowed spots where Jesus has met with us in former
days, where, or ever we were aware, our soul was
made " like the chariots of Ammi-nadib." Lord,
renew Thy former mercies, and we shall rise, like
the phœnix, from our ashes!

It may cost you a great deal to be set right again.
John Bunyan speaks of the pilgrim who lost his roll,
and had to go back for it, so that he travelled three
times over the road, and then found the sun setting
ere he reached his lodging. But cost us whatever it
may, we must get right with God. I read a dream,
the other day, which was the means of a man's conversion. He thought that he was going with his
friend into one of the Eastern towns, and as he was
about to enter, the portcullis above the gate began to
fall. As it descended, he stooped; but it fell so fast
that he could not get through, stooping, kneeling,
crouching, or even lying down. He felt that he must
enter, so he made a desperate effort. He had on a
very fine laced vest, and he pulled that off, but the
portcullis still descended, till he found that the only
thing he could do was to strip himself, and then, close
to the earth, and grazed by the gravel, he crept
through. When he was safely inside the gate, a
shining one covered him from head to foot with
glittering garments. It may be that, in order to get
right with God, we shall have to part with that fine
vest, that splendid theory, that love of popularity, that
rhetorical flourishing; but, oh! if we once get through

that gate, and God covers us with the robe of acceptance in the Beloved, it will well repay us for anything that the struggle may cost us.

I am sorry to say that I am made of such ill stuff that my Lord has to chasten me often and sorely. I am like a quill pen that will not write unless it be often nibbed, and therefore I have felt the sharp knife many times ; and yet I shall not regret my pains and crosses so long as my Lord will write with me on men's hearts. That is the cause of many ministers' afflictions ; they are necessary to our work. You have heard the fable of the raven that wished to drink, but the pitcher had so little water in it that he could not reach it, and therefore he took stone after stone, and dropped them into the vessel until the water rose to the brim, and he could drink. There is so little grace, in some men, that they need many sicknesses, bereavements, and other afflictions to make their graces available for usefulness. If, however, we receive grace enough to bear fruit without continual pruning, so much the better.

It is expected of us, brethren, that from this time we rise to a higher point. It is the Lord's due, if we think of what He has done for us. Some of my comrades in arms, now before me, have gone through battles as hard as any men may wish to fight ; and after such success as they have had, they must never say die. After what the Lord has done for us, we must never strike our flag, nor turn our backs in the day of battle. Sir Francis Drake, when it was feared that he would be wrecked in the Thames, said, " What! have I been round the world, and am I now to be drowned in a ditch? Not I." So say I to you, brethren: you have done business in stormy waters, and will you sink in a village pond? We shall not be worse treated than we have been. We are now in fine fighting trim, for we are hardened by former blows. A great pugilist at Rome was so battered, his nose, eyes, and face were so disfigured, that he was always ready to fight, because he said, " I cannot look worse than I do." Personally, I am in much the same plight. Men cannot say anything worse of me than they have said. I have been belied from head to foot, and misrepresented to the last degree. My good looks are gone, and none can damage me much now.

Some of you have had more to batter you than you are ever likely to endure again; you have had trial and tribulation and affliction as heavy as you can have them; and after having stood in the lists so long, surely you are not going to yield, and slink away like cowards? God forbid it! God forbid it! God grant, on the contrary, that the elder ones among you may have the pleasure, not only of winning battles for Christ, but of seeing others, who have been saved under your instrumentality, trained to fight for Jesus better than you yourselves have fought! The other day, I read a story, and with that I will conclude, desiring that I may, in spiritual things, have the same joy myself, and that it may be the lot of you all. Diagoras the Rhodian had, in his time, won many wreaths at the Olympian games. He had two boys, and he brought them up to the same profession. The day came when his own force abated, and he was no longer able to strive for masteries in his own person; but he went up to the Olympian games with his two sons. He saw the blows they gave and received, and rejoiced when he discovered that they were both victorious. A Lacedæmonian said to him, " You may die now, Diagoras ; " meaning that the old man might be content to die, because he had, in his own person, and in that of his sons, obtained the highest honours. The old man seemed to feel that it was even so, for when his two sons came, and shouldered their father, and carried him through the arena amid the ringing cheers of the great assembly, the old man, flushed with excitement, died under the eyes of the assembled Greeks. It would have been a wiser thing to have lived, for he had a third son, who became more renowned than the other two ; but he passed away on a wave of victory. O brethren, may you have spiritual children who shall win battles for the Lord, and may you live to see them doing it ; then may you say, with old Simeon, " Lord, now lettest Thou Thy servant depart in peace, according to Thy Word."

In the Name of the Ever-blessed, we this day again set up our banners. Our watchword is " Victory." We mean to win for the grand old cause of Puritanism, Protestantism, Calvinism,—all poor names which the world has given to our great and glorious faith,— the doctrine of Paul the apostle, the gospel of our Lord and Saviour Jesus Christ. We can both strike, and bear the strokes which are returned. Through Divine grace, we have given to us both energy and patience ; we can work, and we can wait. May the Divine life in us put forth its mightiest force, and make us strong to the utmost of human possibility, and then we shall gain the victory, and give all the glory of it to our omnipotent Leader. The Lord be with you, beloved ! Amen.

LIGHT. FIRE. FAITH. LIFE. LOVE.

———

I NEVER needed help more than now, and never felt so utterly unfitted to give the key-note to the Conference. As you grow more numerous, more gifted, and more experienced, I feel more and more my unworthiness to stand foremost, and to lead your ranks. However, I will trust in God, and believe that He will, by His Holy Spirit, send a word that shall be encouraging and quickening.

Years ago, an eccentric judge, known as Judge Foster, went upon circuit in extreme old age during a very hot summer; and on one of the most sultry days of that summer, he addressed the grand jury at Worcester in some such terms as these, " Gentlemen of the Jury, it is very hot, and I am very old; you know your duties very well; go and do them." Following his example, I feel inclined to say to you, " Gentlemen, here you are assembled; I have many infirmities to bear, and you will have great difficulty in bearing with my talk; you know your duties; go and do them." Action is better than speech. If I speak for an hour, I shall scarcely be able to say anything more practical than that,—" You know your duties; go and do them." " England expects every man to do his duty," was the rousing signal of Nelson at Trafalgar; need I remind you that our great Lord expects every one of His servants to occupy his post

until his Master comes again, and so to be a good and
faithful servant? Go forth, brethren, and fulfil your
Master's high behest, and may God's Spirit work in
you the good pleasure of your Lord!

Those who truly serve God are made to feel more
and more forcibly that " life is real, life is earnest," if
it be indeed life in Christ. In times of great pain, and
weakness, and depression, it has come over me to
hope that, if I should again recover, I should be more
intense than ever; if I could be privileged to climb the
pulpit stairs again, I resolved to leave out every bit of
flourish from my sermons, to preach nothing but
present and pressing truth, and to hurl it at the people
with all my might; myself living at high pressure, and
putting forth all the energy of which my being is
capable. I suppose you, too, have felt like this when
you have been laid aside. You have said to yourselves,
" Playtime is over with us, we must get to work. Parade
is ended, now comes the tug of war. We must not waste
a single moment, but redeem the time, because the
days are evil." When we see the wonderful activity
of the servants of Satan, and how much they accomplish, we may well be ashamed of ourselves that we
do so little for our Redeemer, and that the little is
often done so badly that it takes as long to set it
right as we spent in the doing of it. Brethren, let us
cease from regrets, and come to actual amendment.

A great German philosopher has asserted that life
is all a dream. He says that " it is a dream composed of a dream of itself." He believes in no actual
existence, not even in his own; even *that* he con-
ceives to be but a thought. Surely, some who are in
the ministry must be disciples of that philosophy, for

they are half-asleep, and their spirit is dreamy. They speak of the eternal truth as though it were a temporary system of belief, passing away like all other visions of earth. They live for Christ in a manner which would never be thought of by a person who meant to make money, or to obtain a degree at the University. "Why," said one, of a certain minister, "if I acted, in my business, as he does in his ministry, I should be in the *Gazette* within three months." It is an unhappy thing that there should be men calling themselves ministers of Christ to whom it never seems to occur that they are bound to display the utmost industry and zeal. They seem to forget that they are dealing with souls that may be lost for ever or saved for ever, souls that cost the Saviour's heart's blood. They do not appear to have understood the nature of their calling, or to have grasped the Scriptural idea of an ambassador for Christ. Like drowsy waggoners, they hope to get their team safely home, though they themselves are sound asleep.

I have heard of ministers who are most lively when playing croquet or cricket, or getting up an excursion, or making a bargain. It was said of one, in my hearing, "What a fine minister he would have been if he had only been converted!" I heard it said of a very clever man, "He would have been a great winner of souls, if he had only believed in souls; but he believed in nothing." It is said of the Russian peasants that, when they have done their work, they will lie on the stove, or around it, and there sleep hour after hour; and there is a current opinion among them that they are only awake when they are asleep, and that their waking and working hours are nothing but a horrible dream. The *moujik* hopes that his dreams are facts, and that his waking sufferings are merely nightmares. May not some have fallen into the same notion with regard to the ministry? They are asleep upon realities, and awake about shadows; in earnest about trifles, yet trifling about solemnities. What God will have to say to those servants who do their own work well, and *His* work badly, I will not attempt to fore-shadow. What shall be done to the man who dis-played great capacity in his recreations, but was dull in his devotions; active out of his calling, and languid in it? The day shall declare it. Let us arouse our-selves to the sternest fidelity, labouring to win souls as much as if it all depended wholly upon ourselves, while we fall back, in faith, upon the glorious fact that everything rests with the eternal God.

I see before me many who are fully aroused, and are eager in seeking the lost; for I speak to some of the most earnest spirits in the Christian Church,—evangelists and pastors whose meat and drink it is to do the will of their Lord. But even these, who are most awake, will not differ from me when I assert that they could be yet more aroused. My brethren, when you have been at your best, you might have been better. Who among us might not have had greater success if he had been ready to obtain it? When Nelson served under Admiral Hotham, and a certain number of the enemy's ships had been captured, the commander said, "We must be contented; we have done very well." But Nelson did not think so, since a number of the enemy's vessels had escaped. "Now," said he, "had we taken ten sail, and allowed the eleventh to escape when it had been possible to have

got at her, I could never have called it *well done.*" If
we have brought many to Christ, we dare not boast,
for we are humbled by the reflection that more might
have been done had we been fitter instruments for
God to use.

Possibly some brother will say, " I have done all that
I could do." That may be his honest opinion, for he
could not have preached more frequently, or held more
meetings. Perhaps it is true that he has held enough
meetings, and the people have had quite enough sermons; but there might have been an improvement in
the spirit of the meetings, and in the sermons, too.
Some ministers might do more in reality if they did
less in appearance. A Bristol Quaker—and Quakers
are very shrewd men,—years ago stepped into an
alehouse, and called for a quart of beer. The beer
frothed up, and the measure was not well filled. The
Friend said to the landlord, " How much trade art
thou doing?" " Oh!" he answered, " I draw ten butts
of beer a month." " Dost thou know how thou
mightest draw eleven butts?" " No, sir; I wish I
did." " I will tell thee, friend; thee can do it by
filling thy pots." To any brother who says, " I do
not know how I can preach more gospel than I do,
for I preach very often," I would reply, " You need
not preach oftener, but fill the sermons fuller of
gospel." The Saviour at the marriage-feast said,
" Fill the waterpots with water." Let us imitate the
servants, of whom we read, " They filled them up to
the brim." Let your discourses be full of matter,—
sound, gracious, and condensed. Certain speakers
suffer from an awful flux of words; you can scarcely
spy out the poor little straw of an idea which has been

hurried down an awful Ganges or Amazon of words.
Give the people plenty of thought, plenty of Scriptural, solid doctrine, and deliver it in a way which is
growingly better,—every day better, every year better,
—that God may be more glorified, and sinners may
more readily learn the way of salvation.

I shall now commend to you, for the perfecting of
your ministry, five things, which should be in you and
abound. You remember the passage which says,
" Salt, without prescribing how much." There is no
need for limiting the quantity of any of the matters
now commended to you. Here they are,—*light, fire,
faith, life, love.* Their number is five, so you may
count them on your fingers ; their value is inestimable,
so grasp them with firm hand, and let them be carried
in your hearts.

I.   I commend to you most earnestly the acquisition
and distribution of LIGHT.

To that end, we must *first get the light.* Get light
even of the commonest order, for all light is good.
Education upon ordinary things is valuable, and I
would stir up certain loitering brethren to make ad-
vances in that direction. Many among you entered
the College with no education whatever ; but when
you left it, you had learned enough to have formed
the resolution to study with all your might, and you
have carried it out. I wish that all had done so. It
is a great advantage to a minister to commence his
public life in a small village, where he can have time
and quiet for steady reading ; that man is wise who
avails himself of the golden opportunity. We ought
not only to think of what we can now do for God,
but of what we may yet be able to do if we improve

ourselves. No man should ever dream that his education is complete. I know that my friend Mr. Rogers, though he has passed his eightieth year, is still a student, and perhaps has more of the true student spirit about him now than ever: will any of the younger sort sit down in self-content? We shall continue to learn even in Heaven, and shall still be looking deeper and deeper into the abyss of Divine love: it were ill to talk of perfect knowledge here below. If a man says, " I am fully equipped for my work, and need learn no more; I have moved here after having been three years in the last place, and I have quite a stock of sermons, so that I am under no necessity to read any more ;" I would say to him, " My dear friend, may the Lord give you some brains, for you talk like one who is deficient in that department." A brain is a very hungry thing indeed, and he who possesses it must constantly feed it by reading and thinking, or it will shrivel up or fall asleep. It is the child of the horseleech, and it crieth evermore, " Give, give." Do not starve it. If such mind-hunger never happens to you, I suspect that you have no mind of any consequence.

But, brethren, see to it that you have, in a sevenfold degree, *light of a higher kind.* You are to be, above all things, students of the Word of God ; this, indeed, is a main point of your avocation. If we do not study Scripture, and those books that will help us to understand theology, we are but wasting time while we pursue other researches. We should judge him to be a foolish fellow who, while preparing to be a physician, spent all his time in studying astronomy. There is a connection of some kind between stars and human bones; but a man could not learn much of surgery from Arcturus or Orion. So, there is a connection between every science and religion, and I would advise you to obtain much general knowledge; but universal information will be a poor substitute for a special and prayerful study of the Scriptures, and of the doctrines contained in the revelation of God. We are to study men and our own hearts; we ought to sit as disciples in the schools of providence and experience. Some ministers grow fast because the great Teacher chastens them sorely, and the chastening is sanctified; but others learn nothing by their experience, they blunder out of one ditch into another, and learn nothing by their difficulties but the art of creating fresh ones. I suggest to you all the prayer of a Puritan who, during a debate, was observed to be absorbed in writing. His friends thought he was taking notes of his opponent's speech; but when they got hold of his paper, they found nothing but these words, " More light, Lord! More light, Lord! " Oh, for more light from the great Father of lights!

Let not this light be only that of knowledge, but seek for *the light of joy and cheerfulness*. There is power in a happy ministry. A lugubrious face, a mournful voice, a languor of manner,—none of these things commend us to our hearers; especially do they fail to attract the young. Certain strange minds find their happiness in misery, but they are not numerous. I once had a letter from a man, who told me that he came to the Tabernacle, but as soon as he entered, he felt that it could not be the house of God because there were so many present, and " strait is the gate, and narrow is the way, which leadeth unto life, and

few there be that find it." When he looked at me, he
felt sure that I was unsound in the faith, for I should
not look so cheerful in the face, neither should I be
so bulky in person, if I belonged to the tried people
of God. Worst of all, when he looked round upon
the congregation, and saw their happy countenances,
he said to himself, " These people know nothing about
the depravity of their hearts, or the inward struggles
of believers." Then he informed me that he wended
his way to a very small chapel, where he saw a minister, who looked as if he had been in the furnace ; and
though there were only eight persons present, they all
looked so depressed that he felt quite at home. I
suppose he sat down, and sang,—

> " My willing soul would stay
> In such a frame as this,
> And sit and sing herself away
> From everything like bliss."

I felt glad that the good man was enabled to enjoy a
little comfortable misery with his brethren. I did not
feel at all envious ; nor do I think that such a ministry
of misery will ever draw to itself a number that no
man can number. The children of light prefer the
joy of the Lord, for they find it to be their strength.

Get plenty of light, brethren, *and when you have
obtained it, give it out.* Never fall into the notion
that mere earnestness will suffice without knowledge,
and that souls are to be saved simply by our being
zealous. I fear that we are more deficient in heat
than in light ; but, at the same time, that kind of
fire which has no light in it is of a very doubtful
nature, and cometh not from above. Souls are saved
by truth which enters the understanding, and so

reaches the conscience. How can the gospel save when it is not understood? The preacher may preach with a great deal of stamping, and hammering, and crying, and entreating; but the Lord is not in the wind, nor in the fire;—the still small voice of truth is needed to enter the understanding, and thereby reach the heart. People must be taught. We must " go, and teach all nations," making disciples of them; and I know of no way in which you can save men without teaching on your part, and discipleship on theirs.

Some preachers, though they know a great deal, do not teach much, because they use such an involved style. Recollect that you are addressing people who need to be taught like children; for, though they are grown up, the major part of our hearers are still in a state of childhood as to the things of God; and if they are to receive the truth, it must be made very plain, and packed up so as to be easily carried away, and laid up in the memory. Therefore, brethren, give forth much holy instruction. Some give little instruction because of their involved style; but many fail for other reasons, and mainly because they aim at something else. Talleyrand defines a metaphysician as a man who is very clever in drawing black lines upon a black ground. I should like to draw black lines upon a white ground, or else white lines on a black ground, so that they could be seen; but certain preachers are so profound that no one understands them. On the other hand, have you not heard sermons with great oratorical display about them, and nothing more? You have looked on while the angel wrought wondrously. The preacher has been like Blondin on the tight-rope; and as we have looked at him, we have trembled, lest he should never reach the end of his lofty period. Yet he has balanced himself admirably, and moved along in his elevated position in a marvellous manner. But, when all is over, your mind is unsatisfied, for these acrobatic feats of rhetoric do not feast the soul. Brethren, we must not make it our aim to be grand orators. Certain men are eloquent by nature, and it is not possible for them to be otherwise than oratorical, any more than for nightingales to help singing sweetly; these I do not blame, but admire. It is not the duty of the nightingale to bring down its voice to the same tone as that of the sparrow. Let it sing sweetly if it can do so naturally. God deserves the best oratory, the best logic, the best metaphysics, the best of everything; but if ever rhetoric stands in the way of the instruction of the people, a curse on rhetoric! If any educational attainment, or any natural gift which we possess, should make it less easy for the people to understand us, let it perish! May God rend away from our thought and style everything which darkens the light, even though it should be like a costly veil of rarest lace! May we use great plainness of speech, that gospel light may shine out very clearly from our ministry!

At this time, there is a great necessity for giving much light, for *a fierce attempt is being made to quench or dim the light*. Many are scattering darkness on all sides. Therefore, brethren, keep the light burning in your churches, keep the light burning in your pulpits, and hold it forth in the face of men who love darkness because it favours their aims. Teach the people all truth, and let not our distinctive opinions be concealed. There are sheep-stealers

about, who come forth in the night, and run away with
our people because they do not know our principles,—
the principles of Nonconformists, the principles of
Baptists, or even the principles of Christianity. Our
hearers have a general idea of these things, but not
enough to protect them from deceivers. We are beset,
not only by sceptics, but by certain brethren who
devour the feeble. Do not leave your children to
wander out without the guardianship of holy knowledge, for there are seducers abroad who will mislead
them if they can. They will begin by calling them
" dear " this, and " dear " that, and end by alienating
them from those who brought them to Jesus. If you
lose your members, let it be in the light of day, and
not through their ignorance. These kidnappers dazzle
weak eyes with flashes of novelty, and turn weak
heads with wonderful discoveries and marvellous doctrines, which all tend towards division, and bitterness,
and the exaltation of their own sect. Keep the light
of truth burning, and thieves will not dare to plunder
your house.

Oh, for a church of believers in Jesus who know
why they believe in Him; persons who believe the
Bible, and know what it contains; who believe the
doctrines of grace, and know the bearings of those
truths; who know where they are, and what they are,
and who therefore dwell in the light, and cannot be
deceived by the prince of darkness! Do, dear friends,
—I speak specially to the younger brethren among
us,—do let there be plenty of teaching in your ministry. I fear that sermons are too often judged by their
words rather than by their sense. Let it not be so
with you. Feed the people always with knowledge

and understanding, and let your preaching be solid, containing food for the hungry, healing for the sick, and light for those who sit in darkness.

II. I have now, in the second place, to plead with you that you gather and use in your ministry much heavenly FIRE. Upon this subject, you will perhaps expect me to speak guardedly; for you have seen the mischief of wild fire, and the perils of strange fire, and possibly you are anxious to know what I think of a certain "army" which abounds in fire, and blazes away most marvellously. I shall express no opinion, except that none of the supposed evils of fire are equal to those of lukewarmness. Even fanaticism is to be preferred to indifference. I had sooner risk the dangers of a tornado of religious excitement than see the air grow stagnant with a dead formality. It is far better for people to be too hot than to be luke-warm. "I would thou wert cold or hot" is Christ's word still, and it applies to preachers as well as to others. When a man is freezingly cold in the things of Christ, we know where he is; and if another is red-hot, or even at a white heat, and is thought to be too enthusiastic, we know where he is; but when a minister preaches in such a way that, at the close of his sermon, you say, "This is neither cold nor hot," you go away feeling that you have had enough, or even too much of it. There was nothing to excite you; you could almost wish to have been made angry rather than to have been lulled by such discoursing. A lukewarm sermon sickens every healthy mind.

Nor is this evil to be found in the pulpit alone. I should gravely question whether, if an angel were to take a thermometer, and go round the Dissenting churches in London, he would not find a large proportion of them certainly not cold, most decidedly not hot, but between the two. How is it with you, dear brother? Do you say, " Well, I am not the warmest of all, but then I am not the coldest of all "? Then I have a suspicion as to your temperature; but I leave the matter to your own judgment, only remarking that I have never yet met with fire that is moderately hot. Should any of you discover such an article, you will be wise to patent it, for it might be of service in many ways. The fire with which I have been acquainted has been such that I have never given it my hand without remembering its warm embrace. Fire has never yet learned moderation. I am told that it is wrong to go to extremes, and upon that ground fire is certainly guilty; for it is not only intensely hot, but it has a tendency to consume and destroy without limit. When it once commenced with this city, in the olden time, it left little of it but ashes; there was no keeping it within bounds. May God grant us grace to go to extremes in His service! May we be filled with an unrestrainable zeal for His glory! May the Lord answer us by fire, and may that fire fall first on the ministers, and then upon the people! We ask for the true Pentecostal flame, and not for sparks kindled by human passion. A live coal from off the altar is our need, and nothing can supply its place; but this we must have, or our ministry will be in vain.

Brethren, we must, first of all, take care that we have *the fire burning in our own souls.* I am happy to know that there are very few, if any, among you who are utterly cold; for you go to be warmed into earnestness if we set about it aright. It is very hard to warm a stone. You may clothe a man in blankets until he is fairly warm, because there is life in him; but you cannot heat a stone in that fashion. Life always begets a measure of warmth, and the possibility of more; and as you have life, there is within you the capacity for heat. Some preachers are of such a cold nature that no known means could warm them.

The attempt to find heat in some men's sermons reminds me of Æsop's fable of the apes and the glow-worm. The apes found a glowworm shining on the bank, and straightway gathered round it to warm themselves. They placed sticks over it, and tried to make a fire; but it did not burn. It was a very pretty thing, and looked like flame; but they could not warm their cold hands with its cold light. So have I known ministers, whose light was destitute of heat; and, consequently, the poor sticks around them have never kindled into a flame, nor have frozen hearts been melted by their influence.

It is dreadful work to listen to a sermon, and feel all the while as if you were sitting out in a snowstorm, or dwelling in a house of ice, clear but cold, orderly but killing. You have said to yourself, " That was a well-divided and well-planned sermon, but I cannot make out what was the matter with it;" the secret being that there was the wood, but no fire to kindle it. A great sermon without heart in it reminds one of those huge furnaces in Wales, which have been permitted to go out; they are a pitiful sight. We prefer a sermon in which there may be no vast talent, and no great depth of thought; but what there is has come fresh from the crucible, and, like molten metal, burns its way. I once knew a lad who, when he used to go home from the smithy where he worked, was roughly handled by the boys of the village, till his master suggested to him a plan of defence, which was wonderfully efficacious. He took a rod of iron, and just before he started to go home, he blew up the fire, and made the iron hot. When the boys came round him, he warned them not to touch his stick; and after once feeling it, they obeyed the admonition, and respectfully kept their distance. I do not quote the example with any commendation of the actual fact, but with this moral in view,—heat your sermon red-hot, and it will be likely to be remembered by all who come into contact with it. Everything gives way before fire.

Energy still remains an essential, whatever else in oratory may have changed since the days of old. It is said that the oft-quoted reply of Demosthenes to the question, " What is the first thing in oratory? " was not " Action," but " Energy." What is the second thing? " Energy." What is the third thing? " Energy." I will not pretend to decide the classical question; but I am sure that, as a matter of fact, energy is the main thing in the human side of preaching. Like the priests at the altar, we can do nothing without fire. Brethren, speak because you believe the gospel of Jesus, speak because you feel its power, speak under the influence of the truth which you are delivering, speak with the Holy Ghost sent down from Heaven, and the result will not be doubtful.

Let it be carefully remembered that *our flame must be kindled from on high.* Nothing is more to be despised than a mere painted fire, the simulation of earnestness. Sooner let us have an honest death than a counterfeit life. The imitation of Baxter is detestable; but to be like Baxter is seraphic. If you would be like Whitefield, I would say *be* Whitefield. Let the fire be kindled by the Holy Ghost, and not by animal passion, the desire of honour, emulation of others, or the excitement of attending meetings. Let the terrible example of Nadab and Abihu for ever put away strange fire from our censers. Burn because you have been in solemn fellowship with the Lord our God.

Recollect also, that *the fire which you and I need will consume us if we truly possess it.* " Spare yourself," may be whispered by friends; but it will not be heeded when this fire is burning. We have given ourselves up to the work of God, and we cannot go back. We desire to be whole burntofferings and complete sacrifices to God, and we dare not shun the altar. " Except a corn of wheat fall into the ground and die, it abideth alone : but if it die, it bringeth forth much fruit." We can only produce life in others by the wear and tear of our own being. This is a natural and spiritual law,—that fruit can only come of the seed by its spending and being spent even to self-exhaustion.

Why are many earnest ministers worn and weary till heart and brain give way? They would be of little use if they did not run such a risk. All men, who are eminently useful, are made to feel their weakness in a supreme degree. Can the Spirit of God, even the Infinite Deity, ride in such frail chariots as these, without straining the axle, and making the whole machine to quiver, as if it would be utterly dissolved beneath its sacred burden? When God visits us with

soul-saving power, it is as though devouring flame
came forth from Heaven, and made its abode in our
bosoms; and where this is the case, there may well
be a melting away of all strength. Yet let it be so:
we humbly invite the sacred burnings. Herod was
eaten of worms, being cursed of God; but to be consumed by God for His own service, is to be blessed
to the full. We have a choice between these two, to
be eaten up by our corruptions, or by the zeal of
God's house. It needs no hesitation, the choice of
every man among us is to be wholly the Lord's,—
ardently, passionately, vehemently the Lord's servants, let the Divine fervour cost us what it may of
brain, and heart, and life. Our only hope of honour,
and glory, and immortality lies in the fulfilment of our
dedication unto God; as devoted things, we must be
consumed with fire, or else be rejected. For us to
turn aside from our life-work, and to seek distinction
elsewhere, is absolute folly; a blight will be upon us,
we shall not succeed in anything but the pursuit of
God's glory through the teaching of the Word. " This
people have I formed for Myself," saith God; " they
shall shew forth My praise;" and if we will not do
this, we shall do less than nothing. For this one thing
we are created; and if we miss this, we shall live in
vain.

Good Dr. Wayland, the other day, walking in my
garden, saw the swans out of the water, and he
remarked that they were the true representation of
persons who are out of their proper sphere, and
attempt to do what they were never made for. How
ungainly the swans are on land, they waddle in a
ridiculous manner; but as soon as they are in the

water, how gracefully they glide along; each one is the model of a ship, the image of beauty; every line about it is perfect. So is it with a man who is content to find in the ministry "waters to swim in." As God's sent servant, he is everything that is beautiful; but as soon as he dabbles in trade, or becomes a secular lecturer, or seeks his own aggrandizement, he ceases to be admirable, he often becomes notorious, and is always awkward. Brethren, you are not meant for anything but God; therefore, surrender yourselves to God, and find in Him your wealth, your honour, and your all. If you do this, you shall be the head, and not the tail; but if you start aside, you shall be lightly esteemed. Let the fire of perfect consecration be heaped upon you, for so shall you glow and shine like molten silver, which brightens amid the heat. Let us not subject ourselves to the shame and eternal contempt which will be the portion of those who quit the service of their Redeemer for the bondage of self-seeking. Jesus said to His disciples, "If any man will come after Me, let him deny himself, and take up his cross, and follow Me."

III. The next thing necessary to us is FAITH; I might say the first, second, third, and last thing is FAITH. "Without faith it is impossible to please God;" and if we are pleasing God, it is not by our talent, but by our faith.

Just now, we much need faith in the form of *fixity of belief*. We know more than we did some time ago; at least, I hope we do. I just now heard one of you say to another brother, "How broad you get!" Well, we do widen out; but not as some men; for we are not of the Broad School, who believe little or nothing aright because they desire to believe everything. We have cast our anchor, it has taken a firm grip; we have ceased to drift; we remain at rest. Some men have no creed, or, if they have, it is altered so often that it is of no use to them. It must be like the blanket of a gentleman who came from the Emerald Isle, of which he said, "See here! Our skipper has given me a shamefully bad blanket. Just look at it: it is too long at the top, and it is too short at the bottom; it gets over my head, and yet my feet are always cold. I cut a whole foot off the top, and I sewed it on to the bottom, but it is not altered a bit; it still comes over my eyes, and is too short to cover my feet." That is what certain "thinkers" do with their creed; they keep cutting it off at one end, and putting it on at the other, but it never gets right; it is always forming, never formed. Modern creeds are like the clothes of Italian peasants, which I have gazed upon with wondering enquiry. It would puzzle the most learned geologist to discover the primary formation of a pair of trousers which have been patched and mended with cloth of all patterns and colours from generation to generation. Such and so varied are some men's beliefs and unbeliefs; an agglomeration of philosophic rags, metaphysical tatters, theological remnants, and heretical cast-offs. Certain thinkers have reached the blessed ultimatum of believing nothing at all with anything like certainty of belief.

When these "cultivated" persons speak of us, they manifest great scorn, and affect to believe that we are natural fools. Ah, dear! People are not always what they are thought to be, and it may happen that

a man sees himself as in a glass when he thinks he is
looking out of the window at a neighbour. It is a sign
of great weakness when persons are full of contempt
for others. If, in any Review or pamphlet, a writer
parades his culture, you may be sure that he has been
lying fallow of late, and his affectations are the weeds
which have come of it. If it came to a fair contest
upon the matter of education and culture, the
orthodox would be quite able to hold their own.
Boasting is sorry work; but, sometimes, persons must
be answered according to their folly, and I say boldly
that, in any sort of mental tournament, we should not
tremble to tilt with the men of "modern thought."
Be it so or not, it is ours to believe. We believe that,
when the Lord our God gave forth a revelation, He
knew His own mind, and that He expressed Himself
in the best and wisest manner, and in terms than can
be understood by those who are teachable and truthful. We therefore believe that no new revelation is
needed, and that the idea of other light to come is
practically unbelief in the light which now is, seeing
the light of truth is one. We believe that, though
the Bible has been twisted and turned about by sacri-
legious hands, it is still the infallible revelation of God.
It is a main part of our religion humbly to accept what
God has revealed. Perhaps the highest form of
adoration possible, on this side the veil, is the bowing
of our entire mental and spiritual being before the revealed mind of God; the kneeling of the understanding in that sacred presence whose glory causes angels
to veil their faces. Let those who please to do so,
worship science, reason, and their own clear judg-
ments; it is our delight to prostrate ourselves before

the Lord our God, and to say, " This God is our God for ever and ever: He will be our guide even unto death."

Brethren, rally to the old standard. Fight to the death for the old gospel, for it is your life. Whatever forms of expression you may use as you advance in knowledge, ever keep the cross of Jesus Christ in the forefront, and let all the blessed truths which gather around it be heartily maintained.

We must have faith, not only in the form of fixity of creed, but also in the shape of *constant dependence upon God.* If I were asked what is the sweetest frame within the whole compass of human feeling, I should not speak of a sense of power in prayer, or abundant revelation, or rapturous joys, or conquest of evil spirits; but I should mention, as the most exquisite delight of my being, a condition of conscious dependence upon God. It has been often associated with great pain of body and deep humiliation of spirit, but it is inexpressibly delightful to lie passive in the hand of love, to die into the life of Christ. It is blessed to feel that you do not know, but your Heavenly Father knows; that you cannot speak, but that "we have an Advocate;" that you can scarcely lift a hand, but that He worketh all your works in you. The entire submission of our soul to our Lord, the full content of the heart with God's will and way, the sure reliance of the mind upon the Lord's presence and power,—this is the nearest approach to Heaven that I know; and it is better than rapture, for one can abide in it without strain or reaction.

> " Oh, to be nothing, nothing;
> Only to lie at His feet ! "

It is not so sublime a feeling as soaring aloft on the wings of eagles; but for sweetness,—deep, mysterious, indescribable,—it bears the palm. It is a blessedness which can bear to be thought of, a joy which never seems to be a stolen one; for surely a poor, frail child of God has an unquestioned right to depend upon his great Father, a right to be nothing in the presence of the all-supporting One.

I love to preach in such a mood, not as though *I* was about to preach at all, but hoping that the Holy Spirit would speak through me. Thus to conduct prayer-meetings, and church-meetings, and all sorts of business, will be found to be our wisdom and our joy. We generally make our worst blunders about things that are perfectly easy, when the thing is so plain that we do not ask God to guide us, because we think our own common sense will be sufficient, and so we commit grave errors; but in the difficulties, the extreme difficulties, which we take before God, He gives young men prudence, and teaches youths knowledge and discretion. Dependence upon God is the flowing fountain of success. That true saint of God, George Müller, has always struck me, when I have heard him speak, as being such a simple, child-like being in his dependence upon God; but, alas! the most of us are far too great for God to use us; we can preach as well as anybody, make a sermon with anybody,—and so we fail. Take care, brethren; for if we think we can do anything of ourselves, all we shall get from God will be the opportunity to try. He will thus prove us, and let us see our inability. A certain alchemist, who waited upon Pope Leo X., declared that he had discovered how to transmute the baser metals into gold. He expected to receive a sum of money for his discovery, but Leo was no such simpleton; he merely gave him a huge purse in which to keep the gold which he would make. There was wisdom as well as sarcasm in the present. That is precisely what God does with proud men; He lets them have the opportunity to do what they boasted of being able to do. I never heard that so much as a solitary gold piece was dropped into Leo's purse, and I am sure you will never be spiritually rich by what you can do in your own strength. Be stripped, brother, and then God may be pleased to clothe you with honour, but not till then.

It is essential that we should exhibit faith in the form of *confidence in God*. Brothers, it would be a great calamity if it could be said of any one of you, "He had an excellent moral character, and remarkable gifts; but he did not trust God." Faith is a chief necessary. "Above all, taking the shield of faith," was the apostolic injunction. Alas! some men go to the fight, but leave their shield at home. It would be dreadful to think of a sermon as being all that a sermon ought to be in every respect except that the preacher did not trust in the Holy Spirit to bless it to the conversion of souls; such a discourse is vain. No sermon is what it ought to be if faith be absent: as well say that a body is in health when life is extinct. It is admirable to see a man humbly conscious of his own weakness, and yet bravely confident in the Lord's power to work through his infirmity. We may glory at large when God is our glory. Attempting great things, we shall not overdo ourselves in the attempt; and expecting great things, we shall not be disappointed in our expectation. Nelson was asked whether a certain movement of his ships was not perilous, and he replied, " Perilous it may be, but in naval affairs nothing is impossible, and nothing is improbable." I make bold to assert that, in the service of God, nothing is impossible, and nothing is improbable. Go in for great things, brethren, in the Name of God; risk everything on His promise, and according to your faith shall it be done unto you.

The common policy of our churches is that of great prudence. We do not, as a rule, attempt anything beyond our strength. We measure means, and calculate possibilities with economical accuracy; then we strike off a large discount for contingencies, and a still larger percentage as provision for our ease, and so we accomplish little because we have no idea of doing much. I would to God we had more " pluck." I know of no fitter word to describe what I mean; though the word may better suit the camp than the church, we will for once borrow from the barracks. Bear in mind that there is nothing like courage even in ordinary things. Sir Richard Sutton, when he was ambassador to Prussia, was taken by Frederick the Great to see his regiment of giants, every one of whom stood six feet six in his shoes. The king said to him, " Do you think any regiment in the English army could fight my men, man for man?" Sir Richard answered, " Please your majesty, I do not know whether the same number could beat your giants, but I know that half the number would try at it."

Let us attempt great things, for those who believe in the Name of the Lord succeed beyond all expectation. By faith, the worker lives. The right noble Earl of Shaftesbury said, the other afternoon, of Ragged-school teachers and their work, " It was evident to all thinking persons that we had a great danger in the ignorance of the children of the lower classes, and so the senators began to think of it, and the philosophers began to think of it, and good men of all sorts began to think of it; but while they were all engaged in thinking, a few plain, humble people opened Ragged-schools, *and did it.*" This is the kind of faith of which we need more and more; we need so to trust in God as to put our hand to the plough in His Name. It is idle to spend time in making and altering plans, and doing nothing else; the best plan for doing God's work is to do it. Brothers, if you do not believe in anybody else, believe in God without stint. Believe up to the hilt. Bury yourselves, both as to your weakness and your strength, in simple trust in God. " Oh ! " said one, " as to that man, there is no telling what mad thing he will start next." Let the sneer pass, though it may be as well to say, " I am not mad, most noble Festus ; but carry out works of truth and soberness." The end of all things will show that faith in God is sanctified common sense, without an atom of folly in it. To believe God's Word, is the most reasonable thing we can do ; it is the plainest course that we can take, and the safest policy that we can adopt, even as to taking care of ourselves ; for Jesus says, " Whosoever will save his life shall lose it : and whosoever will lose his life for My sake shall find it." Let us stake all upon the faithfulness of God, and we shall never be ashamed or confounded, world without end.

You must also have faith in God in the form of

expectancy. Our brethren Smith and Fullerton would not have a blessing on their work if they did not expect the blessing to come; but expecting the blessing, they provide an enquiry-room, and persons to look after the converts. Shall we commence farming, and provide no barn? In many a village, the Lord has saved souls under the preaching of the gospel, but the minister has never said, " I shall be in the vestry on such-and-such an evening to see enquirers," or, " I shall stop after the sermon to talk with the anxious." He has never given the people a chance of telling what the Lord has done for them; and if he should hear that a dozen people have been convinced of sin, he would be surprised, and fear that they were hypocrites. We have not so learned Christ. We expect to take fish in our nets, and to reap harvests in our fields. Is it so with you, my brethren? Let it be more so. " Open thy mouth wide," saith the Lord, " and I will fill it." So pray and so preach that, if there are no conversions, you will be astonished, amazed, and broken-hearted. Look for the salvation of your hearers as much as the angel who will sound the last trump will look for the waking of the dead. Believe your own doctrine! Believe your own Saviour! Believe in the Holy Ghost who dwells in you! For thus shall you see your hearts' desire, and God shall be glorified.

IV. It is time for me to talk of the fourth thing, namely, LIFE. The preacher must have life; he must have *life in himself*. Are you all alive, my brother? Of course you have been quickened as a plain believer; but, as a minister, are you altogether alive? If there is a bone in a man's body which is not alive, it becomes the nidus of disease; for instance, a decayed tooth may cause more serious injury than most people imagine. In a living system, a dead portion is out of place, and is sure sooner or later to create intense pain. It is a wise arrangement that it should be so, for decay has a tendency to spread, and mischief might be caused imperceptibly if pain did not sound the alarm bell. I hope that any part of our soul which is not truly alive may pain us till the evil is removed.

Some brethren never seem to be thoroughly alive. Their heads are alive, they are intelligent and studious; but, alas! their hearts are inactive, cold, lethargic. Many preachers never spy out opportunities, for death seems to have sealed up their eyes; and their tongue also is not more than half quickened, so that they mumble and stumble, and all around them sleep rules the hour. I have been told that, if certain preachers would only for once stamp a foot, or lift a handkerchief, or do anything out of their regular way, it would be a relief to their people. I hope none of you have become quite so mechanical and monotonous as that; but I know that some are heavy and yet not weighty, solemn and yet not impressive. My brother, I want you to be alive from the sole of your foot to the crown of your head, alive in brain and heart, in tongue and hand, in eye and ear. The living God should be served by living men.

Labour to be *alive in all your duties.* John Bradford, the martyr, used to say, " I never go away from any part of the service of God till I feel thoroughly alive in it, and know that the Lord is with me in it." Carry out this rule conscientiously. In confessing sin, go on confessing till you feel that your tears have washed the Saviour's feet. In seeking pardon, continue to seek till the Holy Spirit bears witness to your peace with God. In preparing a sermon, wait upon the Lord until you have communion with Christ in it, until the Holy Spirit causes you to feel the power of the truth which you are to deliver. " Son of man, eat this roll." Before you attempt to give out the Word to others, get it into yourself. Is there not too much dead praying, and dead preaching, and dead church work of all sorts? Do you not know churches which are like the ghostly ship in the legend,—the captain, the mate, and all the crew are dead men?

> " The mariners all do work the ropes
>   As they've been wont to do ;
> They raise their limbs like lifeless tools,—
>   They are a ghastly crew.

> " The body of my deacon's self
>   Stands by me knee to knee :
> The body and I pull at one rope,
>   But nothing of life have we."

This is a grim business, but I have beheld such a sight, though never have I seen a ghost. I recollect, long ago, preaching for a church which was almost defunct externally, and altogether defunct internally ; and after the service, during which I felt a terrible chill of soul, I went into the vestry, and there I saw two important persons leaning heavily against the mantelpiece. I said to them, " Are you the deacons of the church?" They answered, " Yes, sir." I replied, " I thought so!" I did not explain further. These pillars of the church evidently needed propping up ; but sluggish ease will not do in the work of the Lord.

Brethren, we must have *life more abundantly*, each

one of us, and it must flow out into all the duties of our office : warm spiritual life must be manifest in the prayer, in the singing, in the preaching, and even in the shake of the hand and the good word after service. I delight in these Conferences because they are living assemblies ; the room does not feel like a vault, nor do you salute each other like a set of living skeletons without hearts, or a company of respectable mandarins fresh from the tea-shops, who nod and bow mechanically. I cannot endure meetings where the only exhibition of life is seen in heated discussions over points of order, amendments, and movings of " the previous question." One marvels at the little things over which an assembly will waste hours of precious time, contending as if the destiny of the whole world and the fate of the starry heavens depended upon the debate. How the mountain heaves, but how small a mouse is born! Brethren, may you be alive, and keep alive, and disseminate your life ! We read in Plato that the Egyptian priests said concerning the Greeks, " You Greeks are always youths, there is not an old man among you." Neither, sirs, is there an old man among us at this hour ; we are full of youth even unto this day, and if you want to see one whose vigour and cheerfulness prove that his grey hairs are all external, there sits the man [pointing to Mr. George Rogers]. It is a grand thing to be perpetually renewing your youth, never getting into the ruts, but making new tracks with your glowing wheels. Those who are old when they are young, are likely to be young when they are old. I like to see the liveliness of the child associated with the gravity of the father ; but especially do I rejoice to see a godly man keep up the vivacity, the joy, the earnestness of his first love. It is a crime to permit our fires to burn low while experience yields us more and more abundant fuel. Be it ours to go from strength to strength, from life to more abundant life.

Be full of life at all times, and *let that life be seen in your ordinary conversation.* It is a shocking state of things when good people say, " Our minister undoes in the parlour what he has done in the pulpit ; he preaches very well, but his life does not agree with his sermons." Our Lord Jesus would have us perfect even as our Father who is in Heaven is perfect. Every Christian should be holy; but *we* are laid under a sevenfold obligation to it : how can we expect the Divine blessing if it be not so? God help us so to live that we may be safe examples to our flocks !

In such a case, *life will go out of us to others.* The man whom God uses for quickening is the man who is himself quickened. May we and our people become like those ornamental waters which we have seen while travelling in foreign parts ; the water leaps up as a fountain, and descends into a basin ; when that basin is full, the crystal stream runs over the brink in a sparkling sheet, and rolls into another basin, and the process is repeated again and again till the result charms the eye. At our Conference, my brethren, may the living waters flow into us, and then flow from us till thousands shall receive a blessing, and communicate it to others ! This is what your Lord desires, as He said, " He that believeth on Me, as the Scripture hath said, out of his belly shall flow rivers of living water." " This spake He of the Spirit, which they that believe on Him should receive." God fill you to the brim, and cause you to overflow! This is essential: life we must have. If among us there is a slumbering brother, who does everything in a slow way, let him wake up. If anyone among us performs his duty in a lifeless manner, as if he were paid by the pound, and would not give half an ounce over, let him also wake up. Our work requires that we serve the Lord with all our heart, and with all our soul, and with all our mind, and with all our strength. Ours is no place for half-heartedness. Go, ye dead ones, take a chaplain's place at the cemetery, and bury your dead; but work among living men needs life,—vigorous, intense life. A corpse among angelic choirs would not be more out of place than a lifeless man in the gospel ministry. "God is not the God of the dead, but of the living."

V. The last thing, but not the least important, of which I have to speak, is LOVE. Assuredly, we must abound in love. It is a hard thing for some preachers to saturate and perfume their sermons with love; for their natures are hard, or cold, or coarse, or selfish. We are none of us all that we ought to be, but some are specially poverty-stricken in point of love. They do not " naturally care " for the souls of men, as Paul puts it. To all, but especially to the harder sort, I would say,—Be doubly earnest as to holy charity, for without this you will be no more than sounding brass or a tinkling cymbal. Love is power. The Holy Spirit, for the most part, works by our affection. Love men to Christ; faith accomplishes much, but love is the actual instrument by which faith works out its desires in the Name of the Lord of love.

Brethren, *love your work*. You will never preach

well unless you are enamoured of it : you will never
do well in any particular charge unless you love the
people, and I would almost say the village and the
meeting-house. I would have you believe that
Slocum-in-the-Marsh is a gem among villages. Think
that London may be all very well as a city, but as a
village, Slocum bears the palm. Even your chapel,
with all its plainness, should have charms for you ; be
of opinion that the Tabernacle is very well in its way,
but that it has great deficiencies about it ; that it is
too big, for one thing,—at least, too big for you.
Your meeting-house holds only three hundred and
twenty ; but, in your judgment, that is quite as large
a number as one man can see after with any hope of
success ; at least, it involves a responsibility quite as
large as you desire to bear. When a mother's love to
her children leads her to believe that they are the
sweetest in the parish, she takes more care in their
washing and their dressing ; if she thought them ugly,
troublesome beings, she would neglect them ; and I
am sure that, until we heartily love our work, and love
the people with whom we are working, we shall not
accomplish much.

I can truthfully say that I do not know anybody
in all the world with whom I would like to
change places. " Ah ! " say you, " that is very likely,
for you have a fine position." I am quite of that
opinion ; but I thought just the same of my little
pastorate at Waterbeach, and it was with the utmost
reluctance that I removed from the first to the second.
I still retain the belief that there were people in my
first congregation whose like I shall never see again,
and that, as a position of usefulness, there are great

attractions about that Cambridgeshire village. It is a rule to which I know of no exception that, to prosper in any work, you must have an enthusiasm for it.

You must have also *intense love to the souls of men*, if you are to influence them for good. Nothing can compensate for the absence of this. Soul-winning must be your passion, you must be born to it; it must be the very breath of your nostrils, the only thing for which you count life worth the having. We must hunt after souls, even as the Swiss hunter pursues the chamois because the spirit of the chase has mastered him.

Above all, we must feel an *intense love to God.* Our dear brother, who led us in prayer this morning, rightly spoke of the power which girds us when we burn with love to God. Why is it that so many say to children and young people, "You must *love* Jesus in order to be saved"? That is not the gospel. The gospel is, "Believe on the Lord Jesus Christ, and thou shalt be saved." We are careful to state the matter correctly to the grown people; why give it inaccurately to the young? If we make a difference at all, it will be wiser to tell the children to believe, and the old people to love : the error will be less injurious, for love is the great lack of most men. The holy grace of love needs to be more preached among us, and more felt by us. "Oh!" said a woman, when she was speaking of the Lord to her minister, "He has heard my prayer many a time, and I can have what I want of Him, for, by His grace, I am very thick with Him." She meant that communion had wrought sweet fellowship, and so her prayers were heard. Oh, that we lived on familiar terms with the Well-beloved, and

felt His love within our bosoms always! Love to
God will help a man to persevere in service when
otherwise he would have given up his work. " The
love of Christ constraineth us," said one whose heart
was all his Master's. I heard one say, the other day,
that " the love of Christ ought to constrain us." This
is true, but Paul did not so much speak of a duty as
of a fact ; he said, " the love of Christ constraineth us."

Beloved brethren, if you are filled with love to your
work, and love to souls, and love to God, you will
gladly endure many self-denials, which else would be
unbearable. The poverty of our country brethren is
very trying, and ought by all means to be relieved ;
but we may well feel proud that so many men are
forthcoming who, for the sake of preaching the gospel
of Christ, are willing to leave remunerative callings,
and endure hardness. Other denominations might
pay them better, but they spurn the golden bribe, and
remain faithful to Christ and to the ordinances as
they were delivered. All honour to those lifelong
martyrs, who put up with sore privations for the sake
of Christ and His Church! The devil once met a
Christian man, so I have heard, and said to him,
" You call yourself a servant of God; what do you
do more than I do? You boast that you fast, so do I ;
for I neither eat nor drink. You do not commit
adultery; neither do I." The fiend mentioned a long
list of sins of which he is incapable, from which he
could therefore claim exemption. The saint at last
said to him, " I do one thing which thou never didst ;
I deny myself." That is the point in which the
Christian comes out; he denies himself for Christ's
sake. Believing in Jesus, he counts all things but loss

for the excellency of the knowledge of Christ Jesus, his Lord. Brethren, do not leave your charges because the stipend is small. Your poor people must be looked after by somebody. Do not despair when times are hard, for they will be better by-and-by; and, meanwhile, your Heavenly Father knows your need. We have heard of men who have remained in plague-stricken cities, when others fled, because they could be of service to the sick. Abide, then, with your people when work fails them; be as faithful to your God as many a man has been faithful to his philanthropy. If you can anyhow manage to tide over the present distress, stick to the people. God will help you, and reward you, if you have faith in Him. May the Lord confirm your confidence, and comfort you in your tribulations!

Go on, brethren, preaching the same gospel; but preach it with more faith, and preach it better every day. Do not draw back: your place is to the front. Qualify yourselves for larger spheres, you who are in little places; but do not neglect your studies to look after better positions. Be prepared for an opening when it comes, and rest assured that the office will come to the man who is fit for the office. We are not so cheap that we need go hawking ourselves in every market; the churches are always on the look-out for really efficient preachers. Men whose fitness for the ministry is doubtful are at a great discount nowadays; but for men of ability and usefulness there is great demand.

You cannot hide a candle under a bushel, and you cannot keep a really able man in an insignificant position. Patronage is of the smallest importance; fitness for the work, grace, ability, earnestness, and a loving disposition soon push the man into his place. God will bring His servant into his true position, if he has but faith to trust in Him. I put this word at the tail-end of my address, because I know the discouragements under which you labour. Do not be afraid of hard work for Christ; a terrible reckoning awaits those who have an easy time in the ministry, but a great reward is in reserve for those who endure all things for the elect's sake. You will not regret your poverty when Christ cometh, and calleth His own servants to Him. It will be a sweet thing to have died at your post, not turning aside for wealth, or running from Dan to Beersheba to obtain a better salary, but stopping where your Lord bade you hold the fort.

Brethren, consecrate yourselves to God afresh. Bring hither new cords; and bind the sacrifice again to the altar! Struggle as it may, anxious to escape the knife, fearful of the fire, yet bind it with cords, even with cords to the horns of the altar; for until death, and in death, we are the Lord's. Entire surrender of everything to Jesus is our watchword this day. Only may the Lord accept the living sacrifice, for Jesus Christ's sake! Amen.

STRENGTH IN WEAKNESS.

MY DEAR BRETHREN,—I greatly value your prayers, and I feel intensely grateful for that Benjamin's share in them which is ever my portion. I never consciously needed your intercessions more than I do just now, for I may say with the psalmist, "He weakened my strength in the way." After my severe illness, I am trembling like a child who is only just commencing to use his feet. It is with difficulty that I keep myself up; what can you expect from one who can scarcely stand? During the last six weeks, I have considered from day to day what to say to you, but nothing has come of my consideration. My meditations have been a failure. I have gone to the pits and found no water, and returned with my vessel empty. My brain has been so occupied with sympathy for the poor body that it has not been able to mount aloft with the eagle, nor even to plume its wings for the lower flight which I must needs attempt this morning. One thing, however, is clear, —I am in special communion with my subject, and can speak, as the good old people used to say, "experimentally." I cannot, however, draw much aid from that fact; but I cast myself upon the power Divine, which has so many times been displayed in weakness. "The Lord hath been mindful of us: He will bless us."

I draw my subject from the words of Paul in 2 Cor. xii. 10: "When I am weak, then am I strong." I shall not be guilty of uttering anything fresh upon my theme, neither shall I be able to say anything forcible upon it. The weak side of the experience will come out most observably; I can only pray that the strong side may not be hidden. My own feelings supply me with a commentary upon the text, and that is all the exposition I shall aim at. Our text is not only written in the Bible, but it is inscribed upon the lives of the saints. Though we are not apostles, and shall never be able to claim the inspiration of Paul, yet in this one particular we are as instructed as he was, for we have learned by experience, "When I am weak, then am I strong." This sentence has passed into a Christian proverb; it is a paradox which has ceased to perplex any child of God; it is at once a warning and a consolation, bidding the strong behold the weakness of power, and setting before the feeble the strength of weakness.

Let it be understood, at the commencement, that OUR TEXT IS NOT TRUE IN EVERY SENSE IN WHICH IT MIGHT BE READ. Some brethren are weak with an emphasis, and always so; but I have never yet discovered that they are strong, except in the sense of being headstrong and wilful. If obstinacy be strength, they are champions; and if conceit be strength, they are gigantic; but in no other respect are they strong.

Many are weak, and yet not strong: we must alter the text concerning them, and say, "When they are weak, they are weakness itself." There is a kind of weakness which we may well dread, it may steal over us insensibly; but it brings no strength, no honour, no virtue with it; it is evil, only evil, and that continually. With it come unfitness for holy service and want of success; and unless infinite grace shall avert the calamity, there will arise out of it failure of character and defeat in life. May we never know the weakness which befell Samson after he had told his secret, and had lost his locks! He could not say, "When I am weak, then am I strong;" but rather, "When I am shorn, I am weak as other men." See what befalls him! "The Philistines be upon thee, Samson!" He cannot now smite them; he cannot protect his own limbs; he cannot guard his own eyes; he cannot obtain his own liberty. Blinded, he toils at the mill; the hero of Israel is become a slave to the uncircumcised Philistines! Alas, that such weakness should be possible to a man who had slain his thousands, and laid them heaps upon heaps! Oh, that such weakness should be possible to a man who had carried the gates of Gaza away on his shoulders, posts, and bars, and all! And yet it was so, and it may be so with us. "Howl, fir tree; for the cedar is fallen!"

Brethren, we must strive against all weakness which leads to sin, lest to us also some Delilah should bring destruction. Samson's unshorn locks denoted his Nazarite consecration, and *if we ever become weak through failure of consecration*, such weakness will be fatal to true usefulness. If the man who had "none of self, and all of God," grows downward till he craves for "some of self, and some of God," he is in a sad condition. If he, who once lived to win souls, now lives to win silver and gold, his money shall perish with him; if he, who once was famous for devotion to his Master, becomes his own master, he shall be infamous; for I trow that, even if we do nothing wrong in the eyes of man, it is wrong enough to have declined from whole-hearted service for God. It is this that demons laugh at, and that angels marvel at;—a man of God living like a man of the world! Even the Lord Himself stays a while to ask, " What doest thou here, Elijah?" The holy and the zealous grieve if they see a minister of Christ ministering to his own ambition. We are only strong as our consecration is perfect. Unless we live wholly for God, our strength will suffer serious leakage, and our weakness will be of that kind which degrades the believer till the ungodly scornfully enquire, " Art thou also become weak as we? Art thou become like unto us?"

We must, dear friends, never become weak in another sense, namely, *in our communion with God*. David slackened his fellowship with God, and Satan vanquished him through Bathsheba; Peter followed afar off, and soon denied his Lord. Communion with God is the right arm of our strength; and if this be broken, we are weak as water. Without God, we can do nothing; and in proportion as we attempt to live without Him, we ruin ourselves. Alas! that the man who has seen the face of the Strong One, and has been made mighty, should forget where his great strength lieth, and so become sick and enfeebled! He who has suspended his visits to the banqueting-house of hallowed fellowship will be ill-fed, and will have to cry out, " My leanness! My leanness! Woe unto me!" He who walks not with the Well-beloved will soon be a Mephibosheth in the feet, and a Bartimæus in the eyes; timorous in heart, and trembling at his knees. If we are weak in communion with God, we are weak everywhere. If a man can be strong without God, such dangerous strength may fall to the lot of the man who is out of communion; but if it be true that only as we hang upon the Lord are we strong, then broken fellowship will soon bring broken strength.

And, dear friends, there is a kind of weakness which I hope none of you will ever cultivate, though it seems greatly in favour at the present day, namely, *weakness of faith;* for when I am weak in faith, then I am not strong in the Lord. When a man doubts his God, he weakens himself. A little time ago, persons who were full of distrust and unbelief were regarded as the possessors of a deep experience; but I hope the age has for ever gone by in which unbelief shall be regarded as a qualification for eminent saintship. If the gospel message were, "He that doubteth, and is not baptized, shall be saved;" there are many who have made their calling and election sure; but while ours is a gospel of faith, unbelief can never be regarded with complacency. Faith is our battle-axe and weapon of war; woe to the warrior who forgets it! Therefore, brethren, let us separate between weakness *and* weakness,—the weakness which is the token of strength, and weakness in faith which is the indication of spiritual decay.

I pray that we may never be *weak in love,* but that we may become like Basil, "pillars of fire." Love is the greatest of all the powers which can possess the human breast. I must not compare love with other graces so as to depreciate any virtue; yet, of all active powers, love is the most forceful; for even faith worketh by love. Faith does not overcome men's hearts for Jesus until it takes to itself this wondrous weapon, and then believingly loves them to Christ. Oh, for a passionate love, a love which shall be a pure flame, burning to a white heat, and consuming us! May this sacred fire burn in the very centre of our being! May we love our God intensely, and love the people for His sake! Brethren, be strong there! Depend upon it, if you leave off loving the people to whom you preach, and the truth you are ordained to proclaim, the state of the church will be "as when a standard-bearer fainteth." There may remain to you strength of passionate temper, strength to offend, and strength to scatter; but the power of God will be withdrawn. You will, like Phaeton, try to drive the horses of the chariot of the sun; but they shall only hurry you to swift destruction.

We want, brethren,—oh, how we would pine for it!—*to be delivered from all weakness of the spiritual life.* We want to outgrow the weakness natural to us as babes in Christ, so that we may become young men who are strong; yea, we need to go beyond this, and to become fully-developed men in Christ Jesus, "strong in the Lord, and in the power of His might." If we are weak in that respect, we are strong nowhere. As ministers, we ought to covet all the spiritual strength which God is ready to bestow. Would to God that the Holy Ghost, who dwelleth in us, found nothing within to impede Him, and nothing to restrain His influences! Oh, that the full Godhead of the blessed Spirit might as much manifest itself in these mortal bodies of ours as once the Godhead of the second Person of the Trinity manifested itself in the person of Christ Jesus, the Son of man! I mean not, of course, miraculously, nor in any way to make us rival the incommunicable glories of our Divine Master; but even to its fulness I would that our nature, like the bush in Horeb, were aglow with the indwelling Deity. Never mind though the bush should be consumed; it were well to be consumed so long as the Spirit of God would dwell in us, and manifest His power.

Thus, you see, there are senses in which we flatly contradict the text, and thereby establish its true meaning. If it were true that all who are weak are strong, we might straightway find a vigorous ministry by ransacking our hospitals, enlisting a troop from our idiot asylums, and calling together all persons of weak brain and garrulous tongue. No, no; it is not given to the fearful and the unbelieving, the foolish and the frivolous, to claim that their mental, moral, and spiritual weaknesses are a fit platform for the revelation of the Divine strength.

A second observation must be brought before you before I actually come to the text. THERE IS ANOTHER FORM OF IT WHICH IS CLEARLY TRUE. "*When I am strong, then am I weak.*" That is true, almost as true as Paul's declaration, "When I am weak, then am I strong;"—of course, not true in all senses, but so nearly correct that I would recommend its acceptation as a proverb worthy to be quoted with the text itself.

Look at the tyro who has just commenced preaching in a village chapel or in a mission-room, and admire his boundless confidence in his own strength. He has collected certain anecdotes and telling metaphors, and he propounds these as if they were the *Summa Theologia*, the very flower and essence of wisdom. He is voluble and energetic, though there is nothing in what he says. See him stamp his feet, and clench his fists! He is a wonder unto many, for they see no sufficient cause for his powerful self-assurance. Possibly he comes to College; he enters the classroom feeling that, for once, *a man* treads the College floor. The inhabitants of London shall know that verily there is a prophet among them. We hear about this gentleman very soon, for he is not appreciated; his brethren are not "willing for a season to rejoice in his light;" they even show a disposition to snuff him out. Yet how perfectly self-satisfied he is! I have heard such a brother deliver himself of nothing at all at extreme length, and sit down full to the brim with satisfaction. I have almost envied and altogether grieved over him. Many an abler man is weeping over his shortcomings, while this poor soul is glorying in his own imagined triumphs Like Cowper's poor believer,—

"Pillow and bobbins all her little store,"

he knows this much, and nothing more,—his abilities transcendent and his knowledge vast. How self-content he is! But he is not strong for all that. Did you fear him when you first came into contact with him? Did you look upon him as an ironclad, utterly impregnable? The delusion did not last long.

" Man being in honour abideth not." If I remember
rightly, you who were in the College classroom began
to try your prows upon this man-of-war. You found
that it was only a wooden ship after all. There is a
grim pleasure in seeing the mighty collapse ; and that
fell to your share. We felt a degree of happiness in
seeing the great man lose, ounce by ounce, his boasted
strength, till he died outright. We never buried the
body of vainglory, for we never knew precisely what
became of it ; but we were glad to find, in its place, a
diffident youth, who needed cheering lest he should
too much depreciate himself,—a lowly spirit, whom, in
due time, the Lord exalted. As he grew consciously
weak, he became strong, and discovered that, when he
was strong in his own opinion, he was in many ways
weak.

Since we left the College benches, we have seen
many strong men. I think I see one sitting down in
his study. He has been reading the Reviews and
Quarterlies, and a little of the latest modern thought :
now he is looking out for a text. He perfectly understands it, whatever it may be. At any rate, if *he* does
not understand it, who does? When he falls upon
his text, he interprets it, not at all desiring to know
what the men of God who lived before him have said
upon it, for they were of a darker age, and he lives in
the nineteenth century, that world of wonders, that
region of wisdom, that flower and glory of all time.
Now you shall see what you shall see when this cultured divine comes forth from his chamber as a giant
refreshed with new wine. No dew of the Spirit of God
is upon him, he does not require it ; he drinks from
other fountains. He speaks with astounding power, his

diction is superb, his thought prodigious! But he is as weak as he is polished, as cold as he is pretentious; saints and sinners alike perceive his weakness, and by degrees the empty pews confirm it. He is too strong to ask to be strengthened of the Lord, and therefore he is too weak to bless a congregation. He seeks another sphere, and another, and yet another; but in no position is he powerful, for he is too strong in self. His preaching is like a painted fire, no one is either cheered or alarmed by it.

We have known other men, who were not so strong, who felt that they could not even understand the Word of God without Divine illumination, and who went to the great Father of lights for that illumination. Trembling and afraid, they have asked to be helped to speak the mind of God, and not their own mind; and God has spoken through them, and they have been strong. They were weak, for they were afraid lest their thoughts should stand in the way of God's thoughts, they were fearful lest their mind should darken the Word of God; and yet they have been truly strong, and humble people have listened to them, and said that God spake through them; and sinners have listened, and though they have become angry, they have come again, and at last have yielded themselves to Christ. Verily, God spoke through that man.

I have known preachers who have been very weak, and yet they have been used of the Lord. For many, many years, my own preaching was exceedingly painful to me because of the fears which beset me before entering the pulpit. Often, my dread of facing the people has been overwhelming. Even the physical feeling, which came of the mental emotion, has been painful; but this weakness has been an education for me. I wrote, many years ago, to my venerable grandfather, and told him of many things that happened to me before preaching,—sickness of body, and terrible fears, which often made me really ill. The old gentleman wrote back, and said, " I have been preaching for sixty years, and I still feel many tremblings. Be content to have it so; for when your emotion goes away, your strength will be gone." When we preach and think nothing of it, the people think nothing of it, and God does nothing by it. An overwhelming sense of weakness should not be regarded as an evil, but should be accepted as helpful to the true minister of Christ.

Look at *the preacher who has no burdens.* His sermon is in his pocket; there cannot happen any mischief to it unless a thief should steal it; he has rehearsed all his action, he is as safe as an automaton. He does not need to pray for the Spirit of God to help him in his preaching; and though he uses the form, one wonders what the prayer can mean. He surveys the congregation with the complacency of a gardener looking at a bed of flowers. He has something to say, and he knows what it is going to be, every word of it, and therefore he says it with ease, and comes down the stairs as pleased with himself as heart could desire; the notion of trembling is far from him, he is not so weak. Yonder is a poor brother, who has been tugging away with his brains, wrestling on his knees, and bleeding at his heart; he is half-afraid that he may break down in the sermon, and he is fearful that he will not reach the hearts of the people; but he means to try what can be done by the

help of God. Be you sure that he will get at the
people, and God will give him converts. He is looking up to God, for he feels so feeble in himself. You
know which of the two preachers you would sooner
hear, and you know who is the really strong man of
the two; the weak man is strong, and the strong man
is weak.

An American divine, who says a great many things
that are wise, and a few which are otherwise, says
that the best preparation for preaching is to get a
good night's rest, and to eat a good breakfast.
According to his opinion, a fine constitution is a most
efficient help to preaching the gospel. If you know
nothing of the headache, and nothing of the heartache, and never allow anything to disturb the equilib-
rium of your mind, you may expect to be a very successful minister. It may be so. I would not depreciate health, appetite, a bounding spirit, and a good
Saturday night's sleep; but these things are not all,
nor much. *Mens sana in corpore sano*, by all means;
but where that has been a good deal relied upon, it
has displayed itself in fine sensational sermons; but,
brethren, I question whether the next generation will
say that it has proved itself fruitful in spiritual teaching which will feed the soul or move the conscience.
Many of the noblest specimens of our sermonic literature have come from men who were patient sufferers.
Men who have had the most touching pathos, the
highest spirituality, the most marvellous insight into
the deep things of God, have often known little of
bodily health. Calvin laboured under many fierce
disorders, yet shall we ever see his like? Robert
Hall was rarely free from pain, but who ever spoke

more gloriously? And here I would mention one whom all of us love, Charles Stanford, who grows sweeter and sweeter as he grows weaker and weaker, and who sees all the more clearly now that his eyes grow dim. My brethren, physical force is not our strength; it may be our weakness. Health is to be desired, and carefully preserved where we have it; but if we lose it, we may count it all joy, and look forward to be able to exclaim with Paul, "When I am weak, then am I strong." In some form or other, we must be tried. A preacher who has no cross to carry, a prophet of the Lord without a burden, is an unprofitable servant and a burden to the church.

It would be a dreadful thing to be a pastor without cares. I do not address any such, I am happy to believe; but I do address some who, as pastors, are overloaded with cares, and overweighted with sorrows. Perhaps the largeness of your church, or, more likely, the smallness of it, may be to you a daily trouble. Do not ask to be otherwise than troubled. The shepherd who can always go to bed regularly at night, and who is able to say, "I do not have much trouble with my flock," is not the man to be envied. He coolly says, "A few lambs died last winter; we must expect that kind of thing. It is true that some sheep died of starvation; but if the meadows failed, I could not help that." That is the kind of shepherd who deserves to be eaten by the next wolf; but the man who is able to say with Jacob, "In the day the drought consumed me, and the frost by night," is the true shepherd. He is most irregular as to his rest; the only thing regular about him is his labour and his disappointment, and yet faith makes him a happy man.

When you grow very weak as a pastor, and your charge utterly overcomes you, do not repine at such weakness, for then you will be at your full strength; but when you are strong as a pastor, and say, " I think that, to be a minister, is an easy matter," you may depend upon it that you are weak.

Permit me here to say that, *whenever a brother gets to be so strong as to talk much of his own holiness,* then also he is weak. I have not observed yet that anybody who has had grace to make into flags has won the more victories in consequence. I have required, as far as I am concerned, all my grace to make into a sword; I have wanted all my power for real fighting; but, as to making a single banner out of it to display before men, I have not yet attained unto that, and must still take a very lowly position among the servants of God. Coleridge was once asked whether he believed in ghosts, and he said that he did not, for he had seen too many of them! If anyone asked me if I believed in perfect men, I should have to say that I have seen too many of them to believe in them. A ghost is a wonderful affair, and when you see it at first, it makes each particular hair of your head " to stand on end, like quills upon the fretful porcupine." But this does not occur a second time, for a suspicion of hollow turnip and candle steals over you. We heard of one, the other day, who even dared to squirt carmine over a spirit which had been conjured from the vasty deep at a *séance.* I have sometimes ventured to oppose a perfect man, and the warmth of his temper has been evidence to me that, while he may have been upon the verge of perfection among his own friends, he had not absolutely reached that consummation when exposed to the colder judgment of strangers. The pretender to perfection has usually avoided me from a distaste to my protestantism against his holiness; and I have not bewailed my loss. I am not in love with that perfection which talks about itself. There is little virtue in the beauty which calls attention to itself; modest beauty is the last to extol its own charms. A number of persons, in company, were boasting of their graces and attainments, and only one brother sat silent. At last, one said to him, "Have you no holiness?" "Yes," he said, "but I never had any to boast of." All the holiness that can be had let us have, and let us press on toward perfection; but let us still recollect the fact that, when we are strong, then we are weak; that, when we think we have reached perfection, the blue mould of pride is coming over us. We have not afforded ourselves a complete inspection, or we should have found some fault to repent of, some evil yet to struggle against.

Hitherto, we have been going round the text, after the example of Rowland Hill; now let us come fairly up to it: "When I am weak, then am I strong."

I. Here is, first, A DEPRESSING EXPERIENCE: "When I am weak." When is that? Truly we are so always. Is there ever a time when the strongest Christian is not comparatively weak?

But there are certain seasons when we are consciously weak. Take Paul's case as an illustration. He had been caught up to the third heaven, but he could not bear revelations so well as John, who had enough of them to fill a book, and yet was never elated by them; but Paul was not so well qualified to be a seer, for he was more at home with arguments than with visions; and, therefore, when he saw a vision, he set great store by it. He kept his secret for fifteen years; but it was such a very remarkable thing for him, and so much out of his natural line of things, that the tendency in him was to "be exalted above measure through the abundance of the revelations;" and therefore the Lord sent, not Satan, but "the messenger of Satan,"—a mean, despicable spirit,—not to fight with him with sword and buckler, but to "buffet" him, as boys do their playmates. Have you never had an insignificant thing to vex you, like a fly buzzing around you? Have you not felt the trial to be intensely worrying, and yet meanly trifling? You could have girded yourself to meet a lion; but this trouble was a mere yelping cur, and it irritated you to the last degree, and inflicted a pain upon you. Paul does not describe his trial as the cut of a sword, else he would have bound it up; it was only the prick of a thorn; he could scarcely see the cause of the pain, or he would have taken a needle, and extracted it; but it was a little thorn which had buried itself in the flesh, and festered there.

This was Paul's worry, and it was sent to keep him humble. Paul might have gloried in wrestling with the devil; but this "thorn in the flesh" was a wretched business. To grapple with a great temptation, and to hurl it to the ground, has a grandeur in it which inspires you; but it is very different when you are assailed by a thing so small that you despise yourself for taking notice of it, and yet it frets your soul. You say to yourself, "How weak I am! Why am I thus irritated and disturbed? If anyone else made half this fuss about a little thorn, I should say, ' You ought to know better;' and yet here am I, a preacher of the gospel, greatly tried by a trifle, and beseeching the Lord thrice to take it away from me, for I cannot bear it." Do we ever get into such a condition? I wish that, at such a time, we would confess our abject weakness, and cast ourselves upon God, for then should we be made strong.

This festering of the thorn does not afflict us all, because it does not happen to all of us to see visions; but many servants of God are made to feel their weakness in another way, *by an oppressive sense of responsibility.* Brethren, I speak to you as unto wise men, who will not misunderstand me. I hope you will always feel your responsibility before God; but do not carry the feeling too far. We may feel our responsibility so deeply that we may become unable to sustain it; it may cripple our joy, and make slaves of us. Do not take an exaggerated view of what the Lord expects of you. He will not blame you for not doing that which is beyond your mental power or physical strength. You are required to be faithful, but you are not bound to be successful. You are to teach, but you cannot compel people to learn. You are to make things plain, but you cannot give carnal men an understanding of spiritual things. We are not the Father, nor the Saviour, nor the Comforter of the Church. We cannot take the responsibility of the universe upon our shoulders. While vexing ourselves with fancied obligations, we may overlook our real burdens. I could sit down, and meditate, until I felt the responsibility of the whole South of London upon my back, and this would render me unable to look after my own church. What is the practical result of making yourself, as one man, responsible for the work of twenty men? Will you do any more? Will you do it any better? I saw a horse, this morning, which was pulling at a three-horse load. How he tugged! How he strained himself! I thought to myself, " There is a good horse being ruined. His master ought to take off part of his load, or else put more horses to pull with him." Does our Lord and Master treat us in this fashion? No; we overload ourselves. We get tugging away as if the salvation of the world depended upon our straining ourselves to death. Now, I do not want you to get away from feeling a due measure of responsibility; but then you are not God, and you do not stand in God's place; you are not the rulers of providence, and you have not been elected sole managers of the covenant of grace; therefore do not act as if you were.

But, dear brethren, having said this much by way of caveat, lest I should lead any of you to despair, let me now ask,—Have we any of us fully felt the measure of our responsibility? If there be one such here, let him speak; but I shall not believe him. We have not done what we should have done, what we could have done, nor what we ought to have done, nor what we will yet do in God's strength. Perhaps we have worked up to the full of what was expected of us in quantity, but how about the quality? It may be we have attended quite enough meetings, and delivered quite enough sermons; but then, has this been done in an apostolic spirit, and night and day with tears have we warned men, and pleaded with them as in the

sight of God? Our responsibilities, when they are
thoroughly felt, crush us, and then are we weak indeed; but this weakness is the road to strength.
" When I am weak, then am I strong."

And do we not often feel weak *in the sense of utter
unfitness for being ministers at all by reason of our
own sinfulness?* Paul said of his calling to the
ministry, " Woe is unto me, if I preach not the
gospel! " We can say that, too; yet, sometimes, we
feel as if we would speak no more for Christ, and we
should sink into silence were it not that His Word is
as a fire in our bones, and we cannot refrain. Then
we think we will go away into the far West, and in
some log cabin teach a few children the way of
salvation, for we do not feel fit for anything higher.
Our shortcomings and our failures stare us out of
countenance, and then are we painfully weak; but this
also is the highway to strength: " When I am weak,
then am I strong."

Sometimes we grow depressed and weak *because
our sphere of labour seems specially difficult.* This
is not the time to dilate upon the peculiar trials of
cur pastorates. Ministers in London could tell a tale
that would astonish you, for they see things which are
their burden day and night. As for our country
brethren, what some of them have had to put up with!
They cannot move the deacons and the church at all,
perhaps the deacons wish to move them; they cannot
get at the people, and though they preach their hearts
out, they preach to empty pews. If we could only put
certain men into the positions which their brethren
faithfully occupy under great discouragement, they
would know themselves better, and leave off boasting,

and instead of finding fault, they would wonder that so much has been accomplished under such circumstances. By that way also we become strong; when God makes us feel that our work is impossible to us without His aid, then are we driven to His strength.

Some of you are *quite alone* as to the helpful fellowship of kindred spirits. This is a trying deprivation, and may well depress you. Beside this, many of you are *poor*, and you hardly know how to support your families. As I listened to the prayer of the brother who led our devotions just now, and remembered what he is suffering, and how he has actually worked in the harvest-fields, with workingmen, so that he might earn his bread, and preach the gospel, I felt that I could rejoice in him. Still, I know that poverty often makes a man feel sadly weak; when his children are without shoes, and the wife's dress is nearly worn-out, and he knows not where any more are to come from, his heart sinks within him.

In addition to this, it may be that *reproach comes undeservedly.* A scandalous story from the father of lies may be forged against you, and you may be quite unable to defend yourself. You fear lest, in trying to erase the blot, you might spoil the page. Hearts are broken over this matter. Oh, how weak a man becomes when this is the case; he may half feel himself guilty after having heard the accusation repeated again and again, although all the while he is as pure as the driven snow. This brings a weakness which may paralyze a man. Oh, to be strong in the Lord at such times!

I suppose you do not think *that I ever get dried up,*

and find it difficult to say anything fresh in my sermons; yet so it is. Think, dear brethren; I have already so many volumes of sermons in print. It grows harder to say anything new as those volumes increase. "Where will the next sermon come from?" is the question we have asked ourselves again and again; we have feared that we could not keep up the supply, and we have felt our own weakness to a terrible degree; but this, also, is the way to strength. So prepare yourselves, my younger brethren, to become weaker and weaker; prepare yourselves for sinking lower and lower in self-esteem; prepare yourselves for self-annihilation, and pray God to expedite the process.

Certain brethren know nothing of this experience, they are not weak at all; but despise such confessions. Have you never met with preachers who can keep on and on, though they never did say anything, and never will? Yet they never know what it is to be weak; they are just as able to-day as ever they were. I have heard of an old Scotch preacher, whose divisions were very numerous, and whose subdivisions were almost innumerable; so one day the people, one by one, went away, until at last the boy took the keys up, and said to him, "You can lock the church up when you have done." Some are so very long in saying nothing, and are so surely emptying their places, that it would be wise to hand them the keys so that they might retire when they are quite through.

As for some of us, we are consciously feeble; and when we prose, we know it. We come out of the pulpit, at times, feeling that we are less fit than ever for the holy work. Our last sermon we judge to be our worst, and frequently for that reason it is our best ; we grow, and among other growths we grow downwards. We shall go on feeling less fit, and still less fit, and all the while we shall be becoming more ready to be used of the Lord. I know one who said, the other night, when she was reading, that it seemed as if her eyes had dropped out. The truth was, her spectacles had fallen off. Go on losing your spectacles, and be sure that you get rid of all those holy tones and whines, and grotesque methods, and stiffnesses and mannerisms, which are not your eyes, but only shockingly bad spectacles.

II. I conclude by speaking upon THE BLESSED EXPERIENCE : " When I am weak, then am I strong." How is it, and how can it be?

Well, first, it is when I am weak that *I am sure to flee to God for succour and help.* The little conies mentioned in Scripture were poor, puny creatures, yet they baffled the sportsman. Learn a lesson from them : " The conies are but a feeble folk, yet make they their houses in the rocks." Brethren, because I cannot think, I hide behind a doctrine which God has thought out for me ; and because I cannot invent a hypothesis, I rest my soul on a self-evident fact ; and because I cannot even be consistent with myself, I get behind the plain teaching of the text, and there I abide. It is wonderful how strong a man feels in such a hiding-place. When you cannot lay a stone, and cannot lift a trowel by yourself, then you may begin to build for God, for He will make you a worker together with Him, your feebleness will be linked to the eternal strength, and then the wall will rise with speed.

Next, we are strong when we are weak *because we gain our strength by prayer, and our weakness is our best argument in supplication.* Jacob never conquered until he limped, nay, until he fell. When the sinew shrank, the suppliant triumphed. When you are engaged in prayer, plead your strength, and you will get nothing ; then plead your weakness, and you will prevail. There is no better plea with Divine love than weakness and pain ; nothing can so prevail with the great heart of God as for your heart to faint and swoon. The man who rises in prayer to tears and agony, and feels all the while as if he could not pray, and yet must pray,—he is the man who will see the desire of his soul. Do not mothers always care most for the tiniest child, or for that one which is most sick? Do we not spend the greatest care upon that one of our children which has the least use of its limbs ; and is it not true that our weakness holds God's strength, and leads Him to bow His omnipotence to our rescue?

There is another strength in weakness which it is well for us to have. I believe that, *when we preach in conscious weakness, it adds a wonderful force to the words we utter.* When Mr. Knill went out to distribute tracts among the soldiers, he tells us that there was one wicked man who said to his comrades, " I will cure him of coming to us with his tracts ; " so, when a ring was made around the minister and the blasphemer, he cursed Mr. Knill with awful oaths. Hearing those profane words, Mr. Knill burst into tears, and said how he longed for the man's salvation. Years after, he met that soldier again, when the man said to him, " I never took notice of your tracts, or of anything that you said; but when I saw you cry like a child, I could not stand it, but gave my heart to God." When we tell our people how we are hampered, but how much we long for their souls' salvation; when we ask them to excuse our broken language, for it is the utterance of our hearts, they believe in our sincerity, for they see how our hearts are breaking, and they are moved by what we say. The man who grinds out theology at so much a yard has no power over men; the people need men who can feel,—men of heart, weak and feeble men, who can sympathize with the timid and sorrowful. It is a blessed thing if a minister can weep his way into men's souls, or even stammer a path into their hearts. So, brethren, do not be afraid of being weak, but rejoice to be able to say, with the apostle, "When I am weak, then am I strong."

Besides this, another form of strength comes of weakness, for by it *our sympathy is educated*. When you and I become weak, and are depressed in spirit, and our soul passes through the valley of the shadow of death, it is often on account of others. One Sabbath morning, I preached from the text, "My God, My God, why hast Thou forsaken Me?" and though I did not say so, yet I preached my own experience. I heard my own chains clank while I tried to preach to my fellow-prisoners in the dark; but I could not tell why I was brought into such an awful horror of darkness, for which I condemned myself. On the following Monday evening, a man came to see me who bore all the marks of despair upon his countenance. His hair seemed to stand upright, and his eyes were ready to start from their sockets. He said to me, after a little parleying, " I never before, in my life, heard any man speak who seemed to know my heart. Mine is a terrible case; but on Sunday morning you painted me to the life, and preached as if you had been inside my soul." By God's grace, I saved that man from suicide, and led him into gospel light and liberty; but I know I could not have done it if I had not myself been confined in the dungeon in which he lay. I tell the story, brethren, because you sometimes may not understand your own experience, and the perfect people may condemn you for having it; but what know they of God's servants? You and I have to suffer much for the sake of the people of our charge. God's sheep ramble very far, and we have to go after them; and sometimes the shepherds go where they themselves would never roam if they were not in pursuit of lost sheep. You may be in Egyptian darkness, and you may wonder why such a horror chills your marrow; but you may be altogether in the pursuit of your calling, and be led of the Spirit to a position of sympathy with desponding minds. Expect to grow weaker, brethren, that you may comfort the weak, and so may become masters in Israel in the judgment of others; while, in your own opinion, you are less than the least of all saints.

More than this, I believe that my text is true when a man becomes weak *through love to the particular place in which he is called to labour.* Suppose a brother placed in the midst of a dense, poor population, and he feels the responsibility of his work, and the misery of souls around him, until it gets such a hold upon him that he cannot escape from it He tries to think of more cheerful subjects, but he cannot shake off the nightmare of the people's poverty and sin. It is with him by day, and it is with him by night; he hears the crying of the children, and the wailing of the women; he hears the sighing of the men, and the groans of the sick and dying, and he comes to be almost a monomaniac in his desperate zeal for his own part of the great field of service. Yes, that man may kill himself with anxiety; but, meanwhile, it is evident that he is the man whom God has sent to bless the people. He will go on thinking, and praying, and planning, until, at last, he will hit on a method which outsiders may judge to be as odd as the man; but he will carry it out, and the whole district will be the better for it.

Oh, it is a blessing when God casts a godly man into the middle of a mass of misery, and keeps him there! It may not be a pleasant thing for him, but it will bring a sevenfold reward in the end. I am glad that Howard felt that he must go through all the prisons in Europe. He had a comfortable home of his own, and yet he must roam through France, and Germany, and Russia, poking his nose into every pestilential doghole where prisoners were to be found. He makes himself familiar with the unimaginable horrors of dungeon life, and suffers fevers born of the jail-filth. He has a choice nose for the worst atmosphere; the fouler it is, the more needful that he should breathe it, for he has a passion for the discovery and destruction of prison cruelty. He comes home, and writes a book upon his pet subject; and then, after a little while, he is off again, and at last he dies a martyr to the cause he has espoused; yet it was worth while to be a Howard who could live and could die to rescue his fellow-men. Mr. Howard, it is because you are so very weak, and suffer so much from *prison-on-the-brain*, that you are strong; you will accomplish reforms while others are talking of them. I daresay there were some who said, " These things must be gradually ameliorated by the progress of better principles, and we must try new notions by degrees." Yes, this gradual reform is a prudent idea ; but then Mr. Howard is such a weak-minded man that he goes raking up horrible stories, and insisting upon it that murder by imprisonment must cease at once. Brethren, may you become weak in like fashion,— almost out of your minds with restless resolve to save souls! If you break loose in an absurd way, and set the chill proprieties a-trembling, and the imbecilities ridiculing, it will cause me great joy. Little do I care if you become fools for Christ's sake. When our weakness verges upon fanaticism, it may have all the more power about it. Mr. Plimsoll did nobly when he stood up and pleaded against coffin-ships; but he was never so strong as when he lost himself, and broke the rules of the House of Commons in the ardour of his passion. It was very weak of him, but in that weakness lay his strength. Give us more of the speech which comes of a burning heart, as lava comes of a volcanic overflow. When the truth conquers us, we shall conquer by the truth.

Once more, weakness is strength because, often, *a man's sense of weakness arouses the whole of him;* whatever there is in the man then comes out, it makes him intense in every part. Certain small animals are much more to be dreaded in fight than larger beasts, because they are so active and furious that they bite

so fast. A man might almost as well face a hyæna
as a rat or a weasel, because these lesser creatures are
all alive, and so intent on the attack, that they fight
with their whole bodies; claws and teeth are all at
work, and thus they become strong through that sense
of weakness which causes them to use every atom of
force which they possess. Have you never seen a
great man, perhaps a Doctor of Divinity, concerning
whom you have felt how mighty he is? We all
acknowledge his strength; but what does he accomplish? A far smaller man, full of grace and ardour,
and all alive in working for the Lord, achieves much
more. The conscious littleness of the man makes him
live intensely unto God.

"When I am weak, then am I strong." Because I
cannot do much, therefore I will do all I can. Because
I have little power, therefore I will use all the power I
have. Do not the tradesmen say that "a nimble nine-
pence is better than a lazy half-crown"? I am sure it
is so. A sense of weakness may bestir us to a bravery
which else we had not known. Look at our own
country, ages ago, when Spain tried to destroy her.
See the Invincible Armada! Huge ships burden the
sea, and Papal warriors are speeding to seize the prey.
England must do her best. On the one side is Spain,
mistress of empires, and on the other is a poor little
island, with a brave queen, it is true, but with an army
and navy slender to the last degree. The monster
ships are off Plymouth; here they come, like a half-
moon, or like jaws opening to swallow us up. What is
happening in Britain? Why, everybody is preparing
for the battle, and every man and every woman on the
island will fight to the death. All the seafaring folk

are on the alert. Our sailors in their diminutive
vessels are hovering round the huge galleons, waiting
for an opportunity to strike a blow, and the opportunity comes.

" Look how the Lion of the sea lifts up his ancient crown,
 And underneath his deadly paw treads the gay lilies down."

God watches over England. He blows with His wind,
and the sea covers the Armada, and Spain is smitten,
and England is saved. It was a sense of weakness
that aroused the valour of our forefathers, and stirred
the saints to cry to God for help. Go to, ye mighty
ones, ye are not strong. Come ye up, ye weak ones,
to the help of the Lord, to the help of the Lord
against the mighty, for ye are " strong in the Lord,
and in the power of His might."

And this, last of all, is the reason why we are strong
when we are weak, namely, *because the sacrifice is
being consummated*. When was Christ strongest but
when He was weakest? When did He shake the
kingdom of darkness but when He was nailed to the
tree? When did He put away sin for His people but
when His heart was pierced? When did He trample
upon death and the old dragon but when He was
Himself about to die? His victory was in the ex-
tremity of His weakness, namely, in His death; and it
must be the same with His trembling Church. She
has no might; she must suffer, she must be slandered,
and derided, and so the Lord will triumph through her.
The conquering sign is still the cross. Wherefore,
brethren, let us be perfectly content to decrease even
unto the end, that our right royal Lord and King may
gloriously increase from day to day. Amen.

WHAT WE WOULD BE.*

THIS assembly begins to be venerable. For years, we were a band of young men; but now, our own sons are with us, comrades of our ministry, and we feel that we are no longer striplings. We have not yet reached the sere and yellow leaf, nor have we come to our dotage, or our anecdotage; but we are tending toward maturity, and are impressed with the conviction that, if ever we are to do anything for our Lord Jesus, we must do it at once. To us remains no time for loitering, or even for leisure. To me, at least, eternity seems so near that I cannot frame an excuse for delay. "*Now or never,*" sounds sternly in my ears.

RETROSPECT.

Coming together, as we do now, after more than twenty years of brotherly Conferences, and some of us after more than thirty years of ministry, what recollections surround us! In the crystal glass of memory,

---

* This address was delivered in great pain. It is not what we desired it to be. Our anguish made it hard to think, and almost impossible to think connectedly. Almost all that had been prepared was forgotten, and no new springs of thought could make channels for themselves while the mind was smothered up in physical suffering. The address may be regarded as a literary curiosity,—the talk of a man who could with difficulty keep himself from tears through acute suffering, and yet was resolved to take his part in a meeting which he had anticipated with solemn interest for months before. We may add that the revising of the address was accomplished under much the same conditions as the delivery of it.—C. H. S.

we see the past living and moving. Far be it from me, though racked with pain, to cloud that glass with the hot breath of my own anxiety; yet I must say this,—*Never do I look back upon my own past without regret.* I am among the most favoured of my Lords' servants, and I sink into the dust while I joyfully confess it. I have no complaints to make against my God, yet I have nothing else but complaints to make against myself. It seems to me that, wherein by Divine grace I have succeeded, I might have succeeded on a far larger scale had I been a better man. Want of faith on my part may have hampered and hindered my Lord. If I have fed the saints of God, I might have fulfilled that sacred pastorate far more to my Lord's praise had I only been more fit to be used by His Spirit. How can I take a vain-glorious complacency in the little which has been accomplished, when before my eyes I see an immeasurable mass of possibilities which I have missed?

This will be a healthy feeling for the younger brethren, who are flushed with their first victories. Let them rise to a higher scale of expectancy, lest they readily become self-satisfied, and thus destroy all hope of a great life. Believe me, young brother, as our years sober us, we become more and more aware of our imperfections, and feel less and less inclined to admire our own performances. To me, a retrospect means a hearty psalm of praise, and a deep sigh of regret. Unto the Lord be glory for ever; but unto me belong shame and confusion of face.

But what is the use of regret unless we can rise by it to a better future? Sighs, which do not raise us higher, are an ill use of vital breath. Chasten yourselves, but be not discouraged. Gather up the arrows which aforetime fell wide of the mark, not to break them in passionate despair, but to send them to the target with direct aim, and a more concentrated force. Weave victories out of defeats. Learn success from failure, wisdom from blundering. Through grace, if we have done well, we will do better. We will more fully acquaint ourselves with God, that, being more in harmony with Him, our life may be pitched to a Diviner key. Mayhap, the cure for these ill days may lie near to our own mending. When our own torches have less of smoke, and more of heavenly flame, the night may not seem quite so drear.

PROSPECT.

With regard to the prospect before us, I may be supposed to be a prophet of evil; but I am not. I mourn the terrible defections from the truth which are now too numerous to be thought of in detail; nevertheless, I am not disquieted, much less dispirited. That cloud will blow over, as many another has done. I think the outlook is better than it was. I do not think the devil is any better: I never expected he would be; but he is older. Brethren, whether that is for the better or for the worse, I do not know; but, assuredly, the arch-enemy is not quite such a novelty among us as he was. We are not quite so much afraid of that particular form of devilry which is raging now, because we begin to perceive its shape. The unknown appeared to be terrible; but familiarity has removed alarm. At the first, this "modern thought" looked very like a lion; the roaring thereof was terrible, though to some ears there was always a suspicion of braying about it. On closer inspection, the huge king of beasts looked more like a fox, and now we should honour it if we likened it to a wild cat. We were to have been devoured of lions, but the monsters are not to be seen. Scientific religion is empty talk without either science or religion in it. The mountain has brought forth its mouse, or, at any rate, the grand event is near. Very soon, "advanced thought" will only be mentioned by servant girls and young Independent ministers. It has gradually declined till it may now be carried off with the slops. There is nothing in the whole bag of tricks.

At this hour, I see the tide turning;—not that I care much for that, for the rock on which I build is unaffected by ebb or flood of human philosophy. Still, it is interesting to remark that the current is not setting in quite the same direction as heretofore. Young men, who have tried modern doubt, have seen their congregations dwindle away beneath its withering power; and they are, therefore, not quite so enamoured of it as they were. It is time they should make a change; for Christian people have observed that these advanced men have not been remarkable for abundant grace, and they have even been led to think that their loose views on doctrine were all of a piece with looseness as to religion in general. Want of soundness in the faith is usually occasioned by want of conversion. Had certain men felt the power of the gospel in their own souls, they would not so readily have forsaken it to run after fables.

Lovers of the eternal truth, you have nothing to fear! God is with those who are with Him. He reveals Himself to those who believe His revelation. Our march is not to and fro, but onward unto victory. "The Egyptians whom ye have seen to-day, ye shall see them again no more for ever." Other enemies will arise, even as Amalekites, Hivites, Jebusites, Perizzites, and all the rest of them, rose up against Israel; but, in the Name of the Lord, we shall pass on to possess the promised heritage.

PROPOSAL.

Meanwhile, it is for us quietly to labour on. Our day-dreams are over: we shall neither convert the world to righteousness, nor the church to orthodoxy. We refuse to bear responsibilities which do not belong to us, for our real responsibilities are more than enough. Certain wise brethren are hot to reform their denomination. They ride out gallantly. Success be to the champions! They are generally wiser when they ride home again. I confess great admiration for my Quixotic brethren, but I wish they had more to show for their valour. I fear that both church and world are beyond us; we must be content with smaller spheres. Even our own denomination must go its own way. We are only responsible so far as our power goes, and it will be wise to use that power for some object well within reach. For the rest, let us not worry and weary about things beyond our line. What if we cannot destroy all the thorns and thistles which curse the earth; we can, perhaps, cleanse our own little plot. If we cannot transform the desert into a pasture, we may at least make two blades of grass grow where only one grew before; and that will be something.

Brethren, let us look well to our own steadfastness in the faith, our own holy walking with God. Some say that such advice is selfish; but I believe that, in truth, it is not selfishness, but a sane and practical love of others which leads us to be mindful of our own spiritual state. Desiring to do its level best, and to use its own self in the highest degree to God's glory, the true heart seeks to be in all things right with God. He who has learned to swim has fostered a proper selfishness, for he has thereby acquired the power of helping the drowning. With the view of blessing others, let us covet earnestly the best blessings for ourselves.

PERSONAL AMBITION.

I want to make the most of myself. I may not even yet know the way to be most useful, but I would like to know very soon. At least, I can honestly go the length of saying that, if I felt that I could be more useful outside of the pulpit than within it, I would hurry out of it at once. If there was a street corner where I was Divinely assured that, by my blacking of shoes, God could be more glorified than He is by my bearing witness before the great congregation, I would welcome the information, and practically obey it. Some men never can do much for God in the way which they would prefer, for they were never cut out for the work. Owls will never rival falcons by daylight; but, then, falcons would be lost in the enterprise of hunting barns at night for rats and mice, and such small deer. Each creature is not only good, but "very good" in its own place, fulfilling its own office: out of that place, it may become a nuisance.

Friend, be true to your own destiny! One man would make a splendid preacher of downright hard-hitting Saxon; why must he ruin himself by cultivating an ornate style? Another attempting to be extremely simple would throw himself away, for he is florid by nature; why should he not follow his bent? Apollos has the gift of eloquence; why must he copy blunt Cephas? Every man in his own order. It seems to me that, nowadays, every man prefers his own *dis*order. Let each man find out what God wants him to do, and then let him do it, or die in the attempt. In what way can I bring my Lord most glory, and be of most service to His Church while I am here? Solve that question, and pass into the practical.

MORE GRACE.

One thing is past all question; we shall bring our Lord most glory if we get from Him much grace. If I have much faith, so that I can take God at His word; much love, so that the zeal of His house eats me up; much hope, so that I am assured of fruit from my labour; much patience, so that I can endure hardness for Jesus' sake; then I shall greatly honour my Lord and King. Oh, to have much consecration, my whole nature being absorbed in His service; then, even though my talents may be slender, I shall make my life to burn and glow with the glory of the Lord! This way of grace is open to us all. To be saintly is within each Christian's reach, and this is the surest method of honouring God. Though the preacher may not collect more than a hundred in a village chapel to hear him speak, he may be such a man of

God that his little church will be choice seed-corn, each individual worthy to be weighed against gold. The preacher may not get credit for his work in the statistics which reckon scores and hundreds; but in that other book, which no secretary could keep, where things are weighed rather than numbered, the worker's register will greatly honour his Master.

NEED OF GREAT CARE.

Brethren, my desire is *to do everything for the Lord in first-rate style.* We are all of us eager to do much for the Lord, but there is a more excellent way. With ringing trowel we strike away and build a wall, and girdle a city in six months: the aforesaid wall will be down in six days afterwards. It would be better to do more by doing less. Thoroughness is infinitely preferable to superficial area. It is well to work for God microscopically; each tiny bit of our work should bear the closest inspection. The work of the Church had need be done in perfect fashion; for her flaws are sure to show themselves in exaggerated form before long. The sins of to-day are the sorrows of ages. Look at those straths in the Highlands which remain to this day Roman Catholic. Had they, at the time of the Reformation, been carefully visited by a Protestant ministry, they could not have remained for centuries in bondage to old Rome. How slight a deviation from the right line may involve ages of dreary labour! Our Puritan forefathers raised their walls, and laid their stones in fair colours, building well the city of God. Then that greatest of heroes, Oliver Cromwell, looked upon them, and lent his aid He handled the sword of

steel as few have ever done, but his carnal weapon
agreed not with the temple of the Lord. The Lord
seemed to say to him, even as He said unto David,
" Thou shalt not build an house for My Name, because thou hast been a man of war, and hast shed
blood." Therefore Puritanism had to come down,
with all its exceeding stateliness of holiness, because
its sons saw not that the Kingdom of the Lord is
not of Church and State, nor of the law of nations,
but purely of the Spirit of the Lord. We, upon
whom the ends of the world are come, must be careful
that we do not send the armies of the Lord wandering for another forty years in the wilderness, when
Canaan else had been so near. The Lord help us to
be workmen that need not to be ashamed, rightly
dividing the Word of truth! May we live in the eye
of the ages, past and future; above all, may we live
as seeing Him who is invisible!

AROUSAL.

Need I affectionately call upon you, my brethren,
to *stir up the gifts which are in you?* Cultivate
your natural and gracious qualifications for the
ministry. The pastor knows far more than when he
left College; has he learned all he ought to have
learned in that interval? No doubt many of our
brethren—

> " Grow wiser than their teachers are,
>   And better know the Lord."

I am not so sure about those who are the most eager
to assert this of themselves. Real progress may be
usually reckoned by the gauge of humility. He

knows most who is most aware that he knows little. We have all great need of much hard study if our ministry is to be good for anything. We have heard of the French peasants who sent to the Pope for a *curé* " who had finished his education." They complained that their pastor was always studying, and they wanted a man who knew all that was necessary, and consequently needed no time for books and thoughts. What fools they must be in that part of France! We need exactly the kind of preacher whom they despised. He who has ceased to learn has ceased to teach. He who no longer sows in the study will no more reap in the pulpit.

My earnest desire is that all of us may really be—

SOUL-WINNERS.

I hope it will never get to be your notion that only a certain class of preachers can be soul-winners. Every preacher should labour to be the means of saving his hearers. The truest reward of our life-work is to bring dead souls to life. I long to see souls brought to Jesus every time I preach. I should break my heart if I did not see it to be so. Men are passing into eternity so rapidly that we must have them saved at once. We indulge no secret hope which can make it easy to lose present opportunities. From all our congregations a bitter cry should go up unto God, unless conversions are continually seen. If our preaching never saves a soul, and is not likely to do so, should we not better glorify God as peasants, or as tradesmen? What honour can the Lord receive from useless ministers? The Holy Ghost is not with us, we are not used of God for His gracious purposes, unless souls are quickened into heavenly life. Brethren, can we bear to be useless? Can we be barren, and yet content?

Remember that, if we would win souls, we must act accordingly, and lay ourselves out to that end. Men do not catch fish without intending it, nor save sinners unless they aim at it. The prayer of a certain minister before his sermon was, that God would bless souls by his discourse. After hearing that discourse, I wondered at the prayer. How could the man ask for that which he seemed never afterwards to have thought of? His discourse unprayed his prayer. He might as well have poured water on a fire, and have prayed God to make the fire burn thereby. Unless the Lord had caused the people to misunderstand what the preacher said, they could not have been converted by his utterances. God works by means,—by means adapted to His ends; and this being so, how can He bless some sermons? How, in the name of reason, can souls be converted by sermons that lull people to sleep; by sermons containing mere frivolities; by sermons which say plainly, "See how cleverly I put it;" by sermons which insinuate doubt, and cast suspicion upon every revealed truth? To ask for the Divine blessing on that which even good men cannot commend, is poor work. That which does not come from our inmost soul, and is not to us a message from the Lord's own Spirit, is not likely to touch other men's souls, and be the voice of the Lord to them.

TEACHERS.

Brethren, I long that we may all be " apt to teach."

The Church is never overdone with those whose "lips feed many." It should be our ambition to be "good stewards of the manifold grace of God." We all know certain able ministers who are expositors of the Word, and instructors of believers. You always bring something away when you hear them. They trade in precious things; their merchandise is of the gold of Ophir. Certain passages of Scripture are quoted and set in a new light; and certain specialities of Christian experience are described and explained. We come away from such preaching feeling that we have been to a good school. Brethren, I desire that we may each one exercise such an edifying ministry! Oh, that we may have the experience, the illumination, the industry needful for so high a calling! Oh, for more richly-instructive sermons! Brethren, look at many modern sermons! What fire and fury! What flash and dash! What is it all about? To what purpose is this display? We often meet with sermons which are like kaleidoscopes, marvellously pretty, but what is there in them? See, there are several bits of coloured glass, and one or two slips of mirror, and other trifles, and these are put into a tube! How they sparkle! What marvellous combinations! What fascinating transformations! But what are you looking at? You have not seen any more after twenty displays than you saw at first; for indeed there is no more. Some preachers excel in quotations of poetry; and others excel in apposition and alliteration, or in the quaintness of the division of their texts. Many are great in domestic sorrows, and death-bed spectacles, and semi-dramatic picturings. Very telling, very sensational; and, under gracious direction, useful in its own measure; but when souls are to be saved, and saved souls are to be fed, more solid matters must take a prominent place. We must *feed* the flock of God. We must deal with eternal verities, and grapple with heart and conscience. We must, in fact, live to educate a race of saints, in whom the Lord Jesus shall be reflected as in a thousand mirrors.

FATHERS.

The apostle Paul truly says, " Though ye have ten thousand instructors in Christ, yet have ye not many fathers." He calls the general run of teachers pedagogues, and says that we have myriads of such ; but we have not many " fathers." No man has more than one natural father, and in the strictest sense we have each one *spiritual* father, and no more. How singularly true are the apostle's words at this present hour! Still have we a lack of spiritual fathers. I would suggest to this Conference of brethren who have been for years in the ministry, that we have come to that point of age and experience in which each of us should set before him the image of a father as that to which he should approach more and more. We are already fathers in the sense of having around us converts who are our children in the Lord. We have already heard the penitential cries, and the believing prayers, of those born to God through our preaching. Many of us, beloved brethren, without boasting, can rejoice that the Lord has not left us without witness. Ours has been an imperfect and feeble ministry ; but the Lord has given life to many by our words.

The parental relation is one which requires much

of us. *A father should be a stable and established man.* Something of solid worth and substantial judgment is looked for in a father. Many a preacher we could not call "father"; it would seem too ridiculous. The trifler, the brother of many ways of thinking, and the man who is of an angry spirit, are out of the list when we read over the roll of fathers. Something of weight, kindliness, dignity, steadiness, and venerableness, goes to make up our idea of the father. Great truths are very dear to him, for he has had experience of their power for many years. When some of the boys tell him that he is behind the times, he smiles at their superior wisdom. Now and then, he tries to show them that he is right, though it is hard to make them see it. The boys think the fathers fools; the fathers do not *think* that of *them*, —there is no need. True fathers are patient; they do not expect to find old heads on young shoulders. They have the knack of waiting till to-morrow, for time brings with it many instructions; and while it may demonstrate the true, it may also explode the false. Father is not blown about by every wind of doctrine, neither does he run after every new thing which is cried up by the sceptical or by the fanatical. A father knows what he does know, stands by what he has verified, and is rooted and grounded in the faith.

But, with all his maturity and firmness, *the spiritual father is full of tenderness,* and manifests an intense love for the souls of men. His doctrinal divinity does not dry up his humanity. He was born on purpose to care for other people, and his heart cannot rest until it is full of such care. Along our coast, in certain places, there are no harbours; but, in other spots, there are bays into which vessels run at once in the time of storm. Some men present an open natural harbourage for people in distress: you love them instinctively, and trust them unreservedly; and they, on their part, welcome your confidence, and lay themselves out for your benefit. They were fashioned by nature with warm human sympathies, and these have been sanctified by grace, so that it is their vocation to instruct, to comfort, to succour, and in all ways to help spirits of a feebler order. These are the kingly men who become nursing fathers of the church. Paul says of Timothy, " I have no man like-minded, who will naturally care for your state." He himself had this natural care; but he could not just then put his hand upon another of like mind to himself, except Timothy. This natural care may be illustrated by the feeling of birds towards their off-spring. See how diligently they work for them, and how boldly they defend them! A hen with chicks beneath her wings is bravery itself. She becomes a very griffin for her little ones. She would fight the Emperor of Russia, ay, and all the great powers of Europe. The man of God, who feels the force of holy fatherhood, would do anything and everything, possible and impossible, for the sake of his spiritual children; he gladly spends and is spent for them. Though the more he loves the less he may be loved, yet by the force of inward prompting he is impelled to self-denying labour.

Does any brother exclaim, " I should like to fill a father's place in my church, for then I could rule it "? This is a sorry motive, and one which will

disappoint you. The father of a family usually finds
that *his pre-eminence is one of superior self-denial,
rather than of self-assertion.* The best of fathers
do really rule, but they never raise the question of
"Who is master?" In a well-ordered house, "baby
is king." Have you not seen how everything is set
aside for him? The warmest welcome is for that
little stranger, and the movements of the household
are guided by his needs. If you were as great an
autocrat as the King of the Cannibal Islands, it would
make no difference,—baby must be attended to.
What means this? Why, that the poorest, weakest,
and most easily-offended person in the whole church
must rule you if you are a true father! You will
study the most wayward, and yield your personal
pleasure for the good of the most faulty. Somebody
asked, "Why should we deny ourselves alcoholic
drink because weak-minded persons are overcome by
it? That would be to make the weakest persons the
virtual rulers of our conduct, which would be absurd."
Just so; but the absurdity appertains to the family of
love. Our domestic affairs must seem absurd to un-
sympathetic strangers. Who likes to tell them to
the uninitiated? It would be casting pearls before
swine. I would say,—All hail to the absurdities of
holy love: long may they reign! Baby is king: the
weakest rule our hearts. The pace of the whole
flock is slackened, lest we overdrive the lambs. Our
ruling is carried out by seeing that none tread down
the weak, and by setting the example of the greatest
self-forgetfulness. He is not fit to be a father who
does not see that this is the imperative law of love,
and is, indeed, the secret of power. We lay ourselves

down for all men to go over us if thus they may come to Jesus.

Our place is to be the servants of all. The father earns the daily bread, brings it home, and divides it. *We* blend father and mother in one, and lay ourselves out to fulfil all needful offices for those committed to our charge. If you desire to be a father in the church that you may have his special honour, you see the way to it : it comes of self-denial, patience, forbearance, love, zeal, and diligence. " Whosoever will be chief among you, let him be your servant."

A father must possess wisdom. But in this matter many are deceived, for they aspire to it from a wrong motive, and so become foolish. If you had wisdom, my brother, what would you do with it ? Would you so use it as to make others feel your superiority ? If so, you have little wisdom as yet. A minister's wisdom lies in endeavouring to be wise for others, not cunning for himself. Some use their wisdom in a very unwise way, and curse the church which they should bless. And so you would go about the church, and put everybody right, being so wise yourself! Herein is often great folly. A man I have heard of said, " I am not at all afraid of thieves breaking into my house. If I heard a burglar, I should touch this button, and in a moment an electric current would explode dynamite in the cellar, and that would blow up the burglar and the whole establishment." You laugh ; but we have met with ministers who have acted in much the same manner. I am sorry to know a brother who has performed this feat in five or six churches. The moment he thinks that a member, especially a deacon, has gone wrong, he blows the whole thing to pieces, and calls it faithfulness. This is not acting the part of a wise father. If we have wisdom, we shall maintain peace, and shall attempt reforms with gentleness. Fathers do not kill their children because they are unphilosophical, or unsound in theology, or somewhat disobedient in conduct.

If we would be fathers, *we must aim at a high degree of holiness.* The query is often proposed,— Is it possible for believers to be perfectly holy here on earth? That question sounds strangely from some lips. I saw a man, the other day, who had no shoes on his feet, and was only half covered by his rags. Suppose he had asked me whether I thought it was possible that he could become a millionaire, I should have answered that he had better first go and earn sixpence for his night's lodging, and then save up enough to buy a decent suit of clothes. Thus, those who are eager to dispute about perfection had better see that their lives are first of all decently consistent with the profession they have made. Brethren, we can be much more holy than we are. Let us attain first to that holiness about which there is no controversy. At the time of the Council of Trent, there was a controversy between the Church of Rome and the Protestants as to whether it was possible for the laws of God to be kept. The question was awkwardly put, and when Luther endeavoured to show that it was impossible, he seems to me to have advocated one truth at the cost of another. At any rate, we dare not set limits to the power of Divine grace, so as to say that a believer can reach a certain degree of grace, but can go no further. If a perfect life be possible, let us endeavour to obtain it. If a faith that never staggers can be ours, let us seek it. If we can walk with God as Enoch did throughout a long life, let us not rest short of it. We dare not straiten the Lord in this matter; if we be straitened at all, it is in ourselves. Let us aspire to saintliness of spirit and character. I am persuaded that the greatest power we can get over our fellow-men is the power which comes of consecration and holiness. More eyes than we wot of are fixed upon our daily life at home, and in the church, and in the world. We claim to be the Lord's ministers, and we must not wonder that we are watched at every turn; ay, watched when we think that no observer is near. Our lives should be such as men may safely copy.

You know *the weighty responsibility of a father towards his children;* such is ours. I do not think that any of us would dare to say to our people, "Follow me in all things." And yet their tendency is to follow the pastor. In this tendency lies influence for the holy, and ·a dreadful power for mischief for the careless. Many beginners take readily to an earthly model; they find it more natural to copy a godly man, whom they have seen, than to imitate the Lord Jesus, whom they have not seen. I do not commend them in this; but so it is, and we must be tender toward this weakness so that it may not become the occasion of evil. Children first obey their parents, and so learn the law of the Lord, and no doubt many of the weaker sort learn the way of holiness from their spiritual guides. A painter, who afterwards becomes a great original, is in his earliest days a disciple of a certain school of art; it is so in religion. The babe in grace is taught to walk by an older brother, and afterwards takes his own path. I believe that many weak ones in our churches are seriously injured, if not entirely broken down, by following the example of their ministers in matters wherein they come short of the Lord's mind. How grievous it would be if any believers were dwarfed through our conduct! May we not fear that there are some in our churches to-day who are not what they might have been had we properly guided them? No doubt some have been coddled into weakness, and others have been allowed to grow more in one direction than in others. Do you say, "We cannot help this; it is no business of ours"? I tell you it is our business. Strangers may talk in a careless way, but fathers are conscious of great responsibility as to their children. If a family is not well-ordered, a wise father begins to mend his own ways. If our people do wrong, we fret and blame ourselves. If we were better, our church-members would be better. It is little use to scold them; our wiser way is to humble ourselves before God, and find out the reason why our ministry does not produce better results.

I don't think I can say much more, I am so greatly overcome by pain. I was going to say that, as an earthly father stands in the place of God to his children, so do we in a certain measure. We do not aim at it, nor wish for it; but we are placed, by many weak and ignorant persons, in a position from which we would gladly escape if we could, for we abhor everything which wears the semblance of priestcraft. Alas! there are simple souls who forget to look to the

Lord's mind as revealed in the Scriptures, but they look to us as their teachers and guides. I grant you that there may be an evil superstition in it, but there it is, and it must not be trifled with. In many instances, however, through their grateful respect, the members of our congregation gather lessons from what we do as well as from what we say, and this should make us very careful lest we lead them astray. Be holy, that others may be holy.

We had need be kind and courteous, for even such a small thing as shaking hands, or giving a nod, may have an influence. One who is now a member of our church told me that he had often stood to shake hands with me at the back gate, as I left the building, long before he had come inside to hear me preach. The mere fact of a kindly notice which I gave him on going out had made him think of me, and inclined him to hear. He assured me that this simple matter was the first link between him and religion. He was drunken, and wretched, and ungodly; but he had, by a happy accident, become the friend of a minister of Christ, and this bond, though slight as a spider's thread, was the beginning of better things. Never be stiff and proud. " Be pitiful, be courteous." Children expect kindness from a father ; let them not be disappointed. It is ours to be all things to all men, if by any means we may save some.

Even to those who are without, we must show a tender consideration. *Even to those who reject our gospel, we must display unbounded tenderness.* It should fill us with deep sorrow that men refuse the Saviour, and follow the way of destruction. If they will persist in ruining themselves, we must weep for them in secret places. Having lovingly preached the gospel to them, if they will not repent, we must break *our* hearts because we cannot break *their* hearts. If Absalom has perished, we must go with David to the chamber over the gate, and bitterly lament him, crying, " O my son Absalom, my son, my son Absalom! would God I had died for thee, O Absalom, my son, my son!" Do you ever mourn over your hearers as one that weepeth for the slain of his people? Can you bear that they should pass away to judgment unforgiven? Can you endure the thought of their destruction? I do not know how a preacher can be much blessed of God who does not feel an agony when he fears that some of his hearers will pass into the next world impenitent and unbelieving.

On the other hand, survey the picture of a father who sees his child returning from the error of his way. In the New Testament, you see the portrait Divinely drawn. When the prodigal was a great way off, his father saw him. Oh, to have quick eyes to spy out the awakened! The father ran to meet him. Oh, to be eager to help the hopeful! He fell upon his neck, and kissed him. Oh, for a heart overflowing with love, to joy and rejoice over seeking ones! As that father was, such should we be; ever loving, and ever on the outlook. Our eyes, and ears, and feet should ever be given to penitents. Our tears and open arms should be ready for them. The father in Christ is the man to remember the best robe, and the ring, and the sandals; he remembers those provisions of grace because he is full of love to the returning one. Love is a practical theologian, and takes care to deal practically with all the blessings of the covenant, and all the mysteries of revealed truth. It does not hide away the robe and ring in a treasury of theology; but brings them forth, and puts them on.

O my brethren, as you are the sons of God, be also fathers in God! Let this be the burning passion of your souls. *Grow to be leaders and champions.* God give you the honour of maturity, the glory of strength! But courageously expect that He will then lay upon you the burden which such strength is fitted to bear. We need you to quit yourselves like men. In these evil days, when the shock of battle comes, it will have to be sustained by the fathers, or not at all. Our young and immature brethren are invaluable as light troops, leading the way, and advancing into the enemy's territory; but the solid squares, which stand firm against the fury of the charge, must mainly be composed of the Old Guard. You of experience in the things of God; you experts, who have fought the battles of the Lord over and over again; you must stand fast, and having done all, you must still stand. I call upon you fathers to hold the fort till Jesus comes. *You* must be steadfast, unmovable, always abounding in the work of the Lord. If you fail, where are we to look? It will be "as when a standard-bearer fainteth."

But lest you should feel pleased with the fact that you desire this high honour, and fancy that the mere aspiration will fulfil itself, let me remind you how the Saviour lived. He never settled down in desires and resolves, but girded Himself for constant service. He said, "My meat is to do the will of Him that sent Me, and to finish His work." Soul-winning must be meat and drink to us. To do the Lord's work must be as necessary as food to us. *His* Father's work is that in which we also are engaged, and we cannot do better than imitate our Lord. Tell me, then, how Jesus set about it. Did He set about it by arranging to build a huge Tabernacle, or by organizing a monster Conference, or by publishing a great book, or by sounding a trumpet before Him in any other form? Did He aim at something great, and altogether out of the common line of service? Did He bid high for popularity, and wear Himself out by an exhausting sensationalism? No; He called disciples to Him one by one, and instructed each one with patient care. To take a typical instance of His method, watch Him as He paused in the heat of the day. He sat upon a well, and talked with a woman, —a woman who was none of the best. This looked like slow work, and very common-place action. Yet we know that it was right and wise.

To that single auditor, He did not deliver a list of clever maxims, like those of Confucius, or profound philosophies, like those of Socrates; but He talked simply, plainly, and earnestly with her about her own life, her personal needs, and the living water of grace by which those needs could be supplied. He won *her* heart, and through her many more; but He did it in a way of which many would think little. He was beyond the petty ambitions of our vain-glorious hearts. He cared not for a large congregation; He did not even ask for a pulpit. He desired to be the spiritual Father of that one daughter; and, for that purpose, He must needs go through Samaria, and must, in His utmost weariness, tell her of the water of life. Brethren, let us lay aside vanity. Let us grow more simple, natural, and father-like as we mature ; and let us be more and more completely absorbed in our life-work.

As the Lord shall help us, let us lay our all upon the altar, and only breathe for Him. Certain of you will go abroad, some of you may find a grave on the banks of the Congo. We cannot all do this; but, brethren, we must all live unto the Lord, and lay down our lives for the brethren. The Thames and the Clyde must have their consecrated ones as well as the Congo and the Ganges. London and Bristol must witness to as true a heroism as Canton and Calcutta. Because we belong to Christ, the zeal of the Lord's house must eat us up.

I wish I could have spoken to you with all my strength, but it may be that my weakness may be used of God to greater purpose. My thoughts are few by reason of pain, which disorders my head ; but they are all on fire, for my heart remains true to my Lord, to His gospel, and to you. May He use every man of us to the utmost of our capacity for being used, and glorify Himself by our health and our sickness, our life and our death! Amen.

STEWARDS.

MY BELOVED BRETHREN,—I might even say with Paul, "My dearly-beloved and longed-for,"—it gives me intense delight to look into your faces once again; and yet I feel weighted with a solemn responsibility in having to direct your thoughts at this time, so as to give the key-note to our solemn Conference. I ask your continued prayers that I may speak aright, saying the right thing in the right way.

There is considerable advantage in the freedom of the usual inaugural address. It may take the methodical form of a sermon, or it may wear looser garments, and come forth in the undress of a speech. Certain freedoms, which are not usually accorded to a set sermon, are allowed me in this discursive discourse. You shall call my talk by what name you choose, when I have done; but it will be a sermon, for I have a very definite and distinct text in my mind, and I shall keep to it with at least an average closeness. I may as well announce it, for it will furnish you with a clue to my intent. You will find the passage in the First Epistle to the Corinthians, in the first and second verses of the fourth chapter :—

"Let a man so account of us, as of the ministers of Christ, and stewards of the mysteries of God. Moreover it is required in stewards, that a man be found faithful."

The apostle was anxious to be rightly accounted of, and well he might be; for ministers are not often estimated rightly; as a rule, they are either gloried in, or else despised. At the commencement of our ministry, when our stories are fresh, and our energies are full; when we blaze and flash, and spend much time in the firework factory, people are apt to think us wonderful beings; and then the apostle's word is needed, " Therefore let no man glory in men " (1 Cor. iii. 21). It is not true, as flatterers insinuate, that in our case the gods have come down in the likeness of men; and we shall be idiots if we think so. In due time, foolish expectations will be cured by disappointment; and then we shall hear unwelcome truth, mingled with unrighteous censure. The idol of yesterday is the butt of to-day. Nine days, nine weeks, nine months, or nine years; be it more or less, time works disenchantment, and changes our position in the world's account. The Primrose-day is over, and the nettle months have come. After the time of the singing of birds has passed away, we come nearer to the season of fruit; but the children are not half so pleased with us as when they wandered in our luxuriant meadows, and strung our daisies and buttercups into crowns and garlands. In our more autumnal years, the people miss our flowers and greenery. Perhaps we are becoming sensible that it is so. The old man is solid and slow; whereas the young man rode upon the wings of the wind. It is clear that some think too much of us, and some think too little of us; it would be far better if they all accounted of us soberly " as the ministers of Christ." It would be for the advantage of the Church, for our own benefit, and for the glory of God, if we were put in our right places, and kept there, being neither over-rated, nor unduly censured, but viewed in our relation to our Lord, rather than in our own personalities. "Let a man so account of us, as of the ministers of Christ."

We are MINISTERS. The word has a very respectable sound. To be a minister, is the aspiration of many a youth. Perhaps, if the word were otherwise rendered, their ambition might cool. Ministers are *servants:* they are not guests, but waiters; not landlords, but labourers. The word has been rendered "under-rowers", men who tug at the oars on the lowest bench. It was hard work to row a galley; those rapid strokes consumed the life-forces of the slaves. There were three banks of rowers: those on the upper bank had the advantage of fresh air; those who were beneath them were more closely shut in; but I suppose that the lowest bank of rowers would be faint with heat, as well as worn out with sore travail. Brethren, let us be content to wear out our lives even in the worst position, if by our labour we can speed the passage of our great Cæsar, and help the progress of the trireme of the Church in which He has embarked. We are willing to be chained to the oar, and to work on through life to make His barque cleave the waves. We are not captains, nor owners of the galley, but only the oarsmen of Christ.

Let us remember that we are the servants in our Lord's house. "Whosoever will be chief among you, let him be your servant." Let us be willing to be door-mats at our Master's entrance-hall. Let us not seek honour for ourselves, but put honour upon the weaker vessels by our care for them. In every well-ordered house,—as I have already reminded you,—it is a matter of fact that " baby is king," because of his weakness. In our Lord's Church, let the poor, the feeble, the distressed have the place of honour, and let us who are strong bear their infirmities. He is highest who makes himself lowest ; he is greatest who makes himself less than the least. " Who is offended, and I burn not? " said the great apostle. If there be any scandal to be borne, let us rather suffer it than allow it to grieve the Church of God. As we are, by office, servants in a special sense, let us cheerfully bear the chief part of the self-denial and travail of the saints.

The text, however, does not call us simply ministers or servants, but it adds, " *of Christ.*" We are not the servants of men, but of the Lord Jesus. Esteemed sir, if you think, because you subscribe to my support, that I am bound to do your bidding, you are under a mistake. Truly, we are " ourselves your servants for Jesus' sake ; " but, in the highest sense, our sole responsibility is to Him whom we call Master and Lord. We obey superior orders ; but we cannot yield to the dictation of our fellow-servants, however influential they may be. Our service is glorious, because it is the service of Christ : we feel honoured in being permitted to wait upon Him whose shoe's latchet we are not worthy to unloose.

We are also said to be " STEWARDS." What are stewards? That is our office. What is required of stewards? This is our duty. We are not now speaking of anybody outside, but of you, brethren, and myself; therefore, let us make a personal application of all that is said.

1. First, *a steward is a servant, and no more.* Perhaps he does not always remember this; and it is a very pitiful business when the servant begins to think that he is " my lord." It is a pity that servants, when honoured by their master, should be so apt to give themselves airs. How ridiculous Jack-in-office makes himself! I do not refer now to butlers and footmen, but to ourselves. If we magnify ourselves, we shall become contemptible; and we shall neither magnify our office nor our Lord. We are the servants of Christ, and not lords over His heritage.

Ministers are for churches, and not churches for ministers. In our work among the churches, we must not dare to view them as estates to be farmed for our own profit, or gardens to be trimmed to our own taste. Some men talk of a liberal polity in their church. Let them be liberal with what is their own; but for a steward of Christ to boast of being liberal with his Master's goods, is quite another matter. As stewards, we are only upper servants; and may the Lord maintain in us the spirit of hearty obedience! If we do not carefully keep our right place, our Master will not fail to chide us, and give our pride a taking down. How many of our afflictions, failures, and depressions, arise out of our being unduly lifted up! I feel sure that no man, who is honoured of God in public, is quite a stranger to that chastening behind the door which keeps proud flesh from being unduly exalted. How often have I prayed, " Dismiss me not Thy service, Lord! " For a dismissed steward is a pitiable object among his lord's servants. He was once great

and mighty, riding the high horse; but when he is
out of a place, he is of less account than the smallest
cowboy. See how glad he is to be received, as a
grateful guest, into the humble cottages of those who
once looked up to him with a sort of awe when he
represented his lordship! Take heed 'that you be
not exalted above measure, lest you come to nothing.

2. *A steward is a servant of a peculiar kind*, for
he has to superintend the other servants, and that is a
difficult thing to do. An old friend of mine, who is
now with God, once said, "I have always been a
shepherd. Forty years I was a shepherd of sheep,
and another forty years I was a shepherd of men, and
the last flock was a deal more sheepish than the first."
This witness is true. I think I have heard that a
sheep has as many diseases as there are days in the
year; but I am sure that the other sort of sheep are
liable to ten times as many. A pastor's work is an
anxious one. All sorts of difficulties occur with our
fellow-servants; and, alas! unwise stewards make a
great many more than there need be by expecting perfection in others, although they do not possess it
themselves. Our fellow-servants are, after all, wisely
selected; for He who put them into His household
knew what He was doing; at any rate, they are *His*
choice, and not ours. It is not our place to find fault
with our Lord's own election. It is very common
with some to revile the Church; but as the Church is
the bride of Christ, it is rather dangerous work to
criticize the Lord's beloved. I feel towards the
Church somewhat as David felt towards Saul; I dare
not lift up my hand against the Lord's anointed.
Better far will it be for us to find fault with ourselves

rather than with our people, when there is anything wrong with them.

Still, our church-members are men, and the best of men are but men at the best : to direct, instruct, console, and aid so many different minds, is no easy task. He who rules among men, for God, should be a man ; and what is more, he should be a man of God. He should be graciously endowed, a kingly man, head and shoulders above his fellows. Men will gladly yield to real superiority, but not to official pretensions. The superior position must be supported by superior attainments. The steward must know more than the ploughman and the thatcher. He must be of higher intelligence than the gamekeeper and the carter, and he should have a more reliable character than Mary and John, who have to take orders from him. Brethren, as stewards, we must have abundant grace, or we shall not fulfil the duties of our office, or earn to ourselves a good degree.

The other servants will take their cue from us. A steward, who is dull, inert, and slow, will have a slow team of servants about him, and the business of his lordship will fare badly. Those who travel must have noticed that the servants in a hotel are very much like the landlord ; if the landlord is cheery, attentive, and obliging, all the maids and waiters partake of his geniality ; but if he looks sourly at you, and treats you with indifference, you will find that the whole establishment is of a disdainful order. A minister soon gets round him people like himself : " like priest, like people." Oh, that we may always be alive and earnest in the service of the Lord Jesus, that our people may be alive also! I have read of a

Puritan divine, that he was so full of life that his people said he lived like one who fed on live things. Oh, for a life sustained by living bread!

We shall not be good stewards in the management of our fellow-servants unless we are ourselves filled with the grace of God. We must set our fellow-servants an example of zeal and tenderness, constancy, hopefulness, energy, and obedience. We must ourselves practise constant self-denial, and select as our own part of the work that which is hardest and most humiliating. We are to rise above our fellows by superior self-forgetfulness. Be it ours to lead the forlorn hopes, and to bear the heaviest burdens. Archdeacon Hare was giving a lecture at Trinity College when a cry of "Fire!" was raised. His pupils rushed away, and formed themselves into a line to pass buckets of water from the river to the burning building. The tutor saw a consumptive student standing up to his waist in the water, and cried to him, "What! you in the water, Sterling?" The reply was, "Somebody must be in it, and why not I as well as another?" Let us say to ourselves, "Some fellows must be doing the drudgery of the Church, and labouring in the hardest places, and why should not we take that post?" Those whom the Lord will promote are those who have no choice of their own, but are ready for anything, and ready for everything. He who has been fearless in one hour of peril shall have for his reward the privilege of exhibiting still greater courage. He who is faithful over a small charge shall be selected for a post of harder work and sterner trial; this is the promotion to which loyal servants of our King aspire.

3. Next, remember that *stewards are servants under the more immediate command of the great Master.* We should be as the steward who daily goes into his lord's private room to receive orders. John Ploughman was never in the squire's parlour, but the steward is often there. If he neglected to consult the squire, he would soon be doing amiss, and involving himself in heavy responsibility. How often ought you and I to say, " Lord, show me what Thou wouldst have me to do! " To cease to look up to God, so as to learn and practise His will, would be to quit our true position. What shall be done to a steward who never communicates with his master? Give him his wages, and let him go. He who does his own will, and not his master's, is of no value as a steward.

Brethren, we must wait upon God continually. The habit of going to Him for our orders must be cultivated. How grateful should we be that our Master is always within call! He guides His servants with His eye ; and with His guidance, He also gives the needful power. He will make our faces to shine before the eyes of our fellows, if we commune with Him. Our example must encourage others to wait upon the Lord. As our business is to tell them the mind of God, let us study that mind very carefully. I trust I do not address a single man who has fallen into the slovenly habit of going to his work without first communing with his Master; for such an unhappy person, being out of touch with his Lord, will exercise an injurious influence over the rest of the household, making them idle, or indifferent, or dissatisfied, or dispirited. If the steward does not care for his master's interests ; or if he is wilful, and would fain alter or reverse his lord's orders, if he dared ; or if he in any way tampers with the estate, as did the unjust steward in the parable, then the servants under him will learn disloyalty. I might indicate how much of this is done in certain churches, but I refrain. The Master will come speedily, and woe to the steward whose account will prove him to have been unfaithful !

4. Again, *stewards are constantly giving account.* Their account is given as they go along. A business-like proprietor requires an account of outgoings and incomings, from day to day. There is great truth in the old proverb that " short reckonings make long friends." If we make short reckonings with God, we shall be long friends with Him. I wonder if any of you keep account of your faults and shortcomings. Perhaps the time will be better spent in constant efforts to serve your Master, and increase His estate. We ought each one to ask himself, " What am I doing by my preaching? Is it of the right kind? Am I giving prominence to those doctrines which my Lord would have me put in the forefront? Am I caring for souls as He would have me care for them? " It is a good thing thus to review one's whole life, and enquire, " Do I give sufficient time to private prayer? Do I study the Scriptures as intensely as I should? I hurry about to many meetings, but am I in all this fulfilling my Master's orders? May I not be grati-fying myself with the appearance of doing much, whereas I should really be doing more if I were more attentive to the quality than to the quantity of the work? " Oh, to go often to the Master, and to be right and clear in our accounts with Him !

5. To come to the main point : *a steward is a trustee of his master's goods.* Whatever he has, belongs to his master ; and choice things are put into his custody, not that he may do as he likes with them, but that he may take care of them. The Lord has entrusted to each one of us certain talents, and these are not our own. Gifts of knowledge, and thought, and speech, and influence, are not ours to glory in, but ours in trust for the Lord alone. It is *His* pound that gains five pounds.

We ought to increase our capital stock. Are all the young brethren doing that? Are you increasing in gift and capacity? My brethren, do not neglect yourselves. I observe that some brethren grow, and others stand still, dwarfed and stunted. Men, like horses, are very disappointing creatures ; good colts drop suddenly lame, or develop a vice of which they were never before suspected. Alas! too many young men destroy our hopes ; they are extravagant in their expenses, make an unfortunate marriage, fall into ill humours, wander after novel opinions, give way to laziness and self-indulgence, or in some other way fail to improve themselves. Yet the most needful and profitable labour is that which we spend upon our own mental and spiritual improvement. Whatever you do, take heed unto yourselves, and to your doctrine. Those who neglect thinking in order that they may be everlastingly " jawing ", are very foolish ; they resemble a bailiff who does nothing on the farm, but talks at great length about what ought to be done. Dumb dogs cannot bark, but wise dogs are not always barking. To be always giving out, and never taking in, tendeth to emptiness.

Brethren, we are "stewards of the mysteries of God;" we are "put in trust with the gospel." Paul speaks of the glorious gospel of the blessed God which was committed to his trust. I hope none of you have ever had the misfortune to be made a trustee. It is a thankless office. In executing a trust, there is little scope for originality; we are bound to carry out the trust with literal exactness. One person wishes to receive more money, and another desires to alter a clause in the deed; but the faithful trustee falls back upon the document, and abides by its provisions. I hear him say, as they worry him, " Dear friends, I did not make this trust; I am simply the administrator of it, and I am bound to carry it out." The gospel of the grace of God needs great improvement;—at least, so I am informed;—but I know that it is no business of mine to improve it, my part is to act upon it. No doubt many would improve God Himself from off the face of the earth, if they could. They would improve the Atonement until it vanished. Great alterations are demanded of us, in the name of "the spirit of the age." Of course, we are warned that the very notion of punishment for sin is a barbarous relic of mediæval ages, and must be given up, and with it the doctrine of substitution and many other old-fashioned dogmas. We have nothing to do with these demands; we have only to preach the gospel as we find it.

As a trustee, if my course of action is disputed, I keep to the letter of the bond; and if any quarrel over it, they must take their complaints to the proper Court, for I have no power to alter the record. We are simply administrators; and if we are not allowed to act, we will throw the whole thing into the heavenly Chancery. The dispute is not between us and modern thought, but between God and the wisdom of men. "Oh!" they say, "it is barbarous to go on prosing with this old, old story." We care not how old the story is; since it came from God, we repeat it in His Name. Call it what you like, it is in the Book from which we derive our authority. "*But you surely have a judgment of your own?*" May be we have, and as much of it as those who oppose us; but our judgment does not invent a trust, it simply guides us in the carrying of it out. Stewards must keep to their orders, and trustees must carry out the terms of their trust.

My brethren, we are at this present hour "set for the *defence* of the gospel." If ever men were called to this office, we are so called. These are times of drifting : men have pulled up their anchors, and are driven to and fro with winds and tides of divers kinds. As for me, I have in this hour of danger not only let down the great bower anchor, but I have cast four anchors out of the stern. That may be quite the wrong place ; but in these times we need anchoring both fore and aft. Now am I fixed. Sceptical reasonings might have moved me at one time, but not now. Do our enemies ask us to lay down our swords, and cease to fight for the old faith? Like the Greeks said to Xerxes, we answer, "Come and take them." The other day, the advanced thinkers were going to sweep the orthodox into limbo ; but as yet, we survive their assaults. These boasters do not know the vitality of Evangelical truth. No, glorious gospel, thou shalt never perish ! If we are to die, we will die fighting. If we shall personally pass away, fresh evangelists will preach upon our graves. Evangelical truths are like the dragon's teeth which Cadmus sowed, they breed men all armed for the fray. The gospel lives by dying. Brethren, at any rate, in this contest, if we are not victorious, we will at least be faithful.

6. *A steward's business is to dispense his master's goods according to their design.* He is to bring forth things new and old; to provide milk for babes and strong meat for men, giving to each one his portion of meat in due season. At some tables, I fear the strong men have been waiting a long time for the meat, and there is small hope of its yet appearing; the milk-and-water is more plentiful by far. Someone went to hear a certain preacher, last Sunday, and complained that he did not preach Christ. Another remarked that perhaps it was not the due season; but, my brethren, the due season for preaching Christ is every time you preach. God's children are always hungry, and no bread will satisfy them but that which comes down from Heaven.

A wise steward will maintain the proportion of truth. He will bring forth things new and old; not always doctrine, not always practice, and not always experience. He will not always preach conflict, nor always victory; not giving a one-sided view of truth, but a sort of stereoscopic view, which shall make truth stand out "evidently set forth" before them. Much of the preparation of spiritual food lies in the correct proportion of the ingredients. One spoke incorrectly of using in his sermons three grains of Calvinism and two of Arminianism; meaning, as I afterwards learned, that he preached both a full gospel and a free gospel: in that which he intended, I fully agree with him. Let us give a wide range of experience, not forgetting that higher life which consists in increased lowliness of mind. To make full proof of our ministry, will require great discrimination; for a want of balance in preaching has done serious injury to many a church. The line of wisdom is as fine as a razor's edge, and we shall need Divine wisdom to keep us to it. We are not always to harp upon one string. Our Master's servants will murmur if we give them nothing but "rabbits hot and rabbits cold." We must bring forth, out of the Master's stores, a rich variety of food fit for the building up of spiritual manhood. Excess in one direction, and failure in another, may breed much mischief; let us therefore use weight and measure, and look up for guidance.

Brethren, take care that you use your talents for your Master, and for your Master only. It is disloyalty to our Lord if we wish to be soul-winners in order to be thought to be so. It is unfaithfulness to Jesus if we even preach sound doctrine with the view of being thought sound, or pray earnestly with the desire that we may be known as praying men. It is for us to pursue our Lord's glory with a single eye, and with our whole heart. We must use our Lord's gospel, and our Lord's people, and our Lord's talents, for our Lord, and for Him alone.

7. *The steward should also be the guardian of his master's family.* Look to the interests of all who are in Christ Jesus, and let them all be as dear to you as your own children. Servants, in the olden times, were often so united to the family, and so interested

in their masters' affairs, that they spoke of *our* house, *our* land, *our* carriage, *our* horses, and *our* children. Our Lord would have us thus identify ourselves with His holy business; and, especially, He would have us love His chosen. We, beyond all others, should lay down our lives for the brethren. Because they belong to Christ, we love them for His sake. I trust we can each one of us heartily say,—

> "There's not a lamb in all Thy flock
> I would disdain to feed."

Brethren, let us heartily love all whom Jesus loves. Cherish the tried and suffering. Visit the fatherless and the widow. Care for the faint and the feeble. Bear with the melancholy and despondent. Be mindful of all parts of the household, and thus shall you be a good steward.

8. I shall cease from this picture when I have said that *the steward represents his master.* When the master is away, everybody comes to the steward for orders. He had need to behave himself well who represents such a Lord as ours. A steward should speak much more carefully and wisely when he speaks for his lord than when he speaks on his own account. Unless he is guarded in his utterances, his lord may be forced to say to him, "You had better speak for yourself: I cannot allow you thus to misrepresent *me*." My beloved brethren and fellow-servants, the Lord Jesus is compromised by us if we do not keep His way, declare His truth, and manifest His spirit Men infer the Master from the servant; are they not to be excused if they so do? Ought not the steward to act after his master's manner? You cannot dissociate the squire from the steward, the Lord from

His representative. A Puritan was told that he was too precise; but he replied, " I serve a precise God." We should be gentle, for we represent the gentle Jesus. We should be zealous, for we represent One who was clad with zeal as with a cloak. Our best guide, when we are uncertain as to what to do, will be found in the answer to the question, " What would Jesus do? " When deliberating about going to a place of amusement, you may end the deliberation by saying, " I will go if my Master would have gone." If moved to speak with warmth, take heed that it is only such warmth as your Lord would have exhibited.

If urged to utter your own thoughts rather than revealed truth, follow Jesus, who spake not His own thoughts, but those of the Father. In this way, you will be acting as a steward should do. Here lies your wisdom, your comfort, and your strength. It was a sufficient vindication for a steward, when one accused him of folly, that he could reply, " Say what you please of what I did, for therein I followed my master's orders." Caviller, do not blame the steward. The man has done according to the command of his superior; what else would you have him do? Our conscience is clear, and our heart is restful, when we feel that we have taken up our cross, and have followed the footprints of the Crucified One. Wisdom is justified of her children. If not to-day, yet in the long run, it shall be seen that obedience is better than originality, and teachableness is more to be desired than genius. The revelation of Jesus Christ will outlive the speculation of man. We are content, nay, anxious, not to be regarded as original thinkers and original doers; we wish to make known the thoughts of God, and finish the work which He worketh in us mightily.

The second part of my address will be occupied with OUR OBLIGATIONS AS STEWARDS. " It is required in stewards, that a man be found *faithful*." It is not required that a man be found brilliant, or that he be found pleasing to his associates, or even that he be found successful. All that is required is, that he be found *faithful ;* and, truly, this is no small matter. It will need the Lord Himself to be both our wisdom and our strength, or we shall surely fail. Many are the ways by which we may come short of this requirement, however simple it may seem to be.

1. We may fail to be faithful *through acting as if we were chiefs instead of servants*. A difficulty arises in the church, which might readily be settled by loving forbearance, but we " stand upon our dignity ; " and then the servant grows out of his livery. We can be very high and mighty, if we please ; and the smaller we are, the more easily do we swell out. No cock is greater in fight than a bantam ; and no minister is more ready to contend for his " dignity " than the man who has no dignity. How foolish we look when we play the grandee ! The steward thinks he has not been treated with proper respect, and he will " let the servants know who he is." The other day, his master was roughly used by an angry tenant, and he took no notice, for he had too much sense to be put out by so small a matter ; but his steward passes by nothing, and fires up at everything : is this as it should be ? I think I see the gentle master lay his hand upon his furious servant's shoulder, and I hear

him say, " Can you not bear it? I have borne far
more than this."

Brethren, our Master " endured such contradiction
of sinners against Himself," and shall we be weary
and faint in our minds? How can we be stewards
of the gentle Jesus if we behave ourselves haughtily?
Let us never ride the high horse, nor attempt to be
lords over God's heritage; for He will not have it so,
and we cannot be faithful if we give way to pride.

We shall also fail in our duty as stewards if we
begin speculating with our Master's money. We may
play " ducks and drakes " with our own, but not with
our Lord's money. We are not bidden to speculate,
but to " occupy " till He comes. Honest trading with
His goods, is one thing; but to play a high game, and
run unlawful risks, is quite another. I do not intend
to speculate with my Master's gospel, by dreaming
that I can improve it by my own deep thinking, or by
soaring aloft with the philosophers. We will not, even
with the idea of saving souls, speak other than the
gospel. If I could create a great excitement by delivering novel doctrine, I would abhor the thought.
To raise a revival by suppressing truth, is dealing
deceitfully; it is a pious fraud, and our Lord wants no
profit which might be supposed to come by such a
transaction. It is ours simply and honestly to trade
with our Master's pounds, and to bring to Him such
increase as they gain in fair dealing.

We are stewards, and not masters, and hence we
must trade in our Master's Name, and not in our own.
It is not ours to fabricate a religion, but to proclaim
one; and even that proclamation is not to be made
by our own authority, but it is ever to be based on that

of our Lord. We are " labourers together with Him."
If a brother sets up in business for himself, he will
make a mess of it, and fall into spiritual bankruptcy
before long. His credit will soon run out when his
Master's Name is gone. We can do nothing in our
heavenly merchandise without our Lord. Let us not
attempt to act on our own account, but keep our place
near our Chief in all lowliness of mind.

2. We may become false to our trust *by acting as
men-pleasers.* When the steward studies the good
pleasure of the ploughman, or the whims of the ser-
vant-maid, everything must go wrong, for everything
is out of place. We are influenced by one
another, and we influence one another. The
greatest are unconsciously affected in some
measure by the least. The minister must be over-
whelmingly influenced by the Lord his God, so that
other influences may not warp him from his fidelity.
We must resort continually to headquarters, and receive the Word from the mouth of the Lord Himself,
so that we may be kept straight and true ; otherwise,
we shall soon be biassed, although we may not be
aware of it. There must be no holding back to please
one person, no rushing forward to satisfy another, no
moving an inch even to gratify the whole community.
We must not harp upon a certain string to win the
approval of this party, neither must we be silent upon
an important doctrine to avoid offending that clique.
What have we to do with idols, dead or alive? O
brethren, if you go in for pleasing everybody, you
have indeed set yourselves a task! The toils of
Sisyphus and the labours of Hercules are nothing to
this! We must not flatter men ; we must speak plain

words, and words which conscience will approve. If we please men, we shall displease our Lord; so that success in our self-imposed task would be fatal to our eternal interests. In trying to please men, we shall not even succeed in pleasing ourselves. To please our Lord, though it may seem very difficult, is an easier task than pleasing men. O steward, have thine eye alone upon thy Master!

3. We shall not be found faithful stewards *if we are idlers and triflers*. Do you ever meet with lazy ministers? I have heard of them; but when mine eye sees them, my heart abhors them. If you plan to be lazy, there are plenty of avocations in which you will not be wanted; but, above all, you are not wanted in the Christian ministry. The man who finds the ministry an easy life will also find that it will bring a hard death. If we are not labourers, we are not true stewards; for we are to be examples of diligence to the King's household. I like Adam Clarke's precept: "Kill yourselves with work, and then pray yourselves alive again." We shall never do our duty either to God or man if we are sluggards.

Yet some, who are always busy, may still be unfaithful, if all that they do is done in a jaunty, trifling manner. If we play at preaching, we have chosen an awful game. To shuffle texts like cards, and make literary essays out of themes which move all Heaven and hell, is shameful. We must be serious as death in this solemn work. There are boys and girls who are always giggling, but who never laugh; and they are the very image of certain ever-jesting preachers. I like an honest laugh; true humour can be sanctified, and those who can stir men to smile can also move them to weep. But even this power has limits which the foolish soon exceed. It is not, however, of the earnest eccentric that I now speak. The men I mean are sardonic and sarcastic. An earnest brother makes a mistake in grammar, and this they observe with a sneer; another devout believer errs in a classical allusion, this also affords them pleasure. The earnestness and the devotion go for nothing; or, rather, these are the secret reasons for the contempt of these superfine and superficial critics. The gospel is nothing to them; cleverness is their idol. As for themselves, these gentlemen are mainly concerned to find out what will bring them most honour in the philosophical school to which they belong. They have neither convictions nor beliefs, but only tastes and opinions, and the whole matter is a sport from first to last. I pray you, above all things, to keep clear of the scorner's chair and the trifler's camp-stool. Be seriously in earnest. Live like men who have something to live for; and preach like men to whom preaching is the highest exercise of their being. Our work is the most important under Heaven, or else it is sheer imposture. If you are not earnest in carrying out your Lord's instructions, He will give His vineyard to another; for He will not put up with those who turn His service into trifling.

4. When we *misuse our Master's property*, we are false to our trust. We are entrusted with a certain amount of talent, and strength, and influence, and we have to use this trust-money with a single purpose. Our purpose is to promote the Master's honour and glory. We are to seek God's glory, and nothing else. By all means, let every man use his best influence

on the right side in politics; but no minister has liberty to use his position in the church to promote party ends. I do not censure workers for temperance; but even this admirable movement must not push out the gospel: I trust it never does. I hold that no minister has a right to use his ability or office to cater for the mere amusement of the multitude. The Master has sent us to win souls: all is within the compass of our commission which tends towards that end; but that is chiefly our work which drives directly and distinctly at that end. The danger lies, at this time, in setting up theatricals, semi-theatricals, concerts, and so forth. Until I see that the Lord Jesus Christ has set up a theatre, or planned a miracle-play, I shall not think of emulating the stage or competing with the music-hall. If I mind my own business, by preaching the gospel, I shall have enough to do. One object is enough for most men: one such as ours is enough for any minister, however many his talents, however versatile his mind.

Do not misapply your Master's goods, lest you be found guilty of embezzlement. If your consecration is true, all your gifts are your Lord's, and it will be a sort of felony to use them for any other than your Lord. You are not to make a fortune for yourself; I do not think you will be likely to do that in the Baptist ministry. In no other way are you to have a second aim or object. "Jesus only" must be the motive and motto of your life-course. It is the duty of a steward to be devoted to the interests of his master; and if he forgets this for any other object, however laudable that object may be, he is not faithful. We cannot afford to let our lives run in two channels; we have not enough life-force for two objects. We need to be whole-hearted. We must learn to say, " One thing I do." In every item and particular of life, the mark of consecration must be seen, and we must never allow it to be illegible. There will come a day in which all details will be gone into at the final audit; and it behoves us, as stewards, to have an eye to our Lord's scrutiny in every item of our lives.

5. If we would be faithful as stewards, *we must not neglect any one of the family*, nor neglect any portion of the estate. I wonder whether we practise a personal observation of our hearers. Our beloved friend, Mr. Archibald Brown, is right when he says that London needs not only house-to-house visitation, but room-to-room visitation. We must in the case of our people go further, and practise man-to-man visitation. By personal intercourse alone, can certain persons be reached. If I had a number of bottles before me, and were to play upon them with a fire-engine, how much of the water would be lost; if I want to make sure of filling them, I must take them up one by one, and carefully pour the liquid into them. We must watch over our sheep one by one. This is to be done not only by personal talk, but by personal prayer.

Dr. Guthrie relates that he called upon a sick man who greatly refreshed his soul, for he told him that he was wont to accompany his minister in his visits. "While I lie here, I shall follow you in your visitation. I keep on remembering house after house in my prayer, and I pray for the man, and his wife, and his children, and all who dwell with him." Thus, without moving a step, the sick saint visited Macfarlane, and Douglas, and Duncan, and all the others whom his pastor called to see. We ought thus to beat the bounds of our parish, and go round and round our congregations, forgetting none, despairing of none, bearing all upon our hearts before the Lord. Especially let us think of the poor, the crotchety, the desponding. Let our care, like the hurdles of a sheepfold, enclose all the flock.

Brethren, let us hunt up destitute localities, and see that no district is left without the means of grace. This applies not only to London, but also to villages, hamlets, and little groups of cottages. Heathenism hides away among the lone places, as well as in the crowded slums of our mammoth cities. May every piece of ground be rained upon by gospel influences!

6. Another thing must not be overlooked; in order to faithfulness, *we must never connive at evil.* This injunction will be warmly commended by certain brethren whose only notion of pruning a tree is to cut it down! A gardener comes to a gentleman's house, and when he is told that the shrubs are a little overgrown, he answers, "I will see to them." In a few days, you walk round the garden. He has seen to them with a vengeance; he has done the garden, and done for it! Some persons cannot learn the balance of virtues; they cannot kill a mouse except by burning down the barn. Did I hear you say, "I was faithful, I never connived at evil"? So far, so good; but may it not happen that, by a bad temper, you yourself produced more evil than that which you destroyed? "Keep that child quiet," says the mother to the nurse, and the nurse immediately throws it out

of the window. She has obeyed her mistress, and effectually quieted the child; but small will be her praise. So you fly into a passion, and you "give it" to the people because they are not all they ought to be: are *you* all *you* ought to be? Do you say, "I will let them know that I am master here"? Is that so? Are you master?

But you are, perhaps, moved to answer me by saying, "Do not you, yourself, hold a high position in your own church?" I do; but how have I gained it? I have no power but that which gentleness and love have brought me. How have I used my influence? Have I sought pre-eminence? Ask those who are round about me. But I forbear, and return to what I was saying: we must not allow sin to go unrebuked. Yield in all things personal, but be firm where truth and holiness are concerned. We must be faithful, lest we incur the sin and penalty of Eli. Be honest to the rich and influential; be firm with the wavering and unsteady; for the blood of these will be required at our hand. Brothers, you will need all the wisdom and grace you can get in order to fulfil your duties as pastors. There is an adaptation to rule men which would seem to be quite absent from certain preachers, and the place of it is supplied by an adaptation to set a house on fire, for they scatter firebrands and burning coals wherever they go. Be ye not like unto them. Strive not, and yet wink not at sin.

7. Some neglect their obligations as Christ's stewards by *forgetting that the Master is coming.* "He will not come *yet*," whisper some; "there are so many prophecies to be fulfilled; and it is even possible that He will not come at all, in the vulgar

sense of the term. There is no particular need for us to make haste." Ah, my brethren! it is the unfaithful servant who says, "My Lord delayeth His coming." This belief allows him to put off labour and travail. The servant will not clean the room by daily duty, because the Master is away; and the servant of Christ thinks that he can have a great clear up, in the form of a revival, before his Lord arrives. If we would each feel that each day may be our last day, we should be more intense in our work. While preaching the gospel, we may some day be interrupted by the blast of the trumpet, and the cry, "Behold, the Bridegroom cometh; go ye out to meet Him."

This expectation will tend to quicken our pace. The time is short; our Lord is at the door; we must work with all our might. We must not be eye-servants except in this sense that we labour in the Lord's presence since He is so near. I am impressed with the rapid flight of time, the swift approach of the last great audit. These Annual Conferences return so speedily: to some of us, it seems only a day or two since last year's gathering, the last of them hastens on. I shall soon be giving in the account of my stewardship; or, if I should survive for a while, others of you may be summoned to meet your Lord; you will soon go home to your Lord if your Lord does not soon come to you. We must work on from hour to hour with our eye upon the audit, that we may not be ashamed of the record which will be found in the volume of the book.

We ought to pray much about this faithfulness to our stewardship, for *the penalty of unfaithfulness is terrible.* In the Doges' Palace at Venice, we have seen the portraits of those potentates ranged in long succession round a great hall; one square is note-worthy, for it is a blank. If you do not look at any one of the portraits with attention, you will be sure to fix your eye upon that blank, and ask, "What meaneth this?" There are the Doges in all their splendour, and there is this vacant place. Marinus Falierus dishonoured his office, and the great council of the city ordered his effigies to be blackened over. Shall this be the portion of any steward here? Shall we be immortal in disgrace? Shall everlasting shame and contempt be measured out to us as traitors to our Redeemer? Remember the word of the Lord Jesus, when He says of the unfaithful servant, that his Lord shall "cut him asunder, and appoint him his portion with the hypocrites: there shall be weeping and gnashing of teeth." Can any of you fathom that abyss of horror?

The reward of all faithful stewards is exceeding great: let us aspire to it. The Lord will make the man who was faithful in a few things to be ruler over many things. That is an extraordinary passage where our Saviour says, "Blessed are those servants, whom the Lord when He cometh shall find watching: verily I say unto you, that He shall gird Himself, and make them to sit down to meat, and will come forth and serve them." It is wonderful that our Lord has already served us; but how can we comprehend that He will serve us again? Think of Jesus rising up from His throne to wait upon us! "Behold!" He cries, "here comes a man who served Me faithfully on earth;

make way for him, ye angels, and principalities, and powers! This is the man whom the King delighteth to honour." And, to our surprise, the King girds Himself, and waits upon us. We are ready to cry, "Not so, my Lord." But He must, and will, keep His Word. This unspeakable honour He will pay to His true servants. Happy man, to have been the poorest and most despised of ministers, to be now served by the King of kings! Oh, to be of the number of those who follow the Lamb whithersoever He goeth! Brethren, can ye abide in your steadfastness? Can ye drink of His cup, and be baptized with His baptism? Remember that the flesh is weak. The trials of the present age are peculiarly subtle and severe. Cry to the Strong for strength, and yield yourselves to His almighty love.

Beloved brethren, we are bound to go forward, cost us what it may, for we dare not go back; we have no armour for our backs. We believe ourselves to be called to this ministry, and we cannot be false to the call. We are sometimes charged with saying terrible things about hell. We will not justify every expression we may have used, but we have never yet described misery so deep as that which will await an unfaithful minister. Ah, my brethren, the future of the lost surpasses all conception, if we view it by the light of the expressions used by the Lord Jesus Christ Himself! The almost grotesque figures of Dante, and the horrors depicted by the mediæval preachers, do not exceed the truth taught by our Lord when He spoke of the worm which dieth not, and the fire which is not quenched. To be cast into outer darkness, to crave in vain for a drop of cold water, or to be cut asunder, are unrivalled horrors. Alas, that men will run the risk of these! A thousand times, alas! that any minister should do so; that any mortal man should climb the pinnacle of the temple, and from thence cast himself down to hell. If I must be a lost soul, let me be lost as a thief, a blasphemer, or a murderer, rather than as an unfaithful steward to the Lord Jesus Christ. This is to be a Judas, a son of perdition, indeed.

Remember, if any of you are unfaithful, you win for yourselves a superfluity of condemnation. You were not forced to be ministers. You were not compelled to enter upon this sacred office. By your own choice you are here. In your youth, you aspired to this holy service, and thought yourselves happy in attaining your desire. Brethren, if we meant to be untrue to Jesus, there was no necessity to have climbed this sacred rock in order to multiply the horrors of our final fall. We could have perished quite sufficiently in the ordinary ways of sin. What need to qualify ourselves for a greater damnation? This will be a dreadful result if this is all that comes of our College studies, and our burning of the midnight oil in acquiring knowledge. My heart and my flesh tremble while I contemplate the possibility of any one of us being found guilty of treachery to our charge, and treason to our King. May the good Lord so abide with us that, at the last, we may be clear of the blood of all men! It will be seven heavens in one to hear our Master say, " Well done, good and faithful servant."

THE EVILS OF THE PRESENT TIME,
AND OUR OBJECT,
NECESSITIES, AND ENCOURAGEMENTS.*

IT is not possible for us to converse together, during such a time of intense excitement, without alluding, or at least seeming to allude, to matters which are just now the subjects of severe controversy. It will be thought that things spoken by me this day are aimed at individuals who may not be in my mind at all. I am awkwardly circumstanced, and I might, therefore, speak with great reserve; but such is not my habit: as a rule, I blurt out my thoughts, for I have nothing to conceal. I have no intent to wound anyone, but I cannot help it if I do. I do not say this by way of apology, for I am now past all need of apology, and I have become a chartered libertine in the speaking of my mind, since I have found it utterly impossible to please, let me say or do what I will. One becomes somewhat indifferent when dealing with those whom every word offends. I notice that, when I have measured my words, and weighed my sentences most carefully, I have then offended most; while some of my stronger utterances have passed unnoticed.

---

* Although this address was delivered before the resolution of the Baptist Union, concerning the " Down-grade " Controversy, was passed, nothing has occurred to require any softening, but much to emphasize it. The evils spoken of were at first denied, but surely none can now question that they exist, abound, and triumph.—C. H. S.

Therefore, I am comparatively careless as to how my expressions may be received, and only anxious that they may be in themselves just and true. Certainly, my criticisms have cost me more pain than they have inflicted. At the first, I said that he who ventured on the task which was laid upon me would get no honour from it: the prophecy has proved to be true, and I am content to have it so.

I have now nothing to gain, and I have nothing to fear. I can never endure worse misrepresentation than has already befallen me. It is not my intention to say anything upon the burning question which distinctly refers to the Baptist Union; and if I go beyond that intent, it will be the current of the hour which bears me away, and no resolve of my own. I make these remarks by way of introduction, that your minds may be led out of the clamour of the fight into the hush of quiet thought.

I would also add a word of caution to heated minds. Can we not draw a distinction between men and their opinions? An old Scotch wife once quarrelled with her minister. I think the difference arose out of some business transaction; perhaps the poor preacher was slow in his payments, or she had not been up to the mark in the goods supplied to him; but, anyhow, she felt bitterly towards him. Yet she came constantly to hear him preach; and when he asked her how she could abuse him as she did, and yet always attend his ministry, she answered, " Man, my quarrel is with *you*, not with the gospel." Our case is exactly opposite to hers. Our quarrel is not with the men, but with that other gospel, which is not another, with which they trouble us. Away with personalities, but let us earnestly contend for the faith once for all delivered to the saints. It may not be easy to keep clear the distinction between the men and their opinions; but, at any rate, let us labour to do so. Let us grind the falsehood to powder, but desire from our inmost souls the good of those who are deluded by it. I have heard of a stone being broken to atoms on the breast of a man, yet he who wielded the hammer hurt not the man in the least degree. We wrestle not with flesh and blood, but with spiritual wickedness. We fight neither with small nor great, save only with the deadly error which seeks to be king in Israel.

I desire so to speak to you, that you may be girded for the battle against all sin and false doctrine, and be prepared to follow your Divine Lord in all His sacred warfare. May you go back to your several spheres of service feeling that you have wasted no time in coming up to this Conference, but that you have been inspirited and stimulated by communion with each other and your Lord. God help me so to speak as to give a healthy tone to our fellowship!

I want to speak to the times. We are exhorted to be "abreast of the age": I will look into its breast, and see whether it has there a sound mind, or an evil heart of unbelief. My subject is—

THE EVILS OF THE PRESENT TIME.

Nobody can question that there are evils which are constant throughout the ages; and, on the other hand, there are certain intermittent fevers which rage only at intervals. There are evils of all seasons: evils of winter, evils of summer, evils of autumn, evils of this springtide. Certain evils abound at this particular

period, with which we were not so familiar twenty
years ago. We meet now with error, and with sin,
in forms which they did not commonly assume in the
early years of our ministry. Truth is one and the
same in all eras, but falsehood changes its shape, and
comes and goes like the fashions of dress. To evil
things also there is a season, and a time for every
doctrine which is not from Heaven.

I suppose you have met, in your pastoral work, with
the great evil of *questioning fundamental truth.*
Brethren have always differed on minor points, and it
has not been unusual for us to meet each other, and
discuss matters of doctrine upon the basis of Holy
Scripture. All were agreed that, whatever Scripture
said, should be decisive ; and we only wished to ascer-
tain what the Lord had revealed. But another form
of discussion has now arisen : men question the Scriptures themselves. A deacon of one of our churches
said, the other day, concerning a certain doctrine,
" Even if the Bible said so, I would not believe it."
This is a new thing in our Israel. To some, the
teaching of Scripture is not of final authority : their
inner consciousness, their culture, or some other unknown quantity, is their fixed point, if they have a
fixed point anywhere. The fount of inspiration is
not now within the Book, and with the Holy Spirit,
but within the man's own intelligence. We have no
longer, " Thus saith the Lord ;" but, " Thus saith
modern thought."

We used to debate upon particular and general redemption, but now men question whether there is any
redemption at all worthy of the name. We used to
converse upon which aspect of the atonement should

be made most prominent, but in the vicarious sacrifice we all believed. Alas! we have fallen upon days in which substitution is denied, and the doctrine of the putting-away of sin by the blood of our Lord Jesus is spoken of in opprobrious terms. We described justification by faith under various figures in days gone by; but now men are among us who set it quite aside. The other day, a certain preacher informed us that, even if a sinner should truly repent and believe on his dying bed, he would yet have to suffer for a while in the next world. Thus salvation by faith is made to give place to a sort of purgatory. This is not to differ about the faith, but altogether to renounce it. It is not in our denomination alone or chiefly that these evils exist, but they are everywhere. I know not what our brethren mean when they deny the general prevalence of unbelief. Are they wilfully deaf and blind? Do they live on the dark side of the moon? You must have noticed, in the newspapers, apologies for Mohammedanism and Buddhism, in which these religions are praised to the disparagement of Christianity: this is a sign of the times. Scribes are taking up their pens to write upon themes which would not have been touched by the secular papers years ago; and they are only touched now because there is an unbelief abroad which creates a market for anti-Christian literature. Those against whom we fight to-day are striking at the life of our religion. They are not cutting off its horns, but tearing out its heart.

When I note the clamour for "progress in theology," and mark the changing nature of modern opinion, I am reminded of the story of a prudent churchwarden who trembled for the spire of the parish church. A vane was to be placed on high; and when he saw it upon the ground, it struck him as being far too large to be safely fixed upon the spire. I suppose it was the image of Peter's cock; and when the good man looked upon it, he did not weep, but he trembled. "Surely," he said, "when the North wind blows, it will tear down the vane, and the steeple, too." He who had to fix the vane endeavoured to cheer him by the fact that, when the wind was blowing, the cock would turn round, so that the full force of the gale would not come upon it. That was a comfortable consideration, and it brought a grand idea into the churchwarden's mind. Those four letters, N., E., S., W., were of considerable size, and would offer a serious opposition to the wind: could not these also be made to revolve? Certainly this might mitigate the danger; but of what use would the vane be? Even so, they are trying, in certain quarters, to make the cardinal points of truth go round with the wind. To this, we object. Let the weathercocks spin round as much as they please, but we must have fixed points of faith. Unless we have infallibility somewhere, faith is impossible. The true faith teaches us facts which cannot be questioned. Where is faith to build if there be no rock, and nothing left us but shifting sand? As for us, we find infallibility in the Scriptures of the Old and New Testament, and our one desire is to have them opened up to our minds by the Holy Spirit. Those who choose to do so may invent a changing gospel; but we believe in " Jesus Christ the same yesterday, and to-day, and for ever."

We are tried, at this time, by the way in which *many attack the truth by misrepresenting it, and wickedly distorting it.* They designedly harp upon some one doctrine as though it were all we believed; or, at least, the chief point of our teaching. They know that we hold much more of truth, and that we do not make this one point prominent; but this they willingly forget, that they may make up a case against us. It is easy to paint all a man's features, and yet to caricature him by putting one feature out of proportion to the rest: this is what our opponents do. To give an instance: the doctrine of eternal punishment has been scarcely raised by me in this controversy; but the "modern thought" advocates continue to hold it up on all occasions, all the while turning the wrong side of it outwards. The terror of "the wrath to come" is brought to the front, as if this was our main teaching, and as if its dread forewarning was peculiar to the orthodox doctrine. Can they assure us that there is nothing terrible connected with their own beliefs as to the future of the wicked? If one who holds either of the new views will state his belief clearly, it will be fairly open to much the same criticism as that by which we are castigated. We, at least, do not teach that sinners, who die penitent and believing, will need to undergo long purgatorial pains before they enter Paradise. Our hope is larger than that hideous dogma. Do any of these gentlemen teach that sin does not entail terrible consequences? If they dare not say as much, why do they turn their spurious humanity in our direction, and grow indignant at *us?* They will claim at other times that, upon the point of future judgment, the difference is a matter of degree; but it is not ingenuous on their part to forget this fact when they are labouring to make us the objects of the world's obloquy. This, however, does not matter much to us, for we do not flinch from truth because it is terrible; but it shows the style of men who oppose us.

It is the same with other doctrines which we hold; they are constantly being misrepresented, or, at least, misinterpreted. If our opponents would state the case fairly, we should not mind it; but this would not serve their purpose. One said, the other day, "I hate that text which says, 'Jacob have I loved, but Esau have I hated.'" "Why?" said a friend; "what is the difficulty to your mind?" The reply was, "I cannot see why God should hate Esau." "Nay," said our friend, "I am not at all surprised that God hated Esau, but I am greatly amazed that God loved Jacob." That is indeed a marvel of grace; the other is one of the common-places of justice. Truth thus has its coat turned inside out, and then is dragged up and down the street in scorn. They make a straw man, and carry him about as a guy, hoping afterwards to burn him. This is fine sport for children, but great folly in men.

While we do preach "the terror of the Lord," I may say of myself, and of you also, that "we persuade men" in all tenderness. We do not worry them to Christ; but, with much gentleness and patience, we endeavour to draw them with love, and urge them on with tearful anxiety. We are under trembling apprehensions of the wrath to come, and therefore we are in downright earnest. We have no pleasure in their death. Do our enemies dare to think that we have?

We grieve to think of their dying in their sins. It is ungenerous to represent us as cruel because we are honest in our interpretation of the threatenings of Scripture.

Yet misunderstanding and misrepresentation form an evil which we have to deal with constantly. I have no doubt that you find it in your churches, weakening your testimony, shaking the unstable, and causing unbelief in many minds. Our gospel is adapted to meet this difficulty. Let us not distrust it; but, at the same time, let us not shut our eyes to the fact that this form of evil is rife among us, and must be met in the Name of the God of truth.

Another great evil is *the want of decision for the truth among truly good men;* those who are our brethren in the faith of our Lord Jesus, but who do not seem to have made up their minds as to separation from error. Good, easy men, they are all for peace! " Sitting on the fence " seems to be a popular position among professors just now. After next Monday's Union Meeting, several brethren may have made up their minds; but, until then, they will sit uneasily upon the fence. I have, with commendable forethought, endeavoured to drive a number of tenterhooks and other useful nails into the top of that fence, to assist them in retaining their hold; but I fear they are not deeply grateful to me. Theirs is a position which I never was able to occupy myself, and therefore I have no very profound sympathy with them. One or two learned divines are trying their utmost to get down on both sides of the fence; but it is a perilous experiment. Some are trying to get down on the winning side, and others would prefer to keep their judicious position world without end. Neutrals, in the end, have the respect of neither party; and, assuredly, they are *the difficulty* in every controversy.

There will always be trouble in the churches so long as men are afraid to denounce sin and error. A negro preacher, in a certain village, said that among his flock he carefully abstained from preaching against the sin of stealing chickens, because it seemed so much to damp brotherly fellowship! Many a preacher touches the matter of strong drink very tenderly because certain of his supporters are in " the trade." Is there not a great deal of this suppression of unpalatable truth? Are not many unfaithful as to the sins around them? They are " all things to all men," but it is not that they may " save some." I have heard it whispered that it is in order that they may save *a sum* to the exchequer of the church. Are not important persons too much consulted? Is not position more valued than piety? Is there enough of downright faithfulness to truth and to Christ at all hazards? Brethren, we want grace to say, " I can be poor; I can be ridiculed; I can be abused; but I cannot be false to my Lord."

I make no personal reference, but I see the spirit of compromise concerning holiness and sin, truth and error, far too prevalent. The spirit of compromise comes not of the Spirit of God, but of the spirit of the world. It is always wisest and best to exhibit clear decision upon fundamental points; we must draw the line distinctly, and then stand to it firmly. Do not alter your course because of winds and currents. Do not try to make things pleasant all round. Do not be like the fellow, in one of the American towns, who saw a traveller leaning against a lamp-post, weary and worn with his journey. The traveller enquired of him how far it was to such a place, and was told that it was ten miles. The weary traveller sighed, and said, "I shall never hold out. I shall faint on the road." "Ah!" said his sympathizing informant, "I did not know you were quite so far gone, I will knock off three miles, and make it seven for you." Of course, this operation in words did not alter the fact, nor really reduce the ten to seven. Yet this is the method of some weakly, amiable souls; they tone down truth, forgetting that their tone does not affect the fact. This obligation is too severe; and, therefore, it is suggested that it may be somewhat relaxed. This doctrine is too stern; so make it wear a milder aspect. This manner of pleasing everybody at any cost is the style of the period. If sin, and human depravity, and so forth, are strongly spoken of in the old theology, run off to the new, and soften matters. If the punishment of the impenitent too much alarms men, treat it lightly, and spirit it away; who wants to win converts by fear? Yes, yes; "make it seven." But what avail your soft words? The distance is all the same for your lying; and when the deceived one finds it to be so, he will pour no blessings upon your heads. May the Lord save us from the doom of deceivers of souls! May we be watchmen who will be clear of the blood of all men! Be decided yourselves; and then, like men who themselves stand fast, you will be able to help others whose feet are slipping.

Another great evil of the times is *the insatiable craving for amusements.* That men should have rest

from labour, and that they should enjoy such amusements as refresh both body and mind, nobody wishes
to deny. Within suitable bounds, recreation is necessary and profitable; but it never was the business of
the Christian Church to supply the world with amusements. Did Christ found His Church that it might
offer to the public *tableaux vivants*, and living wax-
works? A Dissenting congregation, to my own
knowledge, commenced a series of special services
with a social meeting, and the evening was spent in
various silly dissipations; and among other things the
assembled friends played at "Musical Chairs"! I do
not know whether you understand what that childish
game means. Think of ministers of the gospel and
officers of a church playing at "Musical Chairs"!
There is a bill extant which states that, next week,
there is to be a "Punch and Judy" show in the same
place of worship (so-called)! This is to go on side by
side with the preaching of Thy bleeding sacrifice, O
Christ of God! No, brethren, let me correct myself;
the preaching of Christ usually ceases when these
frivolities come in. These things are so opposed in
spirit, that one or the other will have to be dropped;
and we know which it will be.

What is to be next done in our chapels? To what
length of tomfoolery will ministers of the gospel yet
go? Amusements beneath the contempt of idiots
have been tolerated in our schoolrooms. It has not
come to that yet with us, personally; but, brethren,
we ourselves have to battle hard against it, for the
people are all agog for these vanities, and there are
so many societies and institutions more or less re-
motely connected with our churches that it is difficult

for us to keep them all from wandering. Brethren, we are not here to play away our time, but to win souls for Jesus and eternal bliss. By the solemnities of death, and judgment, and eternity, I beseech you, keep yourselves clear of the follies, the inanities of the day. Remark with interest how " the wisdom of this world " and the follies of it seem to be boon companions, and turn from them both with equal loathing.

Another of our difficulties lies in *the lack of intense piety in many of the churches.* Numbers of our brethren and sisters to-day are living, in a high degree, to the glory of God. I thank God that there is now as much of holy activity and hearty consecration as in any former period in the history of the Christian Church. Among us are men and women whose names will go down to posterity as examples of devotion. God has not left Himself without witness. But do you not notice how superficial is the religion of the mass of professors? How many servants might live in so-called Christian families without perceiving any difference between these houses and those of worldlings? Is not family prayer neglected in many instances? Have we not members who are never seen at a prayer-meeting? When enquiry is made, do you not find that the richer sort could not attend because the dinner-hour is at the same time as the gathering for prayer? No doubt they will be most careful to worship the god they favour most. In other cases, you find that busy men, who could not come out to pray, were quite able to attend a concert. Public dinners and sing-songs are more important ceremonials with many than the offering of prayer to God. Do we not meet with church-officers who say openly that they do not care for such old-fashioned things as prayer-meetings? This is a wretched sign of declension, and it is frequently to be seen. Our churches may well cause heartache to their pastors; but, for the most part, in such cases the pastors themselves have so much backslidden that they care nothing about it.

In reference to ministers, many church-members are indifferent as to the personal piety of the preacher; what they want is talent or cleverness. *What* the man preaches does not matter now; he must draw a crowd, or please the *élite*, and that is enough. Cleverness is the main thing. One would think they were looking for a conjuror rather than a pastor. Whether he preaches truth or error, the man is held in admiration so long as he can talk glibly, and keep up a reputation as a speaker. If we had truer piety in members and deacons, pretenders would soon take their wares to other markets. Alas! I fear there has been great laxity in the admission of members, and the quality of our churches has become defiled and debased by "the mixed multitude," among whom all manner of evil finds a congenial dwelling-place. Unhappy leader, who has an Achan in his own camp! Better that Demas should forsake us, than that he should abide with us, and import the world into the church. How many ministers are weak for warfare with sin because they are not supported by a godly people, and their hands are not held up by praying brethren!

Not to make my jeremiad too long, I will mention only one more sad evil of the times; that is, *the stolidity of the people outside with regard to the gospel*. Compared with what it used to be, it is hard to win attention to the Word of God. I used to think that we had only to preach the gospel, and the people would throng to hear it. I fear I must correct my belief under this head. If the gospel does not attract men, nothing will; I mean, nothing which can do them good. Personally, I have no reason to doubt the attractiveness of the old, old gospel; but I am assured that some of my brethren, who faithfully preach the gospel of Christ, do not find the people flocking about them. We all feel that a hardening process is going on among the masses. In this vast city, we have street after street where the people are living utterly regardless of the worship of God. Those who attend church or chapel are marked men; and if you were to enquire for them, they would be pointed out to you as remarkable individuals. A curious circumstance came under my own notice lately; it seems that men may come to hear a preacher on a week-evening with less suspicion than on the Sunday. One who had attended a week-night service was asked to come on the Sabbath, but he replied, "Oh, no; I have not gone so far as that yet!" Attendance at a place of worship on the Sunday has in London become, to many people, a profession of religion. Merely to hear Spurgeon on a Thursday, is a different matter! It is a fact that thousands of persons live close to our notable sanctuaries, and never dream of entering them. Even curiosity seems dulled.

Why is this? Whence this distaste for the ordinary services of the sanctuary? I believe that the answer, in some measure, lies in a direction little suspected. There has been a growing pandering to sensationalism; and, as this wretched appetite increases in fury the more it is gratified, it is at last found to be impossible to meet its demands. Those who have introduced all sorts of attractions into their services have themselves to blame if people forsake their more sober teachings, and demand more and more of the noisy and the singular. Like dram-drinking, the thirst for excitement grows. At first, the fiery spirit may be watered down; but the next draught of it must be stronger, and soon it is required to be overproof. The customary gin-drinker wants something stronger than the pure spirit, deadly though that draught may be. One said, as she tossed off her glass, " Do you call *that* gin? Why, I know a place where, for threepence, I can get a drink that will burn your very soul out!" Yes, gin leads on to vitriol; and the sensational leads to the outrageous, if not to the blasphemous. I would condemn no one, but I confess that I feel deeply grieved at some of the inventions of modern mission work.

Apart from this intoxicating sensationalism, there is a sort of heaviness in the air. Do you not feel it? We are getting into the condition into which Germany fell not long ago. To this day, when talking with a German who is about joining our church, I usually find that he has lived in a country town. The devout German villager still attends public worship, but in the large towns a practical atheism is supreme. Why is this? The ministers have done it. They preached the people out of their faith in the Scriptures; they taught them to be doubters. The most mischievous servant of Satan that I know of is the minister of the gospel, who not only doubts the truth in his own soul, but propagates doubt in the minds of others by his criticisms, innuendoes, and triflings with words. Some ministers believe nothing except that nothing can be believed. Such a man's conscience is withered. In some modern ministers, the faculty wherewith to believe is extinct; they have played with words till they cannot be true if they try. Against this evil I have protested with my whole soul. People say, " Why did you not speak against these things twenty-five years ago? " I answer, " These evils were scarcely apparent then." Things are not now as in our early ministry. There has been a sudden growth of the toadstools of error. I never heard of Universalism then, nor of *post-mortem* salvation, nor of probation in the next state. Until very lately, I have not heard of ministers holding up the blood of Jesus to scorn. I will not, however, repeat the sad facts which have of late come to my knowledge, and pierced my heart. The times are out of joint. The world may well be careless, for the Church in many places is full of unbelief. I trust the present hurricane of evil may soon pass over; but anyone who has his wits about him will sorrowfully admit that the good ship of the Church is now tossed about with contrary winds, and needs that her Lord should come, and say to the winds and the waves, " Peace, be still." So far, I have borne before you " the burden of the Lord."

In these evil times, we have still—

ONE ABIDING OBJECT.

Whatever the season may be, the farmer has still his

land to till. In summer and in winter his work may
vary, but his object is the same. It is the same with
the servants of our Lord Jesus. Whatever others
may do, we have lifted our hand unto the Lord, and
we cannot go back. We are still guided by that one
purpose which brought us first into the sacred
ministry: we dare not look back from the plough,
nor turn aside from the furrow.

How do you, at this time, look at your life's mission? What is that mission? What are you at? I
think I hear you answer, "*Our chief end is to glorify
God.*" We do not regard it as our first business to
convert sinners, nor to edify saints; but to glorify
God. If we have preached God's truth, and on any
one occasion no souls have been saved thereby, we
are still "unto God a sweet savour of Christ," as well
in those that perish as in those that are saved. The
preaching of Jesus Christ is the burning of sweet
odours before the throne of God, and to the Lord it
is evermore an acceptable oblation. The sacrifice of
Jesus is that which makes the world bearable to a
holy God, and the preaching of that sacrifice is a
savour of rest unto Him.

This is a kind of lactometer by which we can test
the quality of any doctrine,—" Does it glorify God?"
If it does not glorify God, it is not genuine gospel,
and it will not benefit us or our hearers.

It is for us to keep to our one object, come what,
may. The fisherman goes forth with his nets upon
a calm, bright, summer's day. "Now, boatman, take
thy guitar. Sit upon the bench, and delight us with
sweet music." He answers, "I am not a musician, but
a fisherman." A storm-cloud darkens the sky, and

L

the rain and sleet drive down. " Now, boatman, quit
the deck. Make all trim above, and shelter thyself
below." He smiles, and answers, " I am no yachts-
man out on a pleasure-trip, but I am here to fish ; and
fish I will." Over go the nets!

Our sacred fishing may be better carried on in a
storm than in a calm. When the waters sleep, the
fish seem to sleep also, or they are hidden in silent
deeps far out of our reach. A dead calm is our
enemy, a storm may prove our helper. Controversy
may arouse thought, and through thought may come
the Divine change. In any case, *we must win souls*.
Whatever comes of it, we are bound to catch men for
Jesus. Repentance and faith must be insisted on ;
the new birth, with its loathing of sin and trust in
Jesus, must be ever set before our people. For this
end were we born, and for this purpose were we sent
into the world, that we might bear witness to grand
soul-saving truths, that by the knowledge of these
things God may be glorified among men.

Besides this, we have an intense desire *to build up
the Church;* and it strikes me that, for this object, it
is of perpetual necessity that we continue to preach
always the same gospel. Is there to be no progress?
Yes, within the lines of revealed truth ; but there must
be no departure from fixed principles. A boy at
school commences with his first book in arithmetic ;
in due time, he needs another ; but suppose that the
second book put into his hand contradicted the first,
where would the scholar find himself? Suppose you
assure him that the multiplication table is worn-out,
and that men now know better than to say that twice
two are four! What progress could he make? A

consistent ministry, carried out through many years' preaching of the same truth, must, with God's blessing, produce a result upon a congregation.

A noble building is possible when the walls rise course upon course upon a fixed foundation; but what result can those produce who constantly change their teaching? What can they do who are "ever learning, and never able to come to a knowledge of the truth"? True progress is out of the question when everything is moving, road as well as carriage. There is a story told of a man who married his fourth wife, who had brought him money. The like had been the case with each of her predecessors. A friend said to him, "You seem to make a good thing of your wives, whether they live or die." "Alas!" answered the much-married man, "what with the expense of marrying them, and the expense of burying them, there is not much profit about them after all." I should think it is much the same with the new creeds with which men fall in love one after the other. What with the trouble of learning the new doctrine, and the trouble of very soon burying it to make room for another, there is not much profit. Weaving comes to nothing if it be constantly pulled out again.

If we would, as wise master-builders, really build up the Church, we must be careful as to our foundation at the first; and upon that foundation we must keep on building to the end. As far as I am concerned, the things which I taught at the first are those wherein I abide until this day. If I had chosen a new object, I might have selected new means for promoting it; but those truths which were for the glory of God thirty years ago, still produce the same result. We work to the same end, and trust in the same power, wherefore we change not our teaching.

Brethren, let me take you further, and speak upon—

OUR URGENT NECESSITIES.

If we are to pursue our holy calling with success, *we need to be better men.* Brethren, I do not depreciate you; far from it. But, personally, I feel that, as the times grow sterner, I must cry to God for more grace, that I may be more able to cope with them. You can always cut a hard thing with something still harder. The granite Alps can be pierced by the diamond. Oh, for grace to be equal to the worst case which can arise! Whatever we already possess of capability or fitness is the Lord's gift, and He is able to grant us far more. He that gave us life can give it to us " more abundantly." The capacities of a man, when God takes him in hand, are not to be estimated by the man, but by God Himself. It was prettily put, at the meeting last night, by one of the brethren, when speaking of the cloud " like a man's hand "; he said that it was the Lord's work, but a man's hand was in it. The blessing comes from the Lord alone, but its sign is often the little cloud, like a man's hand. Oh, to have our hands ready for the Lord's work; neither folded in indolence, nor hanging down in despair, but lifted up in holy pleading and full consecration. Brethren, let it be a main business with us to be our-selves more holy, more gracious, and therefore better fitted for our work. It doth not yet appear what we can be. Oh, for high aspirations!

Let us not judge ourselves by others, and say, with

deadening self-complacency, " We are getting on well as compared with our brethren. There are not many additions to our churches, but we are as successful as others." O brothers, if some are still further behind in the course, that does not increase our hope of winning the race! While I was ill, a friend endeavoured to comfort me by remarking that many suffered far more than I did. He looked unutterable things when I replied, " None but a fiend could derive comfort from the greater agonies of others." Shall we, if we have but little of God's blessing, be thankful that others have still less? Did you tell me that John Johnston's potatoes are smaller than mine? I am not going to have my potatoes judged by John Johnston's; my standard as a gardener is not the worst specimen, but the best. Let us measure ourselves by our Master, and not by our fellow-servants: then pride will be impossible, but hopefulness will be natural. We are capable of much greater things; let us attempt them. It is time for us to live, for we are growing old.

This done, *let us get clearer views of what we believe.* A drunken John Brown gets to his own house at four o'clock in the morning, and says to the servant at the door, " Where does John Brown live? " " O sir, don't talk like that," says the servant, " you know that you are John Brown yourself." " Well," says he, " I know that; but I want to know where John Brown lives." There is an inebriation of " modern thought " which maunders much in that manner. John Brown of the New School does not know where John Brown lives. Where he lived yesterday, he knows; but where he lives to-day, it would be hard to tell. Many are spiritual gipsies. They camp behind any hedge, but they abide nowhere, their theology consists of a few sticks and bits of canvas. It is easily upset, but then it is as easily set up. Well may they sing,—

" We've no abiding city here " !

They prefer the chase after truth to truth itself; it is clear that such a chase has not much of reality in it, for the man is pleased that his prey should perpetually escape him. In olden times, the prophet was a *seer;* but, nowadays, a prophet is one who is too cultured to see anything. A man who protests that he has too much light to be sure that he sees anything is the favourite of certain intellectual hearers. David said, " I believed, therefore have I spoken ; " but he was peculiar : our " thoughtful men " now speak because they doubt, and not because they believe.

The next thing necessary for the present time is that *we should have more faith.* We need to believe more intensely in God, so as to trust Him more practically and more unquestioningly. The things which we believe must become more real to us. I fear we often use words without feeling their true meaning. This is terrible. It is a sort of wilful murder to expel the. soul from pious phrases, and still to use them. Let us be honest about the things of God ; let us mean all that we say, and say only what we mean. It is a shocking thing for a man to talk all manner of Evangelical, gracious, and sanctifying things, and yet to mean nothing by them. I fear our pulpits are not free from such word-mongers. Let us not hold forth shadows before the people. Let them, at

any rate, be no shadows to us, but downright facts.
You have heard of the old Scotch lady who was
making her will. She was leaving £500 to this person, and £1,000 to another, till at length the lawyer
remarked, "Have you as much money as this?"
"May be not," said the old soul, "but it will show them
my liberal intentions." It is to be feared that many
preach Evangelical doctrine, not because they believe
it, but that they may please the Evangelical. This
will never do. Let us never lie open to such a suspicion. Let the doctrines we declare be as dear to us
as our life, and as real as our own flesh and blood.
We believe all Scripture to be true. When the Bible
says that a man is lost, we believe that the loss is real
and tremendous. Heaven and hell are realities with
us, even though to others they may be dreams. To
us, Christ is a real Christ; and the Holy Ghost within
a man brings real life from the dead. If we do not
preach realities, I pray God we may be driven out of
the ministry, in which we are only treasuring up
wrath against the day of wrath.

We need also more love to souls. We shall never
save more till we love more. There is a good story
told by our brother Archibald Brown; I will not
attempt to tell it in his presence; but it was something like this:—A man was accidentally buried by a
fall of earth, and many were greatly energetic to dig
the poor fellow out. One fellow stood by, scarcely as
much concerned about the matter as many others
were, until a woman rushed out of the crowd, and laid
hold on him, and said in his ear, "It's your brother
Bill that's in there!" Those few words wrought a
marvellous change in the man; his coat was off in an

instant, and he was down in the sewer working like a Trojan. If we would save our hearers from the wrath to come, we must realize that they are our brothers. We must have sympathy with them, and anxiety about them; in a word, passion and compassion. May God grant these to us!

There must be also a more thorough spirit of self-sacrifice. I must speak tenderly here, because I am among brethren whose life is one of perpetual sacrifice in a pecuniary sense. With scarcely enough to keep body and soul together, they work on without complaint year after year. If they could gain a hundred times their present income in any other calling, they would not quit the pulpit and the pastorate. The work of Christ is more to them than their necessary food. Thank God, this Conference is well supplied with men who count all things but loss for the excellency of the knowledge of Christ Jesus their Lord. But, my brethren, sacrifice is needed every day, that we may keep up the abundance of our service. Here also we have many who excel. They are not loiterers, but labourers. He who has an easy time of it, in his ministry here, will have a hard time of it in the account to be rendered by-and-by. I fear the idea of the ministry with some men is as much on the down-grade as their doctrine is. Their gentlemanly indifference reminds me of the British workman, who observed, "I have such a good master that I do not know how to do too much for him, *but I'll take precious good care I don't.*" Into that spirit may we never enter! Let us live intensely for our Lord!

But, beyond surrendering ease, we must be prepared to give up everything else: our name, our repute, our friendships, our connections, must all go without reserve, if Christ's cause needs them. Sooner than deny the truth, we must forego every meed of honour, every particle of deserved esteem, every rag of repute. You have heard almost too often the classic story of Curtius leaping into the gulf in the Forum at Rome. There is a chasm in the Forum at this hour. Who will devote himself for his people and his God? Curtius does not stipulate that he shall be wholly engulfed except the pennon upon his lance, which shall remain above ground as his memorial. No, he takes the leap, and finds immortal renown in being completely swallowed up. In the battle for the truth, let your personal comfort and reputation go to the winds. Let not the sacrifice be thought worthy of two thoughts. The weakness of many men is that they *think* so long that they *do* nothing. The blood of the martyrs is scarce among us. It will destroy our ministries if we begin thinking of the cost of honesty. Shall we have before our eyes the fear of a large subscriber, and become afraid of offending him by our fidelity? By that very thought, we have already offended God. Brethren, let us fear no loss, because we have nothing to lose, seeing that all we possess is Christ's already.

> "There, take an inventory of all I have,
>   To the last penny; 'tis the King's."

My Lord, for Thee I will rejoice to be "the offscouring of all things," that I may be found faithful to Thee and to Thy truth, even to the end.

I will give you a little advice, which may be suitable for such a time as this. I would recommend you to *go over the fundamental truths with your hearers very carefully.* The bulk of the people do not know the first principles of the gospel. We assume too much when we take it for granted that our hearers, all of them, understand the gospel. Some of the old-fashioned dame-school teachers had a curious way of treating their scholars. They asked Mary to read a passage from a book, but Mary had not yet mastered her letters, and therefore she could not read as she was bidden to do. She was called a naughty child, and put into a corner, and told to study her book. She could do nothing at it, for she did not know the letters! If we have not taught our people their letters, how can we expect them to understand the truths that we preach? Let us go over the foundation truths again and again.

The simplest doctrines would be great novelties in some pulpits I could mention. A king once asked a courtier what made a certain French preacher so famous. "Your majesty," said the nobleman, "he preaches the gospel, and that is the scarcest thing in France." How true of many English pulpits to-day! Go over the elementary truths with your people. Make them know the first principles of the faith. It will not weary your hearers, it will bless them, and many of them will be delighted. Repeat the fundamentals, too; often, if you can. In the days of old-fashioned farming, they dropped three beans into the hole. And why? One was for the worm, another for the crow, and number three perchance would grow. Let us be liberal with the seed, for the evil powers are liberal with worms, and crows, and thorns. Let others go forth to shine; you are sowers, and must

" go forth to sow." Repeat yourselves if necessary. Paul wrote to the Philippians, " To write the same things to you, to me indeed is not grievous, but for you it is safe."

In the next place, *labour distinctly for the immediate salvation of your hearers.* Take aim. At Waterloo, they say that, for every man who was killed, his full weight in lead had to be fired. We must improve upon this, and use arms of precision. We must get at the people each time we address them. It is wise to make definite characters the point of 'attack. We must look to the application of each sermon. I have known a true doctor, in a very critical case, act the part of nurse as well as surgeon, and personally see his liniments and poultices applied to his patient. This personal care gives surgery its best chance. We have great need to be very specific in applying truth to our hearers. If a doctor should prescribe a bitter medicine for children, to be taken every three hours, and then should leave it to the youngsters to take it themselves, I fear the doses taken would be small and few. Even so is it with unpalatable truth ; we must not only set it forth in general terms, but we must measure it out in doses to each individual. Under the guidance of the Holy Spirit, this must be our daily work. We want our hearers saved, and saved at once ; and towards this design we must drive with all our power.

Let us inculcate with all our might the practice of holiness. Holiness is the visible side of salvation. I thought it no ill sign when the preaching of holiness was pushed even to an extreme. I trembled at the fanaticism, but I thanked God for the earnestness out of which it grew. Let us seek the utmost degree of holiness. The doctrines of grace should be accompanied by ethics of the purest kind. We have been clear upon the fact that good works are not the cause of salvation; let us be equally clear upon the truth that they are the necessary fruit of it. What is the use of our churches if they are not holy? What is the use of ourselves if we are not holy? Holiness is practical orthodoxy, and it should walk hand-in-hand with doctrinal orthodoxy. We must not only have a high-toned morality, but a consecrated morality, quickened by the Spirit of God;—and that is holiness.

To this end, I would exhort you to *be careful about the admission of members into the church.* Doubtless there are some in our ranks who ought not to be there. This is to their own hurt, to the dishonour of the Lord Jesus, and to the injury of the church itself. Unconverted members lower the whole tone of the church. How low that tone has now become, let spiritual men judge for themselves. If the members were converted, they would make short work of many of the ministers; but the people are like their priests. Many are the letters of sympathy which my protests upon this matter have drawn forth. It is clear that lax doctrine and lax living are pretty frequently associated. A weeping Hannah writes me concerning her husband who has been for years a lay preacher, but who now spends his evenings far into night at the billiard-table, for which he acquired a taste when he went in for new theology and religious entertainments. Many have gone from the prayer-meeting to the amateur theatricals of the Mutual Improvement Society, and thence to the playhouse itself. This

seems to be natural, if not inevitable. Oh, that we
had a purer membership to work with! Do what we
may, Judas will come in; but let us not invite him:
let us not make it easy for a betrayer of Christ to be
comfortable with us. To mix up the world with the
church, is a crime; it brings with it an awful curse,
and acts upon godliness as a blast and a mildew. Let
the door of the church be opened to all sincere souls,
but closed against all whose hearts are in the world.
It is not even for the worldling's good that he should
hold the form of godliness while he is a stranger to its
power. As you love your Lord, and value men's souls,
guard well the entrance of the church.

As to yourselves, I would recommend *entire separation from those who would be likely to injure your
spiritual life*. I would no more associate with one
who denied the faith than with a drunkard or a thief.
I would guard my spirituals as jealously as my morals.
A loyal man is not at home in the company of traitors.
There are associations with the ungodly into which
we must needs go, unless we get out of the world
altogether; but there are others which are optional,
and here we should dare to be scrupulous. A godly
minister once said of a certain preacher, " I would not
permit such a man to enter my pulpit. I am as jealous
of my pulpit as of my bed." I do not think he was
too rigid. We should guard ourselves against com-
promising the truth of God by association with those
who do not hold it, especially at such a time as this.

Next, *we must bind ourselves more closely together*,
and seek to render help to each other, and to all who
are of the same mind in the Lord. Denominational
divisions sink in the presence of the truth of God.

To my mind, the grand distinction to be now observed
is found in Evangelical doctrine, of which our Lord's
substitutionary sacrifice is the centre and the soul.
Where we see faithful brethren struggling, we ought
to lay ourselves out to help them, for they are sure to
be the objects of inveterate opposition. Lovers of
the old faith should stand shoulder to shoulder, to
remove the injustice of the past, and frustrate the
opposition of the future. The struggle before us is
severe; let us, at any rate, economize our strength by
union.

Lastly, let me leave with you—

WORDS OF ENCOURAGEMENT.

The times are bad, but they have been bad before.
You have to fight with Apollyon, but many have met
this arch-enemy before your day. Gird up the loins
of your mind, and stand fast, for the Lord is greater
than the times. The days are evil, but evil days are
followed by good days. History repeats itself, and
this is one of the points in which history is very per-
sistent. Let me read you a cheering passage from
Witherspoon :—" Nothing is impossible to the power
of God. I add, that the most remarkable times of the
revival of religion, in this part of the United Kingdom,
immediately succeeded times of the greatest apostasy,
when ' truth ' seemed to be ' fallen in the street, and
equity could not enter.' This was the case immediately before the year 1638. Corruption in doctrine,
looseness in practice, and slavish submission in politics,
had overspread the Church of Scotland; and yet, in
a little time, she appeared in greater purity, and in

greater dignity, than ever she had done before, or, perhaps, than ever she has done since that period. Let no Christian, therefore, give way to desponding thoughts. We plead the cause that shall at last prevail. Religion shall rise from its ruins; and its oppressed state at present should not only excite us to pray, but encourage us to hope for its speedy revival."

Make the most of prayer. I have received much encouragement of late, from friends in many different quarters, by the assurance that our conflict for the gospel is continually mentioned in their prayers. The praying heart of God's people is with us. Prayer is the master-weapon. We should be greatly wise if we used it more, and did so with a more specific purpose.

In New England, a certain church had elected a young man named Mr. Stoddard to be its pastor. After a while, the people found out that their new preacher was not a real Christian. What did they do? Did they find fault, and quarrel? No, they were wiser folks. One Sabbath night, when his day's work was over, the young minister saw the people flocking to the meeting-house. He was surprised at their coming in such numbers to a service at which he was not himself to preside. " Why are they meeting? " he asked. " Sir," said one, " they are coming together to pray that their minister may be converted." Young Stoddard went within doors, sought his chamber, prayed for himself, and found eternal life. Before the hour of prayer was over, he was converted, and went down to the meeting to tell the glad tidings. Was not that a glorious work of grace? Might we not win more victories if we more constantly used this weapon of all-prayer? All hell is vanquished when the believer bows his knee in importunate supplication. Beloved brethren, let us pray. We cannot all argue, but we can all pray; we cannot all be leaders, but we can all be pleaders; we cannot all be mighty in rhetoric, but we can all be prevalent in prayer. I would sooner see you eloquent with God than with men. Prayer links us with the Eternal, the Omnipotent, the Infinite; and hence it is our chief resort. Resolve to serve the Lord, and to be faithful to His cause, for then you may boldly appeal to Him for succour. Be sure that you are with God, and then you may be sure that God is with you.

THE PREACHER'S POWER, AND THE CONDITIONS OF OBTAINING IT.

BRETHREN, we want to do our work rightly and effectively, and WE CANNOT DO IT WITHOUT POWER. Of course, no work of any kind is accomplished in this world without a certain expenditure of force, and the force employed differs according to the matter in hand. The sort of power of which we feel the need will be determined by our view of our work; and the amount of power that we shall long for will also very much depend upon our idea of how that work should be done. I speak as unto wise men, who know their object, and know also whence their strength must come. I speak also to men who mean to use their office as in the sight of God; but yet I think it desirable to stir up your pure minds, by way of remembrance, and put you and myself in mind of the grand design for which we need power.

We could be ministers, as some men are ministers, without any particular power, either natural, or acquired. Merely to perform services (to use an ugly word) "perfunctorily" does not require special endowments. Any speaking machine might do as well. There are ministers whose sermons, and whose whole services, are so much a matter of routine, and so utterly lifeless, that if power from on high were to come upon them, it would altogether bewilder them.

Nobody would know them to be the same persons; the change would seem too great. The same things are said, in the same tone and manner, year after year. I have heard of a preacher, whom one of his people likened to a steeple, which had but two bells in it, for, he said, "It is always, 'Ding dong, ding dong, ding dong, ding dong.'" "Oh!" said his friend, "you ought to be abundantly grateful that you have as much variety as *that*, for our man has only one bell, and his note is for ever, 'Ding, ding, ding, ding.'"

When this is the case among Nonconformists, it ruins the congregations, for it is death to every possibility of collecting people to hear; and still more is it murder to all hope of their being improved if they do hear. I should think it is by no means difficult, with a liturgy, to be read without much alteration all the year round, to become a fine example of either the Ding dong, or the Ding, ding; but with us, whose devotion is of a free sort, there is less excuse for monotony, and if we fall into the fault, the result will be more disastrous. It is possible, even without a liturgy, to pray in a very set and formal style; indeed, it is so possible as to be frequent, and then the long prayer becomes a severe infliction upon an audience, and the shorter prayers are not much better. When I have thought of the preaching of certain good men, I have wondered, not that the congregation was so small, but that it was so large. The people who listen to them ought to excel in the virtue of patience, for they have grand opportunities for exercising it.

I have frequently said of myself that I would not go across the road to hear myself preach; but I will venture to say of certain brethren that I would even go across the road in the other direction *not* to hear them preach. Some sermons and prayers lend a colour of support to the theory of Dr. William Hammond, that the brain is not absolutely essential to life. Brethren, I trust that not even one of you will be content with mechanical services devoid both of mental and spiritual force. You will, none of you, covet earnestly the least gifts, and the dullest mannerisms, for you can obtain them without the exertion of the will. You desire to do your Master's work as it ought to be done, and therefore you long for excellent gifts, and still more excellent graces. You wish that people may attend to your discourse, because there is something in it worthy of their attention. You labour to discharge your ministry, not with the lifeless method of an automaton, but with the freshness and power which will render your ministry largely effectual for its sacred purposes.

I am bound to say, also, that our object certainly is not to please our clients, nor to preach to the times, nor to be in touch with modern progress, nor to gratify the cultured few. Our life-work cannot be answered by the utmost acceptance on earth; our record is on high, or it will be written in the sand. There is no need whatever that you and I should be chaplains of the modern spirit, for it is well supplied with busy advocates. Surely Ahab does not need Micaiah to prophesy smooth things to him, for there are already four hundred prophets of the groves who are flattering him with one consent. We are reminded of the protesting Scotch divine, in evil days, who was exhorted by the Synod to preach to the times. He asked, " Do you, brethren, preach to the times? "

They boasted that they did. " Well, then," said he, " if there are so many of you who preach for the times, you may well allow one poor brother to preach for eternity." We leave, without regret, the gospel of the hour to the men of the hour. With such eminently cultured persons for ever hurrying on with their new doctrines, the world may be content to let our little company keep to the old-fashioned faith, which we still believe to have been once for all delivered to the saints. Those superior persons, who are so wonderfully advanced, may be annoyed that we cannot consort with them ; but, nevertheless, so it is that it is not now, and never will be, any design of ours to be in harmony with the spirit of the age, or in the least to conciliate the demon of doubt which rules the present moment.

Brethren, we shall not adjust our Bible to the age ; but before we have done with it, by God's grace, we shall adjust the age to the Bible. We shall not fall into the error of that absent-minded doctor who had to cook for himself an egg ; and, therefore, depositing his watch in the saucepan, he stood steadfastly looking at the egg. The change to be wrought is not for the Divine chronometer, but for the poor egg of human thought. We make no mistake here ; we shall not watch our congregation to take our cue from it, but we shall keep our eye on the infallible Word, and preach according to its instructions. Our Master sits on high, and not in the chairs of the scribes and doctors, who regulate the theories of the century. We cannot take our key-note from the wealthier people, nor from the leading officers, nor even from the former minister.

How often have we heard an excuse for heresy made out of the desire to impress " thoughtful young men "! Young men, whether thoughtful or otherwise, are best impressed by the gospel, and it is folly to dream that any preaching which leaves out the truth is suitable to men, either old or young. We shall not quit the Word to please the young men, nor even the young women. This truckling to young men is a mere pretence ; young men are no more fond of false doctrine than are the middle-aged ; and if they are, there is so much the more necessity to teach them better. Young men are more impressed by the old gospel than by ephemeral speculations. If any of you wish to preach a gospel that will be pleasing to the times, preach it in the power of the devil, and I have no doubt that he will willingly do his best for you. It is not to such servants of men that I desire to speak just now. I trust that, if ever any of you should err from the faith, and take up with the new theology, you will be too honest to pray for power from God with which to preach that mischievous delusion ; if you should do so, you will be guilty of constructive blasphemy. No, brethren, it is not our object to please men, but our design is far nobler.

To begin with, *it is our great desire to bear witness to the truth.* I believe—and the conviction grows upon me,—that even to. know the truth, is the gift of the grace of God ; and that to love the truth, is the work of the Holy Spirit. I am speaking now, not about a natural knowledge, or a natural love to Divine things, if such there be ; but of an experimental knowledge of Christ, and a spiritual love to Him : these are as much the gift of God in the preacher, as the work of conversion will be the work of God in his hearers. We desire so thoroughly to know, and so heartily to love the truth, as to declare the whole counsel of God, and to speak it as we ought to speak it. This is no small labour. To proclaim the whole system of truth, and to deal out each part in due proportion, is by no means a simple matter. To bring out each doctrine according to the analogy of faith, and set each truth in its proper place, is no easy task. It is easy to make a caricature of the beautiful face of truth by omitting one doctrine and exaggerating another. We may dishonour the most lovely countenance by giving to its most striking feature an importance which puts it out of proportion with the rest; for beauty greatly consists in balance and harmony. To know the truth as it should be known, to love it as it should be loved, and then to proclaim it in the right spirit, and in its proper proportions, is no small work for such feeble creatures as we are.

In this grand, yet delicate labour, we have to persevere year after year. What power can enable us to do this? While so many complain of the monotony of the old gospel, and feel a perpetual itching for something new, this disease may even infect our own hearts. This is an evil to be fought against with our whole being. When we feel dull and stale, we must not imagine that the truth of God is so; nay, rather, by returning more closely to the Word of the Lord, we must renew our freshness. To continue always steadfast in the faith, so that our latest testimony shall be identical in substance with our first testimony, only deeper, mellower, more assured, and more intense,—this is such a labour that for it we must have the power of God. Do you not feel this? I pray you, feel it more and more. O brethren, if you propose to be true witnesses for God, your proposal is a very glorious one, and it will tend to make you feel the truth of what I am about to say, namely, that a more than human power must guide you, and make you sufficient for the difficult enterprise!

Your object is, however, so to bear your personal witness *that others may be convinced thereby* of the truth of what is so sure to your own soul. In this there are difficulties not a few, for our hearers are not anxious to believe the revelation of God; some of them are desirous not to do so. In the reign of Queen Elizabeth, an order went forth that everybody should go to the parish church, at least once on the Sunday. Of course, the bulk of the people were still Romish, and it went much against the grain for them to attend the Reformed service. I have read that, when Romanists did go to the service prescribed by law, many of them put wool into their ears, that they might not hear. In a moral sense, this practice is still in vogue. Certain parts of the truth men will hear, but other portions are disagreeable to them, and their ears are dull of hearing. You know—for you believe in the original sin of men, (about the only thing original there is in many)—how Satan has most effectually blinded the minds of the ungodly, so that, speak we as wisely as we may, and as persuasively as we can, nothing but a miracle can convince men dead in sin of the truth of God. Nothing less than a miracle of grace can lead a man to receive what is so altogether opposite to his nature.

I shall not attempt to teach a tiger the virtues of vegetarianism; but I shall as hopefully attempt that task as I would try to convince an unregenerate man of the truths revealed by God concerning sin, and righteousness, and judgment to come. These spiritual truths are repugnant to carnal men, and the carnal mind cannot receive the things of God. Gospel truth is diametrically opposed to fallen nature; and if I have not a power much stronger than that which lies in moral suasion, or in my own explanations and arguments, I have undertaken a task in which I am sure of defeat. Well said the writer of one of our hymns, when he spake of the Holy Spirit,—

> " 'Tis Thine the passions to recall,
>   And upward bid them rise;
> And make the scales of error fall
>   From reason's darkened eyes."

Except the Lord endow us with power from on high, our labour must be in vain, and our hopes must end in disappointment.

This is but the threshold of our labour: our inmost longing is *to call out a people who shall be the Lord's separated heritage.* A new theory has lately been started, which sets forth as its ideal a certain imaginary kingdom of God, unspiritual, unscriptural, and unreal. The old-fashioned way of seeking the lost sheep, one by one, is too slow: it takes too much time, and thought, and prayer, and it does not leave space enough for politics, gymnastics, and sing-song. We are urged to rake in the nations wholesale into this imaginary kingdom by sanitary regulations, social arrangements, scientific accommodations, and legislative enactments. Please the people with the word

" democratic ", and then amuse them into morality.
This is the last new " fad." According to this fancy,
our Lord's Kingdom is, after all, to be of this world ;
and, without conversion, or the new birth, the whole
population is to melt into an earthly theocracy. How-
beit, it is not so.

It seems to me that the Lord will follow up the
lines of the Old Testament economy still, and separate
to Himself a people who shall be in the midst of the
world as the Lord's kings and priests,—a peculiar
people, zealous for good works. I see, in the New
Covenant, not less, but even more, of the election of
grace, whereby a people is called out, and consecrated
to the Lord. Through the chosen ones, myriads shall
be born unto God ; but, besides these, I know of no
other kingdom. Brethren, the election of grace,
which is so often denounced, is a fact which men need
not speak against, since they do not themselves desire
to be elected. I never can make out why a man
should cavil at another's being chosen when he does
not himself wish to be chosen. If he wishes that he
were chosen to repentance, if he desires holiness, if
he longs to be the Lord's, and if that desire be true,
he is chosen already. But seeing that he does not
desire anything of the kind, why does he rail at others
who have received this blessing ? Ask an ungodly
man whether he will take up the humble, often-
abused, and persecuted position of a lowly follower
of Christ, and he scorns the idea. If it were possible
for him to get into that position for a time, how gladly
would he shuffle out of it ! He likes to be " in the
swim," and to side with the majority ; but to be a live
fish, and to force his way up the stream, is not accord-

ing to his desire. He prefers a worldly religion, with abundant provision for the flesh. Religious worldliness suits him very well; but to be out-and-out for Jesus, called out from the world, and consecrated to obedience, is not his ambition.

Do you not see, in this, your need of an extraordinary power? To call men out to a real separation from the world, and a true union with Christ, apart from the power of God, is an utterly futile effort. Go, and whistle eagles into an English sky, or beckon dolphins to the dry land, or lure leviathan till thou canst play with him as with a bird, and then attempt this greater task. They will not come, they have no wish to come; and even so our Lord and Master warned the Jews when He said, "Ye will not come unto Me that ye might have life." They will read the Bible: "Ye search the Scriptures, for in them ye think ye have eternal life;" but they will not come to the Lord Himself; that is too spiritual a matter for their tastes. No, the command, "Repent ye, and believe the gospel," is too hard, too sharp, too humbling for them. Is not this enough to appal you? Dare you go forward unless your Lord shall gird you with heavenly power?

Stop: we have only yet begun. They are called out; but there is something further to be done through the instrumentality of our ministry: *our hearers have to be born again, and made new creatures in Christ Jesus*, or else our preaching has done nothing for them. Ah, dear friends, we get into deep waters when we come to this great mystery! Does any unregenerate man know the meaning of being born again? Ask the learned doctors whether they know anything about it, and they will try to conceal their ignorance beneath a sneer. Ask them if they think there is anything in it, and they will perhaps reply, " Yes, there must be such a phenomenon, for many respectable and even scientific people have professed to be the subjects of it." Still, they smile, and express their wonder that it is so. The confession of many a candid scientist is that it may be so, but he is not himself able to comprehend it. Why, then, do they not hold their tongues? If they have not experienced the new birth, that fact is no proof that others have not. Why do they sneer as if they were our superiors? The regenerate in this matter are necessarily their superiors. A person who has only one eye is a king among blind men; let not the blind affect to despise him. If any of us have personally experienced the new birth, even though we may be ignorant of many other things, we are in this point better instructed than those who have never felt the Divine change.

But, just in proportion as you know what it is to be born again, you will feel that herein is a task indeed. How sublime a position for you to become, under God, the spiritual parents of men! You could not create a fly, much less could you create a new heart and a right spirit. To fashion a world, has less difficulty in it than to create a new life in an ungodly man; for, in the creation of the world, there was nothing in the way of God; but, in the creation of the new heart, there is the old nature opposing the Spirit. The negative has to be removed as well as the positive produced. Stand and look that matter over, and see if you are at all able, in and of yourself, to work the conversion or regeneration of a single child in your Sunday-school. My brethren, we are at the end of ourselves here. If we aim at the new birth of our hearers, we must fall prostrate before the Lord in conscious impotence, and we must not go again to our pulpits till we have heard our Lord say, " My grace is sufficient for thee : for My strength is made perfect in weakness."

Supposing that to be done, remember that *those who are brought to God are to be kept and preserved to the end;* and your longing is that your ministry should be the means of keeping them from stumbling, and holding them fast in the way of righteousness even to the end. Do you propose to do that of yourself? How presumptuous! Why, look at the temptations which pollute this city; and I suppose that the seductions of evil are much the same in smaller towns, and in the villages, though differing in form. Their name is legion, for they are many. Look at the temptations which assail our youth in the literature of the hour! Have you even a slender acquaintance with popular literature? Do you wonder that weak minds are made to stumble? The wonder is that any are preserved. Yet this is only one of the many death-bearing agencies.

How great is the leakage in our churches! The most faithful minister has to complain of the loss of many who appeared to run well, but have been hindered, so that they do not obey the truth. The great heap that we have gathered upon the threshing-floor is sadly diminished when He comes whose fan is in His hand. But we do propose, nevertheless, to be the means, in the hands of God, of leading the sheep of Christ into green pastures, and continuing to lead them, until they feed on the hilltops of Heaven with the great Shepherd Himself in their midst. But what a task we have undertaken! How shall we present them to Christ as pure virgins? How can we keep them from the pollution of the all-surrounding Sodom? How shall we, at the last, be able to say, " Here am I, and the children Thou hast given me "? Brethren, we cannot do it at all; but the Lord can do it, through us, by the energy of His grace.

If you have half-a-dozen converts, how greatly you will praise God, if you pass, with that half-a-dozen at your side, safely through the gate of pearl! Certain of us know many thousands whom we have, instrumentally, brought to the Saviour; but unless we have a power infinitely greater than our own, how shall we shepherd them to the end? We may announce them as our converts, we may associate with them as workers, and feel thankful for them as fellow-heirs; and yet bitter may be our disappointment, when all comes to all, and they turn aside unto perdition. How grievous to be, to all appearance, rich in usefulness, and on a sudden to find that our converts are like money put into a bag that is full of holes, and that our treasured converts fall out, because they were not truly gathered to the Lord Jesus after all!

" Who is sufficient for these things? " We are weak, exceedingly weak, every one of us. If there is any brother here who is weaker than the rest, and knows that he is so, let him not be at all cast down about *that;* for you see, brethren, the best man here, if he knows what he is, knows that he is out of his depth in his sacred calling. Well, if you are out of your depth, it does not matter whether the sea is forty feet or a full mile deep. If the sea is only a fathom deep, you will drown if you be not upborne; and if it be altogether unfathomable, you cannot be more than drowned. The weakest man here is not, in this business, really any weaker than the strongest man, since the whole affair is quite beyond us, and we must work miracles by Divine power, or else be total failures. We have all set up in the Divine profession of working by omnipotence; or, rather, of yielding ourselves up to omnipotence that it may work by us. If, therefore, omnipotence be not within hail, and if the miracle-working power is not within us, then the sooner we go home, and plough the fields, or open shop, or cast up accounts, the better. Wherefore should we undertake what we have not the power to perform? Supernatural work needs supernatural power; and if you have it not, do not, I pray you, attempt to do the work alone, lest, like Samson, when his locks were shorn, you should become the jest of the Philistines.

This supernatural force is the power of the Holy Ghost, the power of Jehovah Himself. It is a wonderful thing that God should condescend to work His marvels of grace through men. It is strange that, instead of speaking, and saying with His own lips, "Let there be light," He speaks the illuminating word by our lips! Instead of fashioning a new heaven and a new earth, wherein dwelleth righteousness, by the mere fiat of His power, He couples Himself with our weakness, and so performs His purpose! Do you not marvel that He should treasure His gospel in these poor earthen vessels, and accomplish the miracles, which I have very briefly described, by messengers who are themselves so utterly unable to help Him in the essential parts of His heavenly work? Turn your wonder into adoration, and blend with your adoration a fervent cry for Divine power. O Lord, work by us to the praise of Thy glory!

We now purpose to consider the way in which we are to obtain the power we so much desire. WE NEED TO FEEL IT WITHIN OURSELVES WHEN WE ARE RECEIVING OUR MESSAGE. In order to have power in public, we must receive power in private. I trust that no brother here would venture to address his people without getting a message fresh from his Lord. If you deliver a stale story of your own concocting, or if you speak without a fresh anointing from the Holy One, your ministry will come to nothing. Words spoken on your own account, without reference to your Lord, will fall to the ground. When the footman goes to the door to answer a caller, he asks his master what he has to say, and he repeats what his master tells him. You and I are waiting-servants in the house of God, and we are to report what our God would have us speak. The Lord gives the soul-saving message, and clothes it with power; He gives it to a certain order of people, and under certain conditions.

Among those conditions I notice, first, *a simplicity of heart.* The Lord pours most into those who are most empty of self. Those who have least of their own shall have the most of God's. The Lord cares little what the vessel is, whether golden or earthen, so long as it is clean, and disengaged from other uses.

He sees whether there is anything in the cup; and if so, he throws it all out. Only then is the cup prepared to receive the living water. If there was something in it before, it would adulterate the pure water of life; or if what was there before was very pure, it would, at least, occupy some of the room which the Lord seeks for His own grace. The Lord therefore empties us, that we may be clear from prejudice, self-sufficiency, and foregone conclusions as to what His truth ought to be. He would have us like children, who believe what their father tells them. We must lay aside all pretence of wisdom. Some men are too self-sufficient for God to use. 'If God were to bless them largely, they would talk in Wolsey's style of "*Ego et rex meus*" (I and my king); but the Lord will have none of it. That straight-backed, upstart letter "I" must bow itself down into its lower-case shape, and just look like a little pot-hook (*i*) of a thing, and be nothing more. Oh, to be rid of self! Oh, to quit every pretence of wisdom!

Many preachers are very superior persons; and so, when they get God's message, they correct it, and interpolate their own ideas; they dream that the old gospel cannot be quite suitable to these enlightened days, when "everything is done by steam, and men are killed by powder." They not only interpolate, but they omit, because they judge that certain truths have become obsolete by the lapse of time. In this way, what with additions and subtractions, little is left of the pure Word of God. The apostles are generally the first to be sent adrift. Poor Paul! Poor Paul! He has come in for very hard lines just lately; as if the Spirit of God did not speak through

Paul with as much authority as when He spake through the Lord Jesus. Note well how our Lord deigns to put Himself on a level with His apostles when He says, " The Word which ye hear is not Mine, but the Father's which sent Me ; " and in His great intercessory prayer He prayed for those who would believe on Him through the apostles' word, as much as to say that, if they would not believe on Him through the word of the apostles, they would not believe at all. John, speaking of himself and his fellow-apostles, has said by the Holy Ghost, " He that knoweth God heareth us ; he that is not of God heareth not us. Hereby know we the spirit of truth, and the spirit of error." This is *the* test of believers at the present time ; the rejection of the apostles condemns the modern school.

Brethren, may the Lord give us *great humility of mind !* It ought not to be an extraordinary thing for us to accept what God says. It ought not to take much humility for such poor creatures as we are to sit at the feet of Jesus. We ought to look upon it as an elevation of mind for our spirit to lie prostrate before infinite wisdom. Assuredly, this is needful to the reception of power from God.

I have noticed, too, that if God's power comes to a man with a message, he not only has child-likeness of mind, but he has also *singleness of eye.* Such a man, trying to hear what God the Lord shall speak, is all ear. He honestly and eagerly desires to know what God's mind is, and he applies all his faculties to the reception of the Divine communication. As he drinks in the sacred message, with a complete surrender of soul, he is resolved to give it out with the entire concentration of his mental and spiritual powers, and with a single eye to the glory of God. Unless you have but one eye, and that one eye sees Christ and His glory in the salvation of men, God will not use you. The man whose eyes cannot look straight on, must not be admitted as a priest unto the living God.

There are certain defects which cut a man off from the Divine employ, and anything like a sinister motive is one of them. If you aim at making money, winning ease, securing approbation, or obtaining position, or even if you aim at the exhibition of rhetorical talent, you will not be fit for the Master's use. God would not have us entangled with subordinate designs. You do not keep a servant to go to the door that people may say, "What a fine girl she is, and how charmingly she dresses!" You may smile if it is so, and put up with it; but your sole wish is to have your message promptly and faithfully delivered. How contemptible it is when a minister so acts as to give the idea of childish display! He stands up to deliver his Lord's message, but his hope is that people will say, "What a nice young man! How properly he speaks, and how prettily he quotes Browning!" Self-display is death to power. God cannot greatly bless men with such small ideas. It is beneath the dignity of the Godhead for the Lord largely to use an instrument so altogether unadapted for His sublime purposes.

Beloved, I notice that God imparts His messages to those who have *a complete subordination to Him.* I will tell you what has often crossed my mind when I have talked with certain brethren, or have read their lucubrations; I have wondered which was the Master, and which was the servant,—the man or God I have been sorry for the errors of these brethren, but I have been far more distressed by the spirit shown in those errors. It is evident that they have renounced that holy reverence for Scripture which is indicated by such an expression as this, "*that trembleth at My Word.*" They rather trifle than tremble. The Word is not their teacher, but they are its critics. With many, the Word of the Lord is no longer enthroned in the place of honour, but it is treated as a football, to be kicked about as they please; and the apostles, especially, are treated as if Paul, and James, and John, were Jack, Tom, and Harry, with whom modern wise men are on terms of something more than equality. They pass the Books of Scripture under their rod, and judge the Spirit of God Himself. The Lord cannot work by a creature that is in revolt against Him. We must manifest the spirit of reverence, or we shall not be as little children, nor enter the Kingdom of Heaven.

When some men come to die, the religion which they have themselves thought out and invented will yield them no more confidence than the religion of the Roman Catholic sculptor who, on his death-bed, was visited by his priest. The priest said, "You are now departing out of this life;" and, holding up a beautiful crucifix, he cried, "Behold your God, who died for you." "Alas!" said the sculptor, "*I made it.*" There was no comfort for him in the work of his own hands; and there will be no comfort in a religion of one's own devising. That which was created in the brain cannot yield comfort to the heart. The man will sorrowfully say, "Yes, that is my own idea;

but what does God say?" Brethren, I believe in that which I could not have invented. I believe that which I cannot understand. I believe that which compels me to adore, and I thank God for a rock that is higher than I am. If it were not higher than I am, it would be no shelter for me.

"But still," says one, "we must be earnest students of the literature of the period, and of the science of the age." Yes; I did not say you were not to be so; but keep them in subordination to the Word of God. When the Israelites took captives in battle, it sometimes happened that, among the prisoners, there was a woman whom the captor might desire to marry, and the Lord did not forbid the alliance; but have you ever noticed the command for her to shave her head, and pare her nails? This must be done most carefully with all the literature of this period, whether it be secular or religious, whether it deals with fact or with fiction. The shaving will need to be very close, and the paring to be very careful. Even when these operations are performed, a wise man will still see reason to question whether the subject of them had not, after all, be better let alone. There is an instructive precept of the ceremonial law which shuts out some things from ever being used in the service of the Lord. I quote it with trembling: "Thou shalt not bring the hire of a harlot, or the price of a dog, into the house of the Lord thy God." I question whether, in quoting certain poets and authors, we may not be contravening this statute. When men's lives have been foul, and their principles atheistic, there should be great hesitation as to quoting their language. The blasphemer of the living God is hardly to be mentioned in the

Lord's house, however fine may have been the product of his rebellious heart. At any rate, all that is of man, even the best of men, must be altogether subordinate to the Word of the Lord.

I have mentioned simplicity of character, singleness of eye, and subordination of mind; and next to these, I notice, also, that, if God will speak to us, there must be a *deep seriousness of heart*. Let me remind you again of that text which I mentioned a minute ago: " To this man will I look, even to him that trembleth at My Word." When George Fox was called a Quaker, because he trembled at the Name of God, the title was an honour to him. The man was so God-possessed that he quaked, as well he might. Habakkuk describes the same feeling as having been his own, and this is no unusual experience with the true child of God. In fact, God never comes to us without causing us to tremble. The old Romish legend is that the tree that bore the Saviour was the aspen, whose leaves continually quiver; and he that bears Christ within him, and feels the weight of the Divine glory, must be filled with awe. Our brother Williams just now said that he feared and trembled for all the goodness that God had made to pass before him: this is my feeling, and yours also. We are so weak, and these Divine inspirations are so weighty, that we are subdued into awe, and there is no room for levity.

Brethren, avoid anything like trifling over sermon-making. Someone says, " Well, I take very little time over my sermon." Make no boast of that; it may be your sin. Listen! If a man had been put apprentice to cabinet-making, and had worked at it for a lifetime, it may be that he would have a great deal of skill and a store of prepared material, so that he could turn out a choice piece of workmanship in a short time; but you must not, therefore, think that you could do the same, and that cabinet-making is mere child's play. A certain minister may quickly compose a sermon, but you must remember that this is the result of the labour of many years. Even he who, according to common parlance, speaks quite extemporaneously, does not really do so; he delivers what he has in previous years stored up. The mill is full of corn, and, therefore, when you put a sack in the proper place, it is filled with flour in a short time. Do not regard preparation for the pulpit as a trifling thing; and do not rush upon your holy duties without devout preparation for the hallowed service. Make your waiting upon God a necessity of your calling, and at the same time the highest privilege of it. Count it your joy and honour to have an interview with your Master. Get your message fresh from God. Even manna stinks if you keep it beyond its time; therefore, get it fresh from Heaven, and then it will have a celestial relish.

One thing more upon this head. This power, which we so greatly need in getting our message, will only come where there is a *sympathy with God*. Brethren, do you know what it is to be in tender sympathy with God? Perhaps no man among us knows what *perfect* sympathy with God means; yet we must, at least, be in such accord with God as to feel that *He* could not do or say anything which we would question. We could not doubt any truth which He could reveal; neither, in our heart of hearts, would we quarrel with anything which His will could appoint.

If anything in us is not in perfect agreement with the Lord, we regard it as evil, and groan to be set free from it. If anything in us contends against God, we contend against it, for we are one with God in intent and desire. We hear much, nowadays, of sympathy with man; and, in a measure, we agree with it. Sympathy with the fallen, the suffering, the lost, is good; but my sympathies are also with the Lord my God. His Name is dishonoured; His glory is trailed in the mire. It is His dear, bleeding Son who is used worst of all. Oh, to think that He should love so well, and yet be refused! That such beauty as His should be unacknowledged, such redemption rejected, such mercy scorned! What are men, after all, compared with God? If they are like myself, it were a pity that they were ever made! As for God, does He not fill all things with goodness as well as with being?

To me, Calvinism means the placing of the eternal God at the head of all things. I look at everything through its relation to God's glory. I see God first, and man far down in the list. We think too much of God to please this age; but we are not ashamed. Man has a will, and oh, how they cry it up! One said, the other day,—and there is some truth in it, too,—" I attribute a kind of omnipotence to the will of man." But, sirs, has not God a will, too? What do you attribute to that will? Have you nothing to say about its omnipotence? Is God to have no choice, no purpose, no sovereignty over His own gifts? Brethren, if we live in sympathy with God, we delight to hear Him say, " I am God, and there is none else."

I can hardly tell you how high a value I set upon this enthusiasm for God. We must be in harmony with all His designs of love towards men, whilst in secret we receive His message. To become apparently warm in the pulpit, is not of much account unless we are much more intense when alone with God. Heart-fire is true fire. A housewife, who perseveres in the old method of making her own bread, does not want a great blaze at the mouth of the oven. "Oh, no!" she says, "I want to get my faggots far back, and get all the heat into the oven itself, and then it becomes of use to me." Sermons are never baked by the fire and flash at the mouth; they must be prepared through the heating of the inmost soul. That precious Word, that Divine shewbread, must be baked in the centre of our nature by the heat that is put there by the in-dwelling Spirit.

The Lord loves to use a man who is in perfect sympathy with Him. I would not say anything un-becoming, but I believe that the Lord finds pleasure in the sympathy of His children. When you have been very heavy of heart, even to weeping, if your little child has said, "Dear father, don't cry," or has asked, "What are you crying for, father?" and then has broken out into sobbing himself, have you not been comforted by him? Poor dear, he does not under-stand what it is all about; but you say, "Bless you, my dear child;" and you kiss him, and feel comfort in him. So doth the Lord take up His poor weeping minister into His bosom, and hear him cry, "Lord, they will not come to Thee; Lord, they will not believe Thee. They are running after evil, instead of to Thee. Lord, if I gave them a play, or a peepshow, they would come in crowds; but if I preach Thy dear Son, they will not hear me." The great God enters into your sorrows, and finds a sweet content in your heart's love. God is not a man; but as man was made in the image of God, we learn something of Him from ourselves. He loves to clasp a sympathizing one to His heart, and then to say, " Go, My child, and work in My Name; for I can trust My gospel in thy hands." Be with God, and God will be with you. Espouse His cause, and He will espouse yours. There can be no question about this.

Follow me, my brethren, while I speak upon THE POWER THAT IS NEEDED WHEN WE ARE DELIVERING THE MESSAGE ITSELF.

If there is to be a Divine result from God's Word, the Holy Ghost must go forth with it. As surely as God went before the children of Israel when He divided the Red Sea, as surely as He led them through the wilderness by the pillar of cloud and fire, so surely must the Lord's powerful presence go with His Word if there is to be any blessing from it. How, then, are we to get that priceless benediction? Great natural forces are in the world, and when engineers wish to employ those forces, they go to work in a certain manner suitable thereto. They cannot create power by mechanism; but they can utilize it, and economize it. For instance, the wheel and pulley do not produce power; but, by diminishing friction, they prevent the waste of power, and this is a great matter. We, also, can be great gainers by using methods to minimize friction with this present evil world, with which we unavoidably come into contact. Your own experience will teach you the wisdom of this. Look earnestly to that holy separateness of spirit which shall preserve you from the distracting and down-dragging tendencies of things seen. Happily, there is another kind of friction which has great power in developing latent force. Just as a certain form of electricity is produced by friction, so can we obtain power by coming in contact with God, and by means of the spiritual effect of truth as it operates upon a willing and obedient heart. To be touched by the finger of God, yea, to come into contact with even the hem of our Master's garment, is to obtain heavenly energy; and if we have much of it, we shall be charged with sacred strength in a mysterious but very palpable way. Be much with God in holy dialogue, letting Him speak to you by His Word while you speak back to Him by your prayers and praises. So far, you will obtain force.

The greatest generator of force which is available to man is heat. I suppose that nothing produces so much power for human purposes as fire; and even so, the burning and consuming element in the spiritual world is a great factor in the development of spiritual strength. We must be in downright earnest, and *must* feel the burnings of a zeal which consumes us, or we shall have little force. We *must* decrease; we must be burning if we would be shining lights. We cannot save our lives and save others; there must be a destruction of self for the salvation of men.

Many other things suggest themselves to me on this point; but I waive them all, to come distinctly to the one most real and most sufficient power, namely, the Holy Ghost, to whom be glory evermore!

In order to have the Holy Spirit with us, there must be *a very close adhesion to the truth of God,* with clearness, boldness, and fidelity in the utterance of it. Do not dream that, to have a formal creed, or a something which is said not to be a creed, but "a declaration", or some other style of confession,—I know not how to mention the nondescript invention,—is enough. Without intensely hearty belief of truth, these precious documents are wretched affairs. Declarations of the kind I refer to may be compared to flags, which may be useful if carried by brave standard-bearers; or they may be tawdry ornaments, used for meaner ends. A teacher was once instructing a class in patriotism and nationality. He happened to see the national flag hanging up upon the wall, and he asked a child, "Now, my boy, what is that flag?" "It is the English flag, sir." "And what is the use of it?" The truthful boy replied, "It is used to cover the dirty place in the wall behind it." I need not interpret the parable. Let modern ecclesiastical history point the moral.

Do not let it be true of any of you, that a loudly-professed orthodoxy is a mere coverlet for error, which is secretly held. No, dear brethren, stick to the truth, because the truth sticks to you. Wherever it leads you, follow it; down into the valley, or aloft upon the hills. Follow close at its heels, and only fear to be left behind in its course. When the road is miry, never fear that you will ever be hurt by the splashes of truth.

The truth of God is the best of all guests; entertain it, as Abraham did the angels. Spare not the best you have for its maintenance; for it leaves a rich blessing with those who deny themselves for it. But do not entertain any of the inventions of man; for these will betray you, as Judas betrayed Christ with a kiss. Do not be dismayed by the caricatures of truth which are manufactured by malicious minds. Nowadays, it is the policy of men to misrepresent gospel doctrines. They remind me of Voltaire, of whom it is said that he could take any book that he read, and make whatever he liked out of it, and then hold it up to ridicule. Remember the Roman practice in persecuting times; they wrapped the Christians in skins of bears, and then set dogs to tear them to pieces. They treat us the same, morally, if we hold by unpopular truth. I have seen myself in several skins lately; I can only say they were no skins of mine. I return them to those who arrayed me in them. If our declarations of truth are fairly and honestly stated, and then argued against,—well and good; but when they are misrepresented, and tortured to mean what we never meant them to mean, then we are not careful to reply. When this happens to you, count it no strange thing. Reckon that, because they cannot overcome the truth itself, they fashion an image of it stuffed with straw, and then burn it with childish exultation. Let them enjoy their game as they may.

Brethren, I do not believe that God will set His seal to a ministry which does not aim at being strictly in accordance with the mind of the Spirit. In proportion as a ministry is truthful, other things being equal, God can bless it. Would you have the Holy Ghost set His seal to a lie? Would you have Him bless what He has not revealed, and confirm with signs following that which is not truth? I am more and more persuaded that, if we mean to have God with us, we must keep to the truth. It is an almost invariable rule that, when men go aside from the old faith, they are seldom successful in soul-winning. I could appeal to all observers whether it is not so,—whether men, powerful in other ways, do not become barren and unfruitful as to the salvation of others when they become doubters rather than believers. If you enquire into the worm which has devoured the root of their usefulness, you will find that it is a want of faith upon some great, cardinal principle,—a want of faith which may not be displayed in their public ministry, but lurks within, poisoning their thoughts. You must be with the Holy Ghost if you are to have the Holy Ghost with you.

Beloved, *have a genuine faith in the Word of God, and in its power to save.* Do not go up into the pulpit preaching the truth, and saying, " I hope some good will come of it ; " but confidently believe that it will not return void, but must work the eternal purpose of God. Do not speak as if the gospel might have some power, or might have none. God sends you to be a miracle-worker ; therefore, say to the spiritually lame, " In the Name of Jesus Christ of Nazareth, rise up and walk," and men will rise up and walk ; but if you say, " I hope, dear man, that Jesus Christ may be able to make you rise up and walk," your Lord will frown upon your dishonouring words. You have lowered Him, you have brought Him down to the level of your unbelief ; and He cannot do many mighty works by you. Speak boldly ; for if you speak by the Holy Spirit, you cannot speak in vain.

Oh, that we could make our people feel that we believe what we are saying! I have heard of a little girl, who said to her father, who was a minister, and

who had been telling her a story, " Pa, is that real, or
is it preaching?" I cannot object to your smiling at
my anecdote; but it is a thing to weep over, that
preaching should be suspected of unreality. People
hear our testimony, and ask " Is it a matter of fact, or
is it the proper thing to be said?" If they saw a
statement in a newspaper, they would believe it; but
when they see it in a sermon, they say, " It is a pious
opinion."

This suspicion is born of want of fidelity in ministers. I saw, just now, outside the shop of a marine-
store dealer, a placard which runs thus: " Fifty tons
of bones wanted." " Yes," I said to myself, " mostly
backbones." Fifty tons of them! I could indicate a
place where they could take fifty tons, and not be
overstocked. As for us, let us be able to say, " I
believed, therefore have I spoken." Let us have a
genuine faith in everything that God has revealed.
Have faith, not only in its truth, but in its power;
faith in the absolute certainty that, if it be preached,
it will produce glorious results.

Closely adhering to the truth by a dogged faith, we
are in the condition in which God is likely to bless us.
But then, there must be, in the preaching, *a concentration of heart upon the business in which we are
engaged*. We shall never do well in our sacred
calling if half our energy goes to something else.
The man who is doing half-a-dozen things generally
fails in them all. Of course he does. We have not
enough water in our streamlet to drive more than one
mill; if we let it run over one wheel, that one wheel
will turn to purpose; but if we divide the water, it will
do nothing. God's message deserves every fragment

of my ability; and when I deliver it, I ought to be "all there," every bit of me; none of me should go astray or lie asleep. Some men, when they get into the pulpit, are not there. One said to me, in conversation, "I do not know how it is, but I feel so different when I shut that pulpit-door." I answered, "Have the door taken off." That might not, however, produce the effect; it would have been better if it could have been said of him as of Noah, "the Lord shut him in."

Do not some show, by their manner of preaching, that their heart is not in it? They have come to preach, and they will get through what they have to say; but their deepest thoughts and liveliest emotions would come out better at a political meeting. They have not all their wits about them when preaching. They remind me of the legend of the two learned doctors down in the fen country, who thought that they would have a day's shooting of wild ducks. They were extremely learned, but they were not at home in common pursuits. They came to a piece of water, into which it was necessary for them to wade to get at the ducks; and one said to the other, "I have not put on my water-boots." The other replied, "I have forgotten my boots, too; but never mind." They both waded in, for they were keen sportsmen. They reached a sufficient nearness for shooting the ducks. Then one whispered, "Now, brother, fire at them." The brother replied, "I've forgotten my gun; haven't you brought yours?" "No," said the other, "I did not think of it." There were fine sportsmen for you! Their deep thoughts had made them unpractical: their Hebrew roots had displaced their common sense.

Have you never seen such preachers? They are "not there": their minds are in the profound abysses of critical unbelief. The Holy Ghost will not bless men of this sort. He spake by an ass once, but that ass showed its sense by never speaking any more. I know creatures of a similar kind that are not half so wise.

Now, dear friends, see what I am driving at. I hope that I shall not miss it. It is plain to every thoughtful mind that, if we are not altogether in our work, we cannot expect a blessing. God the Holy Ghost does not work by a torso, or a bust; He uses our whole manhood. See a tradesman in one of our poorer districts, on a Saturday night, outside his shop. He walks up and down, and cries, "Buy, buy," with vehemence; he salutes every passer-by; he presses his commodities; he seems to be everywhere at once; he compels men to come in; he urges each one to be a purchaser. So, also, must we serve the Lord with all diligence, if we hope for success in our sacred calling.

If we would have the Lord with us in the delivery of our message, *we must be in dead earnest, and full of living zeal.* Do you not think that many sermons are "prepared" until the juice is crushed out of them, and zeal could not remain in such dry husks? Sermons which are studied for days, written down, read, re-read, corrected, and further corrected and emended, are in great danger of being too much cut and dried. You will never get a crop if you plant *boiled* potatoes. You can boil a sermon to a turn, so that no life remaineth in it. I like, in a discourse, to hear the wild-bird notes of true nature and pure grace; these have a charm unknown to the artificial and elaborate address. The music which we hear of a morning, in the spring, has a freshness in it which your tame birds cannot reach; it is full of rapture, and alive with variety and feeling. It is a treat to hear a really good local preacher tell out his experience of how he came to Christ; and relate it in his own hearty, unaffected way. Nature beats art all to nothing. A simple, hearty testimony is like grapes cut fresh from the vine: who would lay a bunch of raisins by the side of them? Give us sermons, and save us from essays! Do you not all know the superfine preacher? You ought to listen to him, for he is clever; you ought to be attentive to his words, for every sentence of that paper cost him hours of toilsome composition; but somehow it falls flat, and there is an offensive smell of stale oil. I speak advisedly when I say that some speakers want locking out of their studies, and turning out to visit their people. A very good preacher once said to me, "I feel discouraged; for, the other Sunday, I did not feel at all well, and I preached a sermon without much study; in fact, it was such a talk as I should give if I sat up in bed in the middle of the night, and in my shirt-sleeves told out the way of salvation. Why, sir, my people came to me, and said, 'What a delightful sermon! We have so enjoyed it!' I felt disgusted with them. When I have given them a sermon that took a full week, and perhaps more, to prepare, they have not thought anything of it; but this unstudied address quite won their hearts." I replied to him, "If I were you, I would accept their judgment, and give them another sermon of the same sort."

So long as the life of the sermon is strengthened by preparation, you may prepare to the utmost; but if the soul evaporates in the process, what is the good of such injurious toil? It is a kind of murder which you have wrought upon the sermon which you have dried to death. I do not believe that God the Holy Ghost cares one single atom about your classical composition. I do not think that the Lord·takes any delight in your rhetoric, or in your poetry, or even in that marvellous peroration which concludes the discourse, after the manner of the final display at old Vauxhall Gardens, when a profusion of all manner of fireworks closed the scene. Not even by that magnificent finale does the Lord work the salvation of sinners. If there is fire, life, and truth in the sermon, then the quickening Spirit will work by it, but not else. Be earnest, and you need not be elegant.

The Holy Spirit will help us in our message, *if there is an entire dependence upon Him.* Of course, you all accept this truth at once; but do you entirely depend upon the Holy Spirit? Can you, dare you, do that? I would not urge any man to go into the pulpit, and talk out whatever first came into his head, under the pretence of depending upon the Holy Spirit; but, still, there, are methods of preparation which denote the utter absence of any trust in the Holy Spirit's help in the pulpit. There is no practical difficulty in reconciling our own earnest endeavours with humble dependence upon God; but it is very hard to make this appear logical, when we are merely discussing a theory. It is the old difficulty of reconciling faith and works. I heard of a good man who had family prayer, and commended his house and household to the care of God during the night-watches. When burglaries became numerous in the neighbourhood, he said to a friend, "After you have asked the Lord to protect your house, what do you do?" His friend answered that he did nothing more than usual. "Well," said the first, "we have put bolts, top and bottom, upon all the doors, and we have a lock and also a chain; beside that, we have the best patent fastenings on all the windows." "All that is well enough," said his friend; "is not that enough?" "No," said he; "when we go to bed, my wife and I have two bolts on the door of the bed-room, and a lock and chain on the door. I have also got a spear-head fixed on a pole, and my wife has an electric apparatus which will ring a bell, and give an alarm outside." His friend smiled, and said, "And all that is faith in God, is it?" The good man replied, "Faith without works is dead." "Yes," said the other, "but I should think that faith with so many works would be likely to be smothered."

There is a medium in all things. I should not pray God to take care of me, and then leave my front door unfastened and my window open. So I should not pray for the Holy Spirit, and then go into the pulpit without having carefully thought upon my text. Still, if I had prepared thoughts and expressions so minutely that I never varied from my set form, I should think that my faith was, to say the least, en-cumbered with more works than would allow her much liberty of action. I do not see where the opportunity is given to the Spirit of God to help us in preaching, if every jot and tittle is settled before-hand. Do let your trust in God be free to move hand and foot. While you are preaching, believe that God the Holy Spirit can give you, in the self-same hour, what you shall speak; and can make you say what you had not previously thought of; yes, and make this newly-given utterance to be the very arrow-head of the discourse, which shall strike deeper into the heart than anything you had prepared. Do not reduce your dependence upon the Holy Ghost to a mere phrase; make it more and more a fact.

Above all, dear friends, if you want the blessing of God, *keep up constant communion with God.* We get into fellowship with God at this Conference; do not let us get out of communion with God when we go home. When may a Christian safely be out of communion with God? *Never.* If we always walk with God, and act towards Him as children towards a loving father, so that the spirit of adoption is always in us, and the spirit of love always flows forth from us, we shall preach with power, and God will bless our ministry; for then we shall know and utter the mind of God.

I must add here that, if we are to enjoy the power of God, *we must manifest great holiness of life.* I would not ask any brother to profess that he has a higher life than other believers; for, if he did so, we might suspect that he had no very eminent degree of humility. I would not invite any brother to talk about having more holiness than his brother-ministers; for, if he did so, we might fear that he hung out the outward sign because the inward grace was absent. But we must have holiness to a high degree. Unholy living! How can God bless it? I heard of one who, on the Sabbath morning, said to his people,

" I was at the play last night, and I saw So-and-so ; " and he used what he saw as an illustration of his subject. It saddened me to hear the story : may the like never be done again! But, alas! acts of worldly conformity are not only tolerated nowadays; they are, in some quarters, commended as signs of a large mind. If a man can enjoy the theatre, it is his own concern ; but when he invites me to hear him preach, I decline to accept his invitation.

Even worldlings look with scorn upon loose habits in a preacher. I know a certain clergyman who is fond of cards. Speaking to a man-servant, a friend said, " Where do you go on Sunday? I suppose you attend the church ; "—the place being very near. " No," said the man, " I never go and hear that gentleman." " Why not ? " " Well," he said, " you know he is very much taken up with card-playing." " Yes," said my friend, " but you play cards yourself." This was the answer, " Yes, I play cards ; but I would not trust my soul with a man who does it. I want a better man than myself to be my spiritual guide." The remark is open to many criticisms, but there is about it a ring of common sense. That is how the world regards matters. Now, if even men of the world judge trifling preachers to be unfit for their work, depend upon it the Holy Ghost has not a better opinion of them, and He must be sorely vexed with unspiritual, unholy intruders into the sacred office. If we can lie, if we can be unkind to our families, if we do not pay our debts, if we are notorious for levity, and little given to devotion, how can we expect a blessing? " Be ye clean, that bear the vessels of the Lord." As I have said before, He does not mind what the vessel is, even though it be but of earth or of wood; but it must be clean. It is not fit for the Master's use if it is not clean. Oh, that God would keep us pure, and then take us in His own hand for His own purposes!

Once more, if we are to be robed in the power of the Lord, *we must feel an intense longing for the glory of God, and the salvation of the sons of men.* Even when we are most successful, we must long for more success. If God has given us many souls, we must pine for a thousand times as many. Satisfaction with results will be the knell of progress. No man is good who thinks that he cannot be better. He has no holiness who thinks that he is holy enough, and he is not useful who thinks that he is useful enough. Desire to honour God grows as we grow. Can you not sympathize with Mr. Welch, a Suffolk minister, who was noticed to sit and weep; and one said to him, " My dear Mr. Welch, why are you weeping? " " Well," he replied, " I cannot tell you;" but when they pressed him very hard, he answered, " I am weeping because I cannot love Christ more." That was worth weeping for, was it not? That man was noted everywhere for his intense love to his Master; and, therefore, he wept because he could not love Him more. The holiest minister is the man who cries, " O wretched man that I am! who shall deliver me from the body of this death? " No common Christian sighs in that fashion. Sin becomes exquisitely painful only to the exquisitely pure. That wound of sin, which would not be a pin's prick to coarser minds, seems a dagger's wound to him. If we have great love to Jesus, and great compassion for perishing men, we shall not be puffed up with large success; but we shall sigh and cry over the thousands who are not converted.

Love for souls will operate in many ways upon our ministry. Among other things, it will make us very plain in our speech. We shall say to ourselves, " No : I must not use that hard word, for that poor woman in the aisle would not understand me. I must not point out that recondite difficulty, for yonder trembling soul might be staggered by it, and might not be relieved by my explanation." I heard a sentence, the other day, which stuck to me because of its finery rather than its weight of meaning. An admirable divine remarked, " When duty is embodied in a concrete personality, it is eminently simplified." You all understand the expression ; but I do not think that the congregation to which it was addressed had more than a hazy idea of what it meant. It is our old friend, " Example is better than precept." It is a fine thing to construct sounding sentences, but it is only an amusement ; it ministers nothing to our great end. Some would impress us by their depth of thought, when it is merely a love of big words. To hide plain things in dark sentences, is sport rather than service for God. If you love men better, you will love phrases less. How used your mother to talk to you when you were a child? There! do not tell me. Don't print it. It would never do for the public ear. The things that she used to say to you were childish, and earlier still, babyish. Why did she thus speak, for she was a very sensible woman? Because she loved you. There is a sort of *tutoyage*, as the French call it, in which love delights.

Love's manner of addressing men disregards all the

dignities and the fineries of language, and only cares
to impart its meaning, and infuse the blessing. To
spread our heart right over another heart, is better
than adorning it with the paint and varnish of brilliant
speech. If you greatly love, you are the kind of man
that knows how to feel for men, and with them.
Some men do not know how to handle a heart at all.
They are like a stranger at the fish-market, who will
so touch certain fish that they at once erect their
spines, and pierce the hand that touches them. A
fishwife is never hurt in that way, for she knows
where to take them. There is a right way of hand-
ling men and women, and the art is acquired through
intense love. How do the mothers of England learn
to bring up their children? Is there an academy for
maternal tuition? Have we founded a guild of
motherhood? No; love is the great teacher, and it
makes the young mother quick of understanding for
her babe's good. Get much love to Christ, and much
love to immortal souls, and it is wonderful how wisely
you will adapt your teaching to the needs of those
around you.

I will mention a few things more which are necessary to the full display of the power which regenerates
sinners, and builds up saints. *Much care should be
bestowed upon our surroundings.* Brethren, do not
think that if you go, next Lord's-day, to a place you
have never visited before, you will find it as easy to
preach there as it is at home among a loving, praying
people. Are you not conscious, when going into some
assemblies, that they are cold as ice-wells? You
say to yourself, " How can I preach here? " You do
not quite know why, but you are not happy.

There is no quickening atmosphere, no refreshing dew, no heavenly wind. Like your Lord, you cannot do anything because of the unbelief around you. When you begin to preach, it is like speaking inside a steam-boiler. No living hearts respond to your heart. They are a sleepy company, or a critical society; you can see it, and feel it. How they fix their eyes on you, and concentrate their spectacles! You perceive that they are in what a countryman called "a judgmatical frame of mind." No good will come of your warm-hearted address.

I have had great success in soul-winning, when preaching in different parts of the country; but I have never taken any credit for *it*, for I feel that I preach under great advantages; the people come with an intense desire to hear, and with an expectation of getting a blessing; and hence every word has its due weight. When a congregation expects nothing, it generally finds nothing even in the best of preachers; but when they are prepared to make much of what they hear, they usually get what they come for. If a man goes fishing for frogs, he catches them; if he fishes for fish, he will catch them, if he goes to the right stream. Our work is, no doubt, greatly affected, for good or evil, by the condition of the congregation, the condition of the church, and the condition of the deacons.

Some churches are in such a state that they are enough to baffle any ministry. A brother-minister told me of a Congregational chapel in which there has not been a prayer-meeting for the last fifteen years; and I did not wonder when he added that the congregation had nearly died out, and the minister was removing. It was time he should. What a blessing he will *not* be somewhere else! "But," said he, "I cannot say much about this state of things; for, in my own church, I cannot get the people to pray. The bulk of them have not been in the habit of taking public part in the prayers, and it seems impossible to get them to do so. What shall I do?" "Well," I replied, "it may help you if you call in your church-officers on Sunday mornings, before the service, and ask them to pray for you, as my deacons and elders do for me. My officers know what a trembling creature I am; and when I ask them to seek strength for me, they do so with loving hearts." Don't you think that such exercises tend to train men in the art of public prayer? Besides, men are likely to hear better when they have prayed for the preacher. Oh, to get around us a band of men whose hearts the Lord has touched! If we have a holy people about us, we shall be the better able to preach. Tell me not of a marble pulpit; this is a golden pulpit.

A holy people, who are living what you preach, make the best platform for a pleader for Christ. Christ went up into the mountain, and taught the crowd; and when you have a company of godly people around you, you do, as it were, go up into the mountain, and speak with the people from a favoured elevation. We need a holy people; but, alas! there is too often an Achan in the camp. Achan is more generally harboured than he used to be, because goodly Babylonish garments and wedges of silver are much in request, and weak faith feels that it cannot do without these spoils. Carnal policy whispers, "What shall we do with the chapel debt if the wealthy deacon leaves, and his silver goes with him? We should miss the respectability which his wife's goodly Babylonish garment bestows upon the place. We have very few wealthy people, and we must strain a point to keep them." Yes, that is the way in which the accursed thing is allowed to debase our churches, and defeat our ministries. When this pest is in the air, you may preach your tongue out, but you will not win souls. One man may have more power for mischief than fifty preachers have power for good. May the Lord give you a holy, pleading people, whom He can bless!

For large blessing, we must have union among our people. God the Holy Spirit does not bless a collection of quarrelling professors. Those who are always contending, not for the truth, but for petty differences, and family jealousies, are not likely to bring to the church the dove-like Spirit. Want of unity always involves want of power. I know that some churches are greatly at fault in this direction; but certain ministers never have a harmonious people, although they change frequently; and I am afraid it is because they are not very loving themselves. Unless we are ourselves in good temper, we cannot expect to keep the people in good temper. As pastors, we must bear a great deal; and when we think we have borne as much as possible, and cannot bear any more, we must go over it again, and bear the same things again. Strong in the love which " endureth all things, hopeth all things," we must quietly resolve not to take offence; and, before long, harmony will be created where discord reigned, and then we may expect a blessing.

We must plead with God that our people may be

all earnest for the spread of the truth and the conversion of sinners. How blessed is that minister who has earnest men around him! You know what one cold-hearted man can do, if he gets at you on Sunday morning with a lump of ice, and freezes you with the information that Mrs. Smith and all her family are offended, and their pew is vacant. You did not want to know of that lady's protest just before entering the pulpit, and it does not help you. Another dear brother tells you, with great grief, (he is so overcome that it is a pity his voice does not fail him altogether,) that one of the best helpers is very much hurt at your not calling to see him last Friday, when you were a hundred miles away preaching for a struggling church. You ought to have called upon him at any inconvenience, so the brother will tell you, and he does his duty with a heart "as cool as a cucumber."

It may even happen that, when you come down from the mount where you have been with God, and preached with your soul on fire, that you come right down into a cold bath of common-place remark, which lets you see that some of your hearers are out of sympathy both with your subject and yourself. Such a thing is a great hindrance, not only to your spirit, but to the Spirit of God; for the Holy One notices all this unkind and unspiritual behaviour. Brethren, what a work we have to do! What a work we have to do! Unless the Spirit of God comes to sanctify these surroundings, how can it ever be done? I am sure you feel the necessity of having a truly praying people. Be much in prayer yourself, and this will be more effectual than scolding your people for not praying. Set the example. Draw streams of prayer out of the really gracious people by getting them to pray whenever they come to see you, and by praying with them yourself whenever you call upon them. Not only when they are ill, but when they are well, ask them to join in prayer with you. When a man is upstairs in bed, and cannot do any hurt, you pray for him. When he is downstairs, and can do no end of mischief, you do not pray for him. Is this wise and prudent? Oh, for a pleading people! The praying legion is the victorious legion. One of our most urgent necessities is fervent, importunate prayer.

Brethren, in addition to co-operation in service, we need that our friends should be *looking out for souls*. Whenever a stranger comes into the chapel, somebody should speak to him. Whenever a person is a little impressed, an earnest brother should follow up the stroke. Whenever a heart is troubled, some genial voice should whisper words of comfort. If these things were so, our ministry would be quadrupled in effort, and the result would be fourfold. May all our chapels be co-operative stores for zeal and earnestness, wherein not one man only, but every man is at work for Christ!

I have done when I say just this. *Let each man bethink him of the responsibility that rests upon him.* I should not like to handle the doctrine of responsibility with the view of proving that it squares with the doctrine of predestination. It does do so, assuredly. I believe in predestination without cutting and trimming it; and I believe in responsibility without adulterating and weakening it. Before you, the man of God places a quiver full of arrows, and he bids you shoot the arrow of the Lord's deliverance.

Bestir yourself, and draw the bow! I beseech you, remember that every time you shoot there shall be victory for Israel. Will you stop at the third shooting? The man of God will feel angry and grieved if you are thus straitened, and he will say, " Thou shouldest have smitten five or six times, and then Syria would have been utterly destroyed." Do we not fail in our preachings, in our very ideal of what we are going to do, and in the design we set before us for accomplishment? Having laboured a little, are we not very satisfied? Shake off such base content! Let us shoot many times. Brethren, be filled with a great ambition; not for yourselves, but for your Lord. Elevate your ideal! Have no more firing at the bush. You may, in this case, shoot at the sun himself; for you will be sure to shoot higher, if you do so, than if some grovelling object were your aim. Believe for great things of a great God.

Remember, whether you do so or not, great are your responsibilities. There never was a more restless time than now. What is being done to-day will affect the next centuries, unless the Lord should very speedily come. I believe that, if we walk uprightly and decidedly before God at this time, we shall make the future of England bright with the gospel; but trimming now, and debasing doctrine now, will affect children yet unborn, generation after generation. Posterity must be considered. I do not look so much at what is to happen to-day, for these things relate to eternity. For my part, I am quite willing to be eaten of dogs for the next fifty years; but the more distant future shall vindicate me. I have dealt honestly before the living God. My brother, do the same. Who knows but what thou art come to the kingdom for such a time as this? If thou hast grit in thee, quit thyself like a man. If thou hast God in thee, then thou mayest yet do marvels. But if not, bent, doubled up, proven to be useless, thou shalt lie on that foul dunghill which is made up of cowards' failures and misspent lives. God save both thee and me from that disgrace!

I would enhance our sense of responsibility by the remembrance of the death-beds of our people. Unless we are faithful to them, it will be a painful sight to be present when they come to die. Suppose that any one of our hearers should stretch out his bony hand, and say, " I am lost, and you never warned me; you always gave me some idea that it might be a little way roundabout, but I should get right all the same; and I chose the roundabout way of 'the larger hope,' instead of the Divine hope that is set before us in the gospel." I would rather never have been born than have anybody speak thus to me when he shall come to die. My brother said to me, the other day, what Charles Wesley said to John Wesley, " Brother, our people die well! " I answered, "Assuredly they do! " I have never been to the sick-bed of any one of our people without feeling strengthened in faith. In the sight of their glorious confidence, I could sooner battle with the whole earth, and kick it before me like a football, than have a doubt in my mind about the gospel of our Lord. They die gloriously. I saw, last week, a dear sister, with cancer just under her eye. How did I find her? Was she lamenting her hard fate? By no means; she was happy, calm, joyful, in bright expectation of seeing the face of the King in His beauty. I talked with a tradesman, who fell asleep not long ago, and I said, "You seem to have no fears." "No," he said, "how can I have any? You have not taught us what will make us fear. How can I be afraid to die, since I have fed these thirty years on the strong meat of the Kingdom of God? I know whom I have believed." I had a heavenly time with him. I cannot use a lower word. He exhibited a holy mirth in the expectation of a speedy removal to the better world.

Now, dear brethren, suffer one last word. You and I will ourselves soon die, unless our Master comes; and blessed will it be for us if, when we lie in the silent room, and the nights grow weary, and our strength ebbs out, we can stay ourselves upon the pillows, and say, "O Lord, I have known Thee from my youth, and hitherto have I declared Thy wondrous works; and now that I am about to depart, forsake me not." Thrice happy shall we be if we can say, in the last article, "I have not shunned to declare the whole counsel of God."

Brethren, I resolve, God helping me, to be among those that shall walk with our Lord in white, for they are worthy. "These are they," it is said, "who have not defiled themselves,"—entered into no contracts and confederacies that would have stained their consciences, and polluted their hearts. These are they who have walked apart for His dear sake, obeying this word, "Come out from among them, and be ye separate, saith the Lord, and touch not the unclean thing; and I will receive you, and will be a Father unto you, and ye shall be My sons and daughters, saith the Lord Almighty." A special enjoyment of adoption is given to the conscience that is true to the separated path, and is never degraded by compromise. God help you to be faithful in this matter! I believe that, in fidelity, will be your power. "You may well make a little slit in your conscience," said one to a Puritan, "for other people make great rents in theirs." But the godly man thought not so; and I would remind you of that solemn word, "I the Lord thy God am a jealous God." This jealousy burns like coals of fire, and it is cruel as the grave; for God is so sternly jealous of those He loves much, that He will not bear in them that which He will endure in others. The greater His love, the more fierce His jealousy if in any way His chosen depart from Him.

I shall be gone from you ere long. You will meet, and say to one another, "The President has departed. What are we going to do?" I charge you, be faithful to the gospel of our Lord Jesus Christ, and the doctrine of His grace. Be ye faithful unto death, and your crowns will not be wanting. But, oh! let none of us die out like dim candles, ending a powerless ministry in everlasting blackness. The Lord Himself bless you! Amen.

THE MINISTER IN THESE TIMES.

B ELOVED BRETHREN, I desire, on this occasion, to say something that shall be suitable for the times. I have never, according to the current phrase, preached *to* the times, but yet I would speak *for* the times, believing that a timely word now may bless all times to come. The times impress me in so many ways, and in such various modes, that I must take up a roving commission, and touch briefly upon a wide range of matters, instead of confining myself to one subject. Accept from me " here a little, and there a little," instead of much upon one subject.

First, let us reflect upon OUR LORD'S POSITION TOWARDS US. Here we have many points which must be boldly maintained in our preaching. Be assured that we cannot be right in the rest, unless we think rightly of HIM. In forming your system of astronomy, where do you put the sun? If you are not clear on that cardinal matter, your scheme will be a failure. If you have not found out the true " tabernacle for the sun," I am not very particular as to where you put Mars or Jupiter. Where is Christ in your theological system? How does He stand in your thoughts? Whereabouts is Jesus in reference to yourself, and your work, and your fellow-men?

Many are the aspects under which we must regard

our Divine Lord, but I must always give the greatest
prominence to His saving character as *Christ our
Sacrifice and Sin-bearer.* If ever there was a time
when we should be clear, pronounced, and vehement
upon this point, it is now. Now the banner of the
cross must lead the way. We cannot afford to put
the atonement upon the shelf as a truth to be taken
for granted, and left among the curiosities of unpractical belief. We cannot now afford to use
orthodox words and phrases upon this subject as one
might repeat the language of a liturgy; we must
livingly and intensely believe the truth ourselves, and
we must enforce it with the full energy of our being.
The vital truth of our Lord's expiation must be
preached often, clearly, and with emphasis; and, if it
be not so, we have not correctly learned Christ, neither
shall we successfully teach Him. To attempt to
preach Christ without His cross, is to betray Him
with a kiss.

I observe that certain persons claim to believe in
the atonement, but they will not say what they mean
by it. May not this mean that really they have no
clear knowledge of it; and, possibly, no real faith in
it? Every man has a theory of what he knows; at
least, he can give a statement of what he understands.
We have heard of the men of Athens, and of their
altar erected " to the unknown God ": in England,
we have philosophical people who believe in an unknown atonement. We conceive that, in this way,
they " ignorantly worship." Robertson, of Brighton,
was orthodox compared with many in this advanced
age; but one said of him that he taught that our
Lord did something or other, which in some way or

other was more or less connected with our salvation. Flimsy as that was, it is better than the doctrine of this hour. Some now think it absurd to believe that what was done at Calvary, nineteen centuries ago, can have any relation to the sins of to-day. Others, who speak not quite so wildly, yet deny that our sins could be laid on the Lord Jesus, and that His righteousness could be imputed to us; this, they say, would be immoral. The ethical side of the atonement is frequently held, and beautifully and strikingly shown to the people; but we are not satisfied with this one-sided view of the great subject. Whatever may be the shadow of the atonement,—by which we mean its ethical influence,—we believe that there was a substance in the atonement; and if that substance be removed, the shadow is gone also.

We have no home-made theory; but our solemn witness is, that He " His own self bare our sins in His own body on the tree." Even if it be called immoral, as some have impudently asserted, we yet believe that God " hath made Him to be sin for us, who knew no sin; that we might be made the righteousness of God in Him." " The chastisement of our peace was upon Him," for " the Lord hath laid on Him the iniquity of us all." It would do us all good to look through the texts, in the Old and New Testaments, which refer to this fundamental truth; they are many, and definite. If we use language in its natural sense, we cannot get away from the assured belief that the Scripture teaches us to come to God through Jesus Christ, believing that He took our sin upon Himself, and suffered on its account, that He might render to God's moral government a recompense for the dishonour which man's rebellion had put upon it. Through His blood, there is forgiveness; and by reason of His vicarious satisfaction, guilt is put away, and the believer is " accepted in the Beloved."

Those who set aside the atonement as a satisfaction for sin, also murder the doctrine of justification by faith. They must do so. There is a common element which is the essence of both doctrines; so that, if you deny the one, you destroy the other. Modern thought is nothing but an attempt to bring back the legal system of salvation by works. Our battle is the same as that which Luther fought at the Reformation. If you go to the very ground and root of it, grace is taken away, and human merit is substituted. The gracious act of God in pardoning sin is excluded, and human effort is made all in all, both for past sin and future hope. Every man is now to set up as his own saviour, and the atonement is shelved as a pious fraud. I will not foul my mouth with the unworthy phrases which have been used in reference to the substitutionary work of our Lord Jesus Christ; but it is a sore grief of heart to note how these evil things are tolerated by men whom we respect.

We shall not cease, dear brethren, in our ministry, most definitely and decidedly to preach the atoning sacrifice; and I will tell you why I shall be sure to do so. I have not personally a shadow of a hope of salvation from any other quarter: I am lost if Jesus be not my Substitute. I have been driven up into a corner by a pressing sense of my own personal sin, and have been made to despair of ever doing or being such that God can accept me in myself. I must have a righteousness, perfect and Divine; yet it is beyond

my own power to create. I find it in Christ : I read
that it will become mine by faith, and by faith I take
it. My conscience tells me that I must render to
God's justice a recompense for the dishonour that I
have done to His law, and I cannot find anything
which bears the semblance of such a recompense till
I look to Christ Jesus. Do I not remember when I
first looked to Him, and was lightened? Do I not
remember how often I have gone as a sinner to my
Saviour's feet, and looked anew at His wounds, and
believed over again unto eternal life, feeling the old
joy repeated by the deed? Brethren, I cannot preach
anything else, for I know nothing else. New dogmas
may or may not be true; but of the truth of this
doctrine, I am sure.

If anybody here is preaching the atonement, but
does not like it, I dare not advise him to cease preaching it, but the words tremble on my lips. I am firmly
persuaded that the unwilling or cold-hearted preacher
of any doctrine is its worst enemy. It comes
to this, in the long run, that the wounds of truth in
the house of its false friends are worse than those
given it by foes. If you do not love the cross in your
heart's core, you had better let it alone. I can truly
say that I preach the atonement *con amore*, with all
my heart. Some seem to think that we poor souls,
who are of the Puritanic school, are " cabin'd, cribb'd,
confined " by harsh dogmas, from which we would
gladly escape. They imagine that we have to check
every rising aspiration of our nobler selves, so as to
preserve the tyranny of a certain iron system. John
Calvin is supposed to ride us like a nightmare, and we
lead dogs' lives under his lash. Brethren, it is far

otherwise. Little do these slanderers know of our
happiness and peace. If they feel more joy in preaching than we do, their felicity is great ; but, from their
tone and style, I should greatly question it. Observers will have noticed that the joyous element has
gone out of many pulpits. The preacher does not
enjoy his own subject, and seldom speaks of having
been in the Spirit while he was discoursing. He likes
twenty minutes' preaching a great deal better than
forty ; and he is peculiarly apt to merge his two week-
night services into one. Nobody enjoys modern doctrine, for there is nothing to enjoy. The people have
to do their best with that soup of which our friend
spoke last night so admirably,—the soup made from
a borrowed bone, which had been lent out for a similar
purpose on six previous days, so that the flavour of
meat no longer remained upon it. No, my brothers ;
let our opponents dismiss from their minds all pity for
our enslaved condition under the old gospel. We are
the free men, whom the Lord makes free, and all are
slaves besides. I would like to rise from my bed,
during the last five minutes of my life, to bear witness
to the Divine sacrifice and the sin-atoning blood. I
would then repeat those words which speak the truth
of substitution most positively, even should I shock
my hearers ; for how could I regret that, as in Heaven
my first words would be to ascribe my salvation to my
Master's blood, my last act on earth was to shock His
enemies by a testimony to the same fact ?

Next, we hold that Christ Jesus is *the sole Mediator
and High Priest.* And this makes us look with in-
dignation upon the claims of superstition. We have
in England still, what we thought, in our younger

days, had become extinct, namely, the gospel of priestcraft,—the priestcraft of old Rome, without its venerableness of age. There are men among us who claim to be priests in a sense other than that in which all believers are priests unto God. According to this dream, our Lord Jesus is not, in Himself, an all-sufficient Mediator; that is to say, He may go a certain distance Godward; but, manward, between sinful man and the Lord Christ, there is a gap which can only be filled by a participator in a fancied apostolical succession. Of course, the sacraments, duly administered, are described as certain conduits of grace. Still we hear the words, " Baptism, wherein I was made a member of Christ, a child of God, and an inheritor of the Kingdom of Heaven." In priestly hands, bread and wine undergo a miraculous change, very near akin to Popish transubstantiation. Sacraments are magnified, because they are administered by priests, and thus they are but a footstool upon which the priest can mount a little higher. The church, the altar, the priest, these are cried up beyond measure; yet these are not our Lord Jesus, but rivals to His priesthood. We hear it asserted, and our poor are continually taught it, that anyone who undertakes to teach the gospel, though he can prove his doctrine from the Bible, and may have an evident blessing resting on his ministry, is to be denounced as a schismatic, unless he has received episcopal laying on of hands. To break bread together as believers in the Lord Jesus, is not allowable to ordinary Christians; and if they dare to do so, they are guilty of schism,—an awful crime, which would seem to be several degrees worse than adultery or murder. You might be forgiven, and it might even be difficult to keep you from the sacraments, though guilty of fornication ; but schism, if persevered in, puts you beyond hope.

Brethren, let us bear most earnest protests against this revived superstition. Let us tolerate nothing between the soul and Christ. It may be that, in London, this priestly assumption does not come so closely and vexatiously under your notice ; but many brethren in this room have to see it before their eyes every day, and to feel its iron hand laid upon their poorer people. Wherever they go, they find claims put forth which uplift a certain class of men into Brahmins, whose blessing is indispensable. Sinners may not come to Christ directly, on their own account ; the way to salvation is set forth as being by the appointed priest. Earnestly protest against this error. Even when it is accompanied by a measure of gospel teaching, it is deadly.

We must be zealous to have no measure of complicity in this superstition. My brethren, be not priests yourselves. It is very possible to give yourselves the airs of hierarchs, even though you are avowedly nothing more than Nonconformist pastors. There is a style of dress,—the affectation of it is not praiseworthy. There is a style of language,—the imitation of it is not commendable. There is an assumption of superiority, looking down upon the common people as mere laity ; this piece of pompousness is ridiculous. Avoid the way of certain clerics who seem intent on making their people feel that a minister is a dignified individual, and that the rest of the members of the church should hardly venture to

o

differ from him. Say what we like about all believers in Christ being a generation of priests, we still find vain fellows among us who would be thought of as possessors of a mystic speciality. Our office, as pastors, deserves to be respected, and will be if properly carried out; but I have observed that some who are very anxious to magnify their office, really try to magnify themselves. Yet, as the official has gone up, the man has gone down. One has wondered how so small a man has obtained so great an office. I heard, yesterday, a question to which I have not yet found a satisfactory answer; it was this: "Which is worse, the man who can preach and won't preach, or the man who cannot preach and will preach?" We have, I fear, some of the latter sort among us; but if they suppose that the mere fact of their being chosen to a pastorate has endowed them with peculiar powers, they deceive themselves.

Let me say, very softly and whisperingly, that there are little things among ourselves which must be carefully looked after, or we shall have a leaven of Ritualism and priesthood working in our measures of meal. In our revival services, it might be as well to vary our procedure. Sometimes shut up that enquiry-room. I have my fears about that institution if it be used in permanence, and as an inevitable part of the services. It may be a very wise thing to invite persons, who are under concern of soul, to come apart from the rest of the congregation, and have conversation with godly people; but if you should ever see that a notion is fashioning itself that there is something to be got in the private room which is not to be had at once in the assembly, or that God is more at that penitent form than elsewhere, aim a blow at that notion at once. We must not come back by a rapid march to the old way of altars and confessionals, and have Romish trumpery restored in a coarser form. If we make men think that conversation with ourselves or with our helpers is essential to their faith in Christ, we are taking the direct line for priestcraft. In the gospel, the sinner and the Saviour are to come together, with none between. Speak upon this point very clearly, "You, sinner, sitting where you are, believing on the Lord Jesus Christ, shall have eternal life. Do not stop till you pass into an enquiry-room. Do not think it essential to confer with me. Do not suppose that I have the keys of the Kingdom of Heaven, or that these godly men and women associated with me can tell you any other gospel than this, 'He that believeth on the Son hath everlasting life.'"

In the next place, let us see to it that we set forth our Lord Jesus Christ as *the infallible Teacher*, through His inspired Word. I do not understand that loyalty to Christ which is accompanied by indifference to His words. How can we reverence His person, if His own words and those of His apostles are treated with disrespect? Unless we receive Christ's words, we cannot receive Christ; and unless we receive His apostles' words, we do not receive Christ; for John saith, "He that knoweth God heareth us; he that is not of God heareth not us. Hereby know we the spirit of truth, and the spirit of error." We must love and reverence all the teaching of our Lord; and we build our houses on the sand if we do not. It is as important to know Christ as the truth, as it is to know Christ as the way and the life.

Some excellent brethren seem to think more of the life than of the truth; for when I warn them that the enemy has poisoned the children's bread, they answer, "Dear brother, we are sorry to hear it; and, to counteract the evil, we will open the window, and give the children fresh air." Yes, open the window, and give them fresh air, by all means. You cannot do a better thing, in view of many purposes; but, at the same time, this ought you to have done, and not to have left the other undone. Arrest the poisoners, and open the windows, too. While men go on preaching false doctrine, you may talk as much as you will about deepening their spiritual life, but you will fail in it. While you do one good thing, do not neglect another. Instead of saying that the life is more important, or the truth is more important, or the way is more important, let us be united in the firm belief that they are each one equally important, and that one cannot be well sustained and thoroughly carried out without the rest.

Some quit the teaching of Christ out of sheer wantonness, and childish love of novelty. To younger brethren, false doctrine comes as an infantile disease, a sort of inevitable spiritual measles. I wish them well through with the disorder, and I trust it will leave nothing bad behind it. With deep anxiety, I have watched over minds infected with this raging epidemic; and I have rejoiced as I have seen the rash of unbelief come out beautifully, and have heard the patient say, "Thank God, I shall never go back to *that* any more." Still, it is a pity that so many should find it needful to traverse the foul way which has bemired others. They remind me of a certain worldly lady, to whom her minister, remarking her great gaiety, said, "Solomon has said, 'Vanity of vanities; all is vanity.'" "Yes," she replied, "I know what Solomon has said; but he found it out by his own personal experience, and I should like to do the same." She was no Solomon, assuredly; for they who have wisdom will profit by the experience of others. If you have seen others go abroad for wool, and come home shorn, prudence would suggest that you need not go also.

Some fall into doubt through an inward crookedness. Certain men start new doctrines because "something is rotten in the state of Denmark," and out of rottenness fungoid growths must come. You may have read Pliny's "Natural History." If you have not read it, you need not do so, for the history is not generally natural, but fabulous. Pliny tells us that, when the elephant goes to a pool of water, and sees himself in it, he is moved with such disgust at his own ugliness, that he straightway stirs the water, and makes it muddy, that he may not see himself. Such an elephant never lived; but I have seen men who have been very comparable to it. Holy Scripture has not agreed with them,—so much the worse for Holy Scripture! Such-and-such doctrines do not suit their tastes, so they must be misrepresented, or denied. An unregenerate heart lies at the bottom of "modern thought." Men are down-grade in doctrine because they were never put on the up-grade by the renewal of their minds.

Some, I doubt not, have tinkered up Christ's teachings, and Christ's gospel, from a desire to do more good. Things are allowed to be said and done at revivals which nobody could defend. Do you notice, at the present moment, the way the gospel is put? I am uttering no criticism upon anyone in particular, but I continually read the exhortation, " Give your heart to Christ." The exhortation is good, but do not suffer it to cover over the gospel word: " Believe on the Lord Jesus Christ, and thou shalt be saved." In the Sunday-school, the teaching often is, " Dear children, love Jesus." Now, this is not the gospel. The love of Jesus comes as a fruit, but the gospel is, " Believe on the Lord Jesus Christ, and thou shalt be saved." If we think that we shall do more good by substituting another exhortation for the gospel command, we shall find ourselves landed in serious difficulties. If, for a moment, our improvements seem to produce a larger result than the old gospel, it will be the growth of mushrooms, it may even be the growth of toadstools; but it is not the growth of trees of the Lord. Let us keep close to Christ as our infallible Teacher in these days of peril, and be exceedingly jealous of the truth, else we may be duped, as Pompey tricked certain cities that would not admit his troops. He said, " I don't ask you to allow my armies to be billeted upon you; but here are a few sick and wounded men, for whom I ask that you will allow them to rest among you." When the invalids were within the walls, they opened the gates, and the inhabitants were easily subdued. Keep out the little errors for which sympathy is asked; or, if not, your citadel will be captured before you are aware of the attack. Stand fast in the faith once for all delivered to the saints, and let no man spoil you by philosophy and vain deceit.

Next, brethren, we must growingly insist that *Christ is the one Law-giver and only Ruler in the Church.* We have systems of religion among us in which the whole organization is an invention; it could not have been discovered in the Bible, but has been brought to it to have a text hung round its neck as a label. We have, for our neighbours, religionists who would hardly attempt to prove that their system was ever sanctioned by our Lord and His apostles. This has been the case for so long a period that we have been obliged to tolerate all kinds of things; but to tolerate is not the same thing as to approve and imitate. We should, in our own churches, keep to apostolic precedent, and follow the rule of Christ in all things. No venerable name is sufficient authority for going aside from Holy Scripture. "To the law and to the testimony;" if a doctrine or a ceremony is not there, it is nowhere for you and for me. Our sole authority is the Word of the Lord.

Worse still will it be if we dare to make omissions in the known rules of Christ. I am sorry that there are disputes in the Church as to baptism and the Lord's supper; but it is not a moot point in the Church of Christ whether baptism and the Lord's supper are to be practised at all. How, then, can these ordinances be set aside by those who admit that they are Scriptural? I heard of one saying, "If Jesus were here now, He would see the evil that has come from those two institutions, and He would set them aside." We cannot endure such a sentence. Surely, we are not revisers of the teachings and doings of our Lord. Have you not, in your congregations, good people, who will say, "Yes, dear sir, I know that

believers' baptism is in the Word; I am quite clear
upon that; but I have never yet attended to it"?
Have you impressed upon that person's mind the wilful disobedience involved in such neglect? It is not
the case of a person who says, "I do not see such an
ordinance to be commanded in the Word of God;"
that would be a sin of ignorance. But he says, "It is
there," yet he neglects it, and boasts that he can be
saved without it. Do not be in a hurry to confirm
that statement, for it may turn out that the man who
says, "I believe in Jesus," and then wilfully refuses to
keep His known commandments, is not saved.
Assuredly, such a man is not saved from wilful
disobedience. What sort of faith is that which does
not work by love, but sets up its own will in opposition to the precept of Christ? We must protest
against all tampering with the law of the great Head
of the Church. I mention the point of baptism
merely as an example; but upon every other point of
sacred rule we must be earnestly urgent. Christ is
Lord as well as Saviour. He has not come into His
house to be trifled with, and to have His words
shuffled like a pack of cards.

You may quit the rule of your Lord in another
way. A brother is going to decide upon his course
of action on a certain important Christian matter; but
he first wants to know what is the opinion of gentlemen who subscribe considerable sums to church work.
If any one of you does this, I shall cry, "Who is thy
master, after all? Judas with his bag in the corner,
or the Christ whom he kisses with a traitor's kiss?"
Be true, and dare all things. If we do not do so,
Christ Jesus is not Law-giver to us. Scorn the bribe,

though it be a covert one, and lose all for truth, if need be.

Our Lord also stands before us as *our example and pattern*. We preach the grace of God, and the blood of Christ; but if any suppose that we do not preach Christ as an example, they know nothing of our ministry; for we insist upon it that faith must obey her Saviour's will as well as trust His grace. We have had some among us, like the old Scotchwoman, who said, " It was a good sermon, all but the duties at the end." It may be possible that we put the precept in such a way that we countenance the suspicion that we are legal in spirit; this we must carefully avoid. We would preach Christ as the perfect pattern, that saints may long to be conformed to Him. Men must have the spirit of Christ, or they are lost. There is no Heaven to be found in a mere forensic justification, apart from a spiritual work within the soul,—a change of heart, and a renewal of mind.

Once more, I trust that we shall always hold Christ as *Lord and God*. Whatever else He is, He is Lord and God to us. Therefore He is to be spoken of and thought upon with deepest reverence of soul. The spirit that trifles with the Word of God, and the things of Christ, is almost more vicious than the action which comes out of it. I have read many things which I have shuddered at; but I have shuddered much more at the state of mind into which a man must have come to be able to write them. Let us cultivate the highest reverence for our Divine Lord, and the surest confidence in His power, and in His ultimate victory. Trust in that hand which He keeps on the helm. Have no shadow of a doubt that His wisdom and might will cause all things to end well. Go, therefore, and speak in His Name. When you have done stating a doctrine, command your hearers, in the Name of Jesus, to believe it. Be daring enough for that. As the apostles commanded lame men to stand, and even dead men to live, so, in the Name of Jesus Christ of Nazareth, command sinners to turn unto Him, and to live. He who gives you faith will answer to His own word.

Now let us turn our earnest attention to the subject of OUR POSITION TOWARDS OUR LORD. The position of the Christian minister towards Christ is a theme upon which one might speak in many ways, and for many a day, and yet barely do more than touch the fringe of it.

The most striking view of it comes before us in meditating upon the fact, that, as He stood in our stead, *we also stand in His stead.* To our hearers we can truly say, " We pray you, in Christ's stead, be ye reconciled to God." Our Lord Jesus lays His pierced hands upon our shoulders, and He says, " As the Father hath sent Me into the world, even so send I you." We are commissioned to plead for Christ, even as He is commissioned to plead for us. For Him we climb those stairs, to point that sick and ignorant woman to the blood of reconciliation. For Him we stand in the pulpit, and speak of sin, and righteousness, and judgment to come. In His place we cry, " Behold the Lamb of God, which taketh away the sin of the world! " Beloved brethren, do we always feel that we are not only labouring for Christ, but in His stead? Could we set forth some of our sermons as having been preached in Christ's stead? Should we not expect our own conscience to cry out against us if we were to make such a claim for those discourses? Some of our hearers would think, if they did not say so, " If that sermon is in Christ's stead, there is an awful falling off from what it would have been had Jesus spoken on His own account." Of course, there would necessarily be a falling off in Divine authority and ability; but there should be none as to truthful and earnest purpose.

We must plead with men in Christ's stead; and that will prevent partiality. We shall not give all our thoughts to the wealthy and educated few; but, as Jesus did, we shall care for the many. James the Fifth of Scotland was known as "the poor man's king," because every peasant, who desired it, could get an audience with him. The Lord make us the poor men's preachers! for how else can we be in Christ's stead? In His ministry, the poor had the gospel preached unto them. If there be one of our flock more sick, more poor, more ignorant than another, let us, for the Lord's sake, seek him first. Let us assume no upstart dignity, but feel at one with the forlorn, the poor, the fallen, even as Jesus did.

If we be in Christ's stead, we shall not bully, but tenderly persuade. We shall have true sympathy, and so we shall plead with sinners unto tears, as though their ruin were our woe, and their salvation would be our bliss. We shall weep over them, because Jesus would have done so; and we shall be patient with them, because of His Divine long-suffering. We shall watch for opportunities, and use'them with perseverance; for so would Jesus have done.

We shall deal with our hearers as a shepherd with his lost sheep, and we shall never rest till we have brought them home upon our shoulders rejoicing; for so was it with our Lord.

This position of ours, in Christ's stead, is greatly responsible; we shall need great grace to bear its weight. Behave yourselves, Christian brethren, for you bear a great Name. Do not disgrace the Name of the holy Jesus. It was shameful of Sheridan, when he was picked up in the gutter, to give his name to the constable as "*Wilberforce.*" What a cruel wrong to our Lord Jesus, for a harsh, or proud, or idle minister to give in his name as acting in the stead of Christ! God forgive the wrong: it is a very heinous one. If you are indeed in Christ's stead, what manner of persons ought you to be! May God help you to be worthy of the embassage on which you are sent!

Therefore, brethren, *we must love sinners for Christ's sake.* Are there not a great many in your congregation whom you could not love for any other reason? Could the Lord Jesus Christ ever have loved you for your merit's sake? He loved you and me for a reason which He found in His own heart; and so must we love our hearers, from causes which are not so much in them as in our own hearts. He "loved me, and gave Himself for me;" and if now He says to me, "Love others, and give yourself for them," shall I not do it? Every angry temper must be chased out. The fallen, the frivolous, the captious, the indifferent, and even the malicious must share our love. We must love them to Jesus. With cords of a man and bands of love must we draw them.

Our mission is to perpetuate on earth the love of the Saviour.

Further than this, your relation to Christ is of such a sort that you are to " *fill up that which is behind of the sufferings of Christ* for His body's sake, which is the Church." His atoning griefs are finished; into that winepress, none of us can set a foot. But those sufferings by which men are won to Christ are far from being finished. All the martyr host have bled and died to keep the truth alive for us, that by the truth men may still be brought to Jesus. Every sufferer who bears pain, or slander, or loss, or personal unkindness for Christ's sake, is filling up that amount of suffering which is necessary to the bringing together of the whole body of Christ, and the upbuilding of His elect Church. " Oh! " cries one minister, " I have been shamefully treated." Yes, and worthier men have been even more evilly entreated than you have. You need not look among your fellow-soldiers for equals in suffering: consider how your Lord Himself " endured such contradiction of sinners."

When Alexander led his men into Persia, and they had to cut through a very mountain of ice and snow, they were ready to turn back, and therefore Alexander alighted from his horse, and took an ice-axe in his hand, and went forward, often up to his waist in snow, cleaving the blocks of ice, and leading the way. Then the Macedonians felt that they would cut through the world with Alexander in front of them. With Christ your Lord cleaving His way by the agonies on the cross, will not you follow where He leads, and fill up the measure that may be wanted of toil, and labour, and suffering, for the salvation of those whom He has redeemed by blood? Nothing was more affecting in our supplications this morning than the prayers of those who had been great sufferers. Through suffering comes blessing. When our Lord means to give His household wine, that our festivals may be full of gladness, what does He do? He says, " Fill the waterpots with water." We must be filled with affliction to the brim. We must have as much of it as we can hold, and then He will say, " Draw out now." This is His beginning of miracles; and some of us rejoice that it was not only wrought at Cana in Galilee, but it is still wrought in this island of the sea.

Do you not think that we all make mistakes as to what will be a blessing? In the matter of faith-healing, health is set before us as if it were the great thing to be desired above all other things. Is it so? I venture to say that the greatest earthly blessing that God can give to any of us is health, *with the exception of sickness.* Sickness has frequently been of more use to the saints of God than health has. If some men, that I know of, could only be favoured with a month of rheumatism, it would, by God's grace, mellow them marvellously. Assuredly, they need something better to preach than what they now give their people; and, possibly, they would learn it in the chamber of suffering. I would not wish for any man a long time of sickness and pain; but a twist now and then one might almost ask for him. A sick wife, a newly-made grave, poverty, slander, sinking of spirit, might teach lessons nowhere else to be learned so well. Trials drive us to the realities of religion. You may feed on chaff until you have real work to do, or real grief to bear ; but then you want the old corn of the land, and you must have it, or else you will faint and fail.

Our afflictions come to us as blessings, though they frown like curses. I have heard of one who was generous, but extremely eccentric. A man, who was deeply in debt, passed his door, and he knew that the poor debtor was terribly exercised about the matter. One day, this odd man of wealth, generous as he was, was so cruel as to throw a heavy bag at the poor debtor. The man was hurt by the missile, and looked round to see what it was. He saw no man who had inflicted the injury. He picked up the bag. He heard the chink of the coin, and when he opened the bag, he found enough to pay his debt, and he heard a voice saying, " Keep it for yourself." He never summoned that man for an assault; but thanked him for the gift. Ofttimes has Providence, with a rough hand, thrown countless gain in our way in the form of the trial of our faith, which is much more precious than gold. Blessed be the Lord, our temporary bruise is soon forgotten, but the spiritual gain abides for ever. In any case, the cause of our Lord Jesus Christ is our cause, and we are linked with Him in a fellowship which cannot be broken, whatever it may involve. We have counted the cost, and we can say, " From henceforth let no man trouble me. I am the branded slave of Jesus, and my ear is bored for Him."

Furthermore, brethren, *our position towards our Lord will become most practical when we realize what He has done for us.* I do not think that we always clearly perceive what He has actually accomplished on our behalf. We say, "We are poor, but Christ makes us rich." Why do we not say, "We are rich, for Christ has made us so"? Our poverty has passed away, and we have become rich in ·Christ. Brethren, He hath called us "out of darkness into His marvellous light." We are apt, when we preach from the text, to enlarge considerably upon nature's darkness; but would it not be as well to be even more full upon the "marvellous light"? Have we the present experience which would lead us to do so? Why do we make so very vivid that word of the apostle, "When I am weak"? Can we not equally dwell upon the next words, "then am I strong"? Our Lord's blessings are realities, and not fancies; let us so treat them. "Blessed are they which do hunger and thirst after righteousness, for they shall be filled;" why spend all the time on the hunger and the thirst? Are we not filled? If not, Lord, fill us! But if we are filled, let us feel and preach the sweetness of the heavenly bread, and commend it with glad hearts to our hearers. Brethren, let us get on the bright side of our religion, and not be always harping upon what we are in ourselves. "The darkness is past, and the true light now shineth." We are now in Christ Jesus. We were all that is evil, but we are washed, cleansed, sanctified. Oh, for the rich enjoyment of the present blessings of the covenant! Oh, for grace to speak as we find! As Abraham's servant took care to talk largely of his master's riches, and to show the precious things which he had brought with him from his house, so let us try to win hearts for our great Lord, by showing who He is, and what He has, and what we personally know thereof.

I think, again, that *we shall do well to stand towards Christ as those who are conscious of His power and presence.* Brethren, our Lord is with us. The best of all is, that He is with us indeed and of a truth. If we are with Jesus, and preach His truth, Jesus is assuredly with us; for He said, "Lo, I am with you alway, even unto the end of the world." That promise was not a pretty piece of romance: it is true that He is with us at this hour. Let us believe it, and act accordingly. If we do not always feel His brightness, let us, like the flowers, turn towards the sun. When the sun is not shining, the flowers know where there is most of light, and their faces turn that way. Let us be true heliotropes, or turners to the sun. When we get into the pulpit, let us look Christ-ward and lean Christward. What a wondrous place the pulpit is when Jesus is there! In the study, when we sit down, and begin to rub our foreheads, and anxiously enquire, "What shall we preach about?" let us turn towards our Lord, and pray with our window open towards His cross and His throne. May we ever feel an influence drawing us Christ-ward when the Bible is open before us! If it be so, our weakness will all vanish, for His strength will be remembered.

When you are contemplating the great struggle against sin, and are making up your account as to the forces that are on the right side, fail not to remember Jesus. You have put yourself down: that amounts to less than nothing. Now you put down your deacons: after estimating them lovingly, they are as nothing, too. You have made an item of pray-ing friends and workers, and so on; but the total sum is just a line of ciphers. What do all these noughts amount to? Your distrust cries out, " I have here nothing, and nothing, and nothing." That is a poor reckoning for you to rely upon; but you have not done yet. What are you going to put before all these noughts? Where will you place the Infinite One? If you put him after these ciphers, like a figure in decimals, you reduce the one to the ten thousandth! Each nought set before THE ONE robs Him of glory, and diminishes Him. But if HE be put first, before the ciphers, what a sum you have! This is not fancy; it is sound arithmetic. Go and test it, and see if it does not turn out to be mathematically true in the spirit world. Powerless as we are alone, our Lord is with us.

Some preachers evidently do not believe that the Lord is with their gospel, because, in order to attract and save sinners, their gospel is insufficient, and they have to add to it inventions of men. Plain gospel preaching must be supplemented,—so they think. Bridget was very busy catching and killing flies. Her mistress said to her, " Bridget, what are you doing? " She answered, " You see, ma'am, we have bought some fly-papers, and we must have the flies caught on them; and as they don't go on of themselves, I am sticking them on." I should not care for fly-papers of that sort. If the gospel must be a failure unless we attract the people by some extraneous method, it is a poor business. If the fly-paper does not attract the flies, and hold them, we may as well burn the fly-paper. If your gospel cannot bring the people to hear you, and if, when they come, your gospel will not impress and convert them, well, then, give it up.

Open a coffee-shop, or start in the ginger-beer line;
but do not call your useless talk the blessed gospel.
If you are not conscious of a supernatural power and
presence with the Word of the Lord, let it alone. A
man said to me, " You told a dead sinner to believe."
I pleaded guilty, but told him I would do it again.
He said, " I could not do it, I should feel that it was of
no use to do so." I answered, " Possibly, it might be
of no use for you to do it, for you have not the necessary faith; but, as I believe that God bids *me* do so,
I deliver the message in the Name of the Lord, and
the dead sinners believe and live." I do not trust in
the dead sinner's power to live, but in the power of
the gospel to make him live. Now, if your gospel has
not the power of the Holy Ghost in it, you cannot
preach it with confidence, and you are tempted to
have a performance in the schoolroom to allure the
people, whom Christ crucified does not draw. If you
are depending on sing-song, and fiddles, and semi-
theatricals, you are disgracing the religion which you
pretend to honour.

Once more, dear friends, *our position towards our
Lord is that of waiting for His coming.* I do not
know how far the most of you are warmly affected
towards the blessed truth of the Second Advent; but
I trust that many of you believe it, and are enlivened
by faith in it. That great hope is gaining ground
among lovers of Evangelical doctrine. At first,
ministers seemed half-afraid of this grand belief, because of the fanaticism which is supposed to grow out
of it. Certain charlatans also do great harm by
pretending to know the day and the hour when the
Lord will come. Times and seasons are not with us;

but *the Lord will come.* He is on His way even now, for He says, " I am coming quickly." Our Lord may come right soon ; certain signs raise our hopes very high. The love of many waxes cold, and the devil is doubly busy ; and this last is no doubtful sign. When you see a farmer beginning to burn the gates, and break down the hedges, and unroof the barns, and so on, you say, " That fellow's lease has run out." Satan has great wrath when he knows that his time is short. In the case of the demoniac child, we read, " As he was yet a-coming, the devil threw him down, and tare him." He knew that he was about to be expelled, so he did his worst. The double veiling of the heavens only brings on that darkest part of the night which precedes the dawn of day. When the tale of bricks is doubled, Moses appears ; and the same is true of our still greater Deliverer. Let us take courage, and be of good heart ; for while we lift Christ on high, and glorify His Name, He is on the way to take up the quarrel of His covenant, and utterly to rout His foes.

Now for two or three words to finish with, upon OUR POSITION INDIVIDUALLY. Peradventure, some sentence may come with power to this man and to that.

Let me say to you, brethren, *be self-contained.* I would to God that we had among us more men in the fulness of spiritual and mental vigour. The want of the period is brethren who know the gospel for themselves, who have had a personal experience of its power, who have tested it as silver is tried in a furnace of earth, and who set such a value upon it, that they